THAILAND
Travel Atlas

Published By Tuttle Publishing,
an imprint of Periplus Editions (HK) Ltd.
www.tuttlepublishing.com

© 2012 Periplus Editions (HK) Ltd.
First Edition
All Rights Reserved
Printed in Singapore   1111CP
15 14 13 12   1 2 3 4 5
ISBN 978-0-8048-4193-1

Distributors:
North America, Latin America & Europe
Tuttle Publishing
364 Innovation Drive
North Clarendon, VT 05759-9436, USA
Tel: 1 (802) 773 8930
Fax: 1 (802) 773 6993
info@tuttlepublishing.com
www.tuttlepublishing.com

Japan
Tuttle Publishing
Yaekari Bldg. 3rd Floor
5-4-12 Osaki
Shinagawa-ku, Tokyo 141-0032 Japan
Tel: (81) 3 5437 0171
Fax: (81) 3 5437 0755
sales@tuttle.co.jp
www.tuttle.co.jp

Asia Pacific
Berkeley Books Pte Ltd
61 Tai Seng Avenue #02-12
Singapore 534167
Tel: (65) 6280 1330
Fax: (65) 6280 6290
inquiries@periplus.com.sg
www.periplus.com

Indonesia
PT Java Books Indonesia
Jl. Rawa Gelam IV No. 9
Kawasan Industri Pulogadung
Jakarta Timur 13930 Indonesia
Tel: 62 (021) 4682 1088
Fax: 62 (021) 461 0206
crm@periplus.co.id
www.periplus.co.id

HOW TO USE THIS TRAVEL ATLAS

The maps in *Travel Atlas Thailand* are organized into eight chapters, each one covering a major geographical region of the country.

Every chapter begins with an overview map of the region covered, with blue boxes showing the insets detailed on the pages following and a page number to allow the user to go directly to the desired page.

The opening spread of this atlas shows a map of the entire country, in addition to the nearby countries of Malaysia, Myanmar, Laos and Cambodia. This map is keyed with color-coded boxes indicating the region covered by each chapter. Every chapter contains overview maps showing large areas, more detailed maps of smaller regions and detailed inset maps of key cities and towns of particular interest to visitors and travelers. The maps, where possible, are arranged so that towns are shown adjacent to the regional maps allowing the user to look for nearby points of interest and find out how to travel from one town to another.

The Index at the end of the atlas lists names of cities, towns and villages that appear on all the various maps in the atlas. These are keyed to the page number and map title where they are located to help user find the general area where the place is located. There are separate index lists for places of interest, national parks and nature reserves.

TUTTLE Publishing
Tokyo | Rutland, Vermont | Singapore

CONTENTS

How to Use This Travel Atlas ....
Maps Coverage & Contents...2

BANGKOK
Greater Bangkok...4
Central Bangkok...6
Downtown Bangkok...8
Lumphini...10 -
Silom...12 -
Sukhumvit...14 -

CENTRAL THAILAND
Central Thailand...16 -
Around Bangkok...18 -
Nakhon Pathom Town...
Ratchaburi (Ratburi) Town...
Samut Prakan Town...
Samut Sakhon Town...
Around Ayutthaya...
Singburi Town...
Ang Thong Town...
Ayutthaya Town...
Lopburi Town...
Around Nakhon Sawan...
Nakhon Sawan Town...
Uthai Thani Town...
Chai Nat Town...
Kanchanaburi Province...
Sangkhlaburi...
Kanchanaburi Town...
Sai Yok National Park...

scale 1 : 6,700,000

0   100km
0   50miles

THEASTERN THAILAND

theastern Thailand 28
Phe 28
amet 28
aya 29
acha 29
i Chang 29
nburi Town 30
nthaburi (Chanburi) Town 31
hang 31
ng Town 31
Town 31

THERN THAILAND

hern Thailand 32
ng Mai, Mae Hong Son,
amphun Provinces 33
nd Chiang Mai ....34 – 35
tral Chiang Mai ....36 – 37
nd Mae Hong Son 38
Hong Son Town 38
Sariang 38
....38
phun Town 39
gmapha 39
ng Rai Town 40
ng Saen 40
Sai 40
Chan 40
ng Rai Province 41
yao Town 41
ng Khong 41
pang Town 42
e Town 42
pang, Nan, Phrae, Uttaradit Provinces 43
....43
radit Town 43
sanulok, Sukhothai & Phichit Provinces ...44
Sukhothai 44
chanalai-Chaliang National Park..........44
hothai Historical Park 44
sanulok Town 45
hit Town......................................45
Town 46
Sot 46
Phang 46
phaeng Phet & Tak Provinces 47
phaeng Phet Town 47

RTHEASTERN THAILAND

theastern Thailand.........................48
ater Nakhon Ratchasima 49
ater Udon Thani 49
hon Ratchasima City.......................50
und Phanom Rung...........................50
ram Town 51
nai 51
aket Town 52
in Town 52
othon Town 52
n Ratchathani Town 53
nat Charoen Town 53
Et Town 54
on Nakhon Town............................54

Kalasin Town 54
Maha Sarakham Town 54
Nakhon Phanom Town 55
Mukdahan Town 55
That Phanom 55
Phetchabun Town 56
Chaiyaphum Town 56
Khon Kaen Town 57
Loei Town 58
Nong Bua Lam Phu Town 58
Chiang Khan 58
Udon Thani Town 59
Nong Khai Town 59

UPPER GULF COASTS

Upper Gulf Coasts 60
Phetchaburi (Phetburi) Town 61
Ranong Town 62
Hua Hin 62
Cha-am 62
Chumphon Town 63
Prachuap Khiri Khan Town 63

LOWER GULF & ANDAMAN COASTS

Isthmus of Kra 64
Around Samui 64
Nakhon Si Thammarat Town 65
Surat Thani Town 65
Ko Samui 66
Mae Nam 67
Lamai 67
Chaweng 67
Ko Pha-Ngan 68
Hat Rin 68
Ko Tao 69
Khao Lak 70
Similan National Park 70
Phuket Province.............................71
Phuket Island 72
Karon & Kata Beaches 72
Phuket Town 73
Rawai 73
Kamala Beach 74
Bang Tao Beach 74
Patong Beach 75
Ko Lanta 76
Ko Phi Phi Don 76
Ao Nang Beach 76
Railay 76
Krabi Town 77
Trang Town 77

FAR SOUTH

Far South 78
Ko Lipe 78
Tarutao Islands..............................79
Hat Yai Town 80
Satun Town 80
Pattani Town 80
Phatthalung Town 81
Songkhla Town...............................81

INDEX..82 – 96

PHIMON RAT

THAWI WATTHANA

BANG KHU RAT

NONG PHRAO NGAI

BANG YAI

BANG MAE NANG

SALA KLANG

SALAYA

THAWI WATTHANA

NONG KHANG PHLU

NONG KHAEM

SUAN LUANG

BANG BON

BANG KHAE

BANG PHAI

TALING CHAN

BANG KRUAI

BANG RAK PHATTANA

BANG KRANG

MUANG NONTHABURI

PAK KRET

KHLONG KHOI

BANG KHU WAT

BAN

WAT CHALO

BANG SUE

BANG PHEAT

BANG WAEK

PHASI CHAROEN

CHOM THONG

THUNG KHRU

BANG RAK

PATHUMWAN

YANNA

LUMP

NAKON PATHOM / SAMUT SAKHON

BANGKOK / NAKON PATHOM

NONTHABURI / BANGKOK

NONTHABURI / NAKON PATHOM

PATHUM THANI / NONTHABURI

Thanon Phet Kasem

Thanon Bang Waek

Thanon Bang Khae

Thanon Kalapaphruk

Thanon Ratchaphruek

Thanon Nakron In

Thanon Ratchaphruek

Thanon Bang Kruai - Sai Noi

Th. Bang Kruai - Sai Noi

Elevated Borommaratchachonnani

Thanon Thammasop

Thanon Rama II

Thanon Ekkachai

Thanon Suk Sawat

Thanon Chaeng Watthana

Thanon Tiwanon

Thanon Rattanathibet

Thanon Phibun Songkhram

Thanon Wong Sawang

Thanon Nakhon Chai Si

Thanon Krung Thep - Nonthaburi

Chalerm Maha Nakhon Expressway

Thanon Phra Ram III

Western Outer Ring

Kanchanaphisek

Phutthamonthon Sai 3

Phutthamonthon Sai 2

Phutthamonthon Sai 1

Phutthamonthon Sai 4

Si Rat Expressway

Phutthamonthon

Bang Bua Thong Sports Stadium

Thepsirin Nonthaburi School

Premier Golf Driving Range

Golden Jubilee Commemoration Park

Su Wongchai Golf Course

Golf Academy Driving Range

Royal Irrigation Department Golf Court

Sukhothai Thammathirat Open University

Drive Ban Suan Golf

Albatross Driving Range

King Taksin Monument

Floating Market

Wongwien Yai

Grand Palace

National Museum

Royal Barges National Museum

Vimanmek Palace Museum

Dusit Zoo

Chitralada Royal Palace

Anusawari Samoraphum

Jim Thompson's House

Erawan Shrine

Pasteur Institute

National Science Museum

LUMPHINI PARK

Patjamit Fort

Wat Prayun

M.R. Kukrit Pramoj House

King Mongkut's University

Gassan Driving Range

Bang Yai Municipality Office

150,000

0   2.5km   0   1mile

ang Ek Vista
olf Course

KHU KHOT

Thupatemi
Golf Course

Tanya Tanee
Country Club

3004

SAM WA TAWAN OK

Th. Chord Ulha Kari

LAK HOK

Thupatemi Royal
Thai Air Force
Sports Stadium

Th. Tang Luang Chomabotch

3312

Th. Lam Luk Ka

KHLONG SIP

SI KAN

Thanon Techatungkha

LAT SAWAI

Th. Lam Luk Ka

Bueng
Kham
Phroi

9

Soi Khlong Ha

3312

Th. Lam Luk Ka

Thanon Nimit Nai

PAO. PN. 2006

Darustam

anon Song Prapha

Don Muang Toll Way

31

DON
MUANG

SAI MAI

Thanon Sai Mai

Th. Lam Luk Ka

3312

PAO. PN. 2006

PATHUM THANI

Sam Wa
Tawan Ok

Maitri Chit

PAO. PN. 2006

Thanon Phahon Yothin

1

Drive Golf Court

Thanon Sukhaphiban 5

3312

BANGKOK

Sam Wa
Tawan Ok

Navamintharachinuthit
Satree Wittaya School

Don Muang
Airport

Khlong
Thanon

Thanon Phoem Sin

Ao Ngoen

Thanon Vacharaphol

Chalong Rat E-way

Kanchanaphisek National Hway

9

Thanon Hathai Rat

Thanon Nimit Nai

SAI KONG
DIN TAI

31

Uttaphimuk Toll Way

TALAT BANG KHEN

304

Talat Bang
Khen

BANG KHEN

Tha
Raeng

Thanon Rarm Intra

Anusawari

Thanon Lat Phrao

KHLONG SAM WA

Sam Wa
Tawan
Tok

BANG CHAN

Sai Kong
Din

SAI KONG
DIN

Khu Fang
Nuea

Thanon Hathai Rat

Thanon Nimit Nai

Thanon
Golf View

Thanon Pracha Ruam Chai

Thanon Rat Uthit

1

Sena
Nikhom

351

UCHAK

Thanon Prasert Manukitch

Chorakhe
Bua

304

LAT PHRAO

Thanon Nuan Chan

Thanon Navamin

2022

KHANNA YAO

304

Thanon Rarm Intra

Thanon Surao Khlong Nueang

304

Thanon Suwinthawong

SAEN SAEP

Chan
Kasem

351

336

Khlong
Khum

KHLONG KUM

2022

SIAM PARK

BANG CHAN
INDUSTRIAL
ESTATE

Thanon Seri Thai

MIN BURI

Samsen
Nok

Thanon Lat Phrao

Khlong
Chan

3278

Thanon Ramkhamhaeng

3119

Thanon Khum Kiao

DAENG

Huai
Khwang

Thanon Lat Phrao

Wang
Thong
Lang

336

BANG KAPI

Saphan
Sung

SAPHAN SUNG

Perfect Golf
Driving Range

Khlong
Song Ton
Nun

Thanon Rom Klao

LAT KRABANG
INDUSTRIAL
ESTATE

LAT KRABANG

Bang
Kapi

3344

Hua Mak

Thanon Ramkhamhaeng

9

Khlong
Sam
Prawet

Lam
Plathew

Thanon Chalong Krung

ate E-way

Rajamangala
Stadium

Kfung Thep Kritha
Golf Club

Thanon Phatthana Channabot 3

Thanon Rom Klao

Thanon Chao Khun Thahan

3119

Sinagarindra

on Phetchaburi

Si Rat Suburban Network E-way

Prasart
Museum

Unico
Golf Course

7

Krungthep Chon Buri New Line

7

Khlong
Tnei
Nuea

how

Petchaburi
Golf Course

Suan
Luang

Th. Phatthanakan

Stamford
International
University

Lat Krabang

K
VADHANA

PARK

3

Phra
Khanong
Nuea

enter of
cation

3344

SUAN LUANG

Thanon On Nut

BANGKOK

SAMUT PRAKARN

Thanon Lat Krabang

Thanon Lat Krabang

LAT KRABANG
PUBLIC PARK

THAP YAO

Sisa
Chofakhe
Noi

ONG

Phra
Khanong

ON NUT

3

Bang
Chak

Sol Sukhumvit 77

PRAWET

3344

9

Cargo &
Customs

Terminal 1

khon
Khan
cal Park

Bang Ko
Bua

King Rama IX
Royal Park

Thanon Chaloem Phrakiat Ratchakan Thi 9

GEMOPOLIS
INDUSTRIAL
ESTATE

Thanon King Kaeo

Suvarnabhumi
International
Airport

am

BANG NA

Th. Sukhumvit 103

SUAN LUANG
RAMA IX PARK

Thanon
Nong
Bon

Racha
Thewa

Future
Terminal 2

Nong
Prue

3109

3

Samrong

Thanon Bang Na-Trat

CENTRAL BANGKOK 6-7

OOK MAI

9

3256

Sisa
Chorakhe
Yai

A PRADAENG

Samrong
Boxing
Stadium

SAMRONG NUA

3344

Bang
Kaeo

BANG PHLI YAI

Summit Windmill
Country Club

3256

3

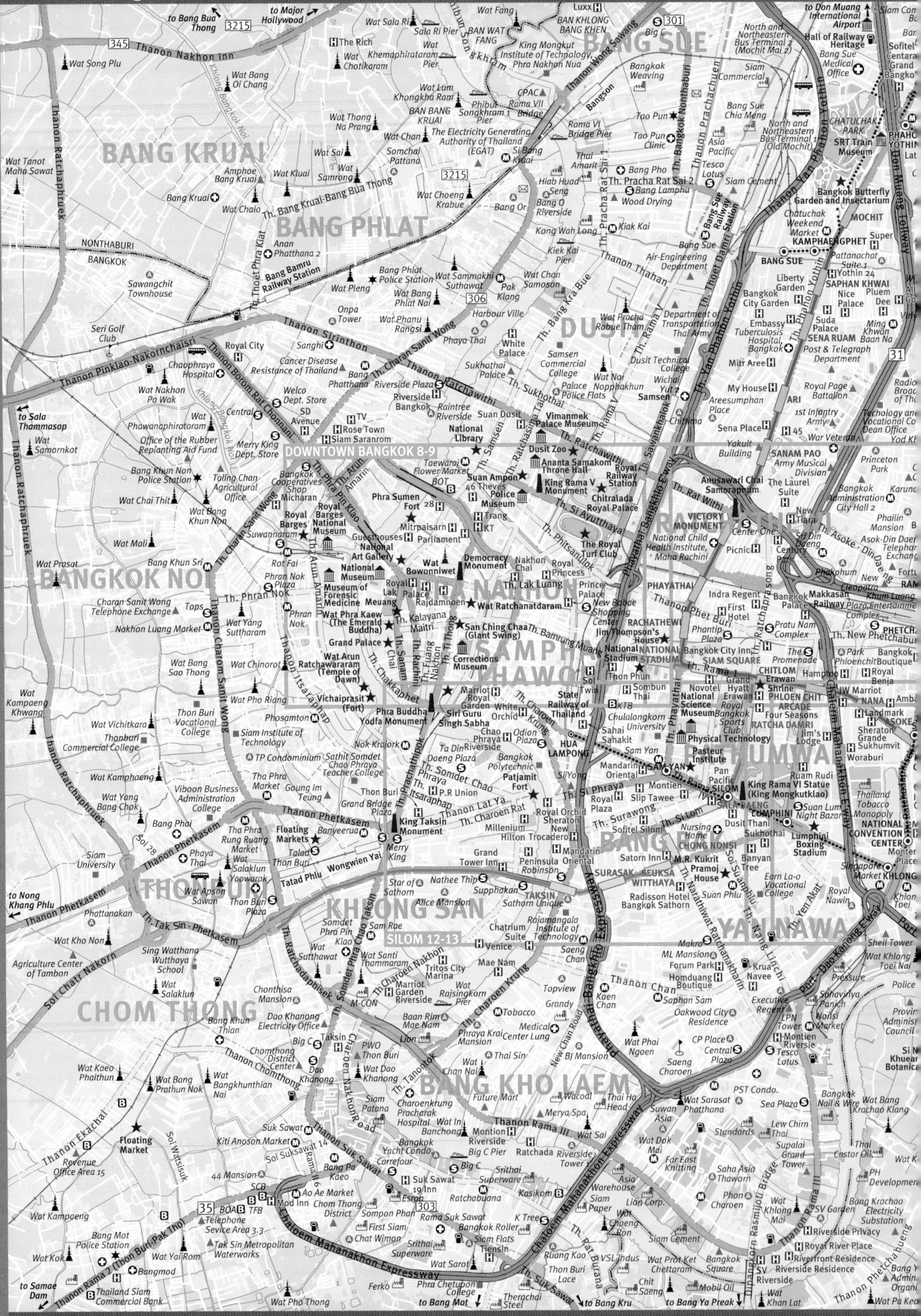

BANG KRUAI

BANG PHLAT

BANG SUE

DUSIT

BANGKOK NOI

NAKHON

SAMPHAN THAWONG

PHAYATHAI

RACHATHEWI

PATHUMWAN

BANG RAK

THONBURI

KHLONG SAN

CHOM THONG

BANG KHO LAEM

YANNAWA

DOWNTOWN BANGKOK 8-9

SILOM 12-13

Thanon Nakhon In

to Bang Bua Thong

to Major Hollywood

to Don Muang International Airport

Thanon Ratchaphruek

Thanon Ratchaphisek

Thanon Phetkasem

Thanon Pinklao-Nakornchaisri

Thanon Charan Sanit Wong

Thanon Rama III

Chaoem Mahanakhon Expressway

Thanon Charoen Krung

Thanon Sukhumvit

Grand Palace

Wat Phra Kaew (The Emerald Buddha)

Wat Arun Ratchawararam (Temple of Dawn)

National Museum

Democracy Monument

Victory Monument

King Taksin Monument

Hua Lamphong

Chatuchak Weekend Market

Chatuchak Park

Dusit Zoo

Vimanmek Palace Museum

National Library

Royal Turf Club

Lumphini Boxing Stadium

Lumphini Night Bazaar

National Convention Center

Port

to Samae Dam

to Nong Khang Phlu

to Bang Mot

to Bang Kru

to Bang Ya Praek

1 : 75,000

0   1km   0   0.5mile

to Anutsawari Thahanasa   to Phayom

KHAN NA YA

Kiattada Golf Course

Thanon Kaset - Nawamin

Sri Siam Hospital   Tesco Lotus   Fashion Island   Big C

304   Bangkok Bank   Th. Ram Intha

Nopparhat Ratchathani Hospital

Wat Patthawikon   Wonder World Fun Park

to Muang Chachoengsao

Thai Suriya Ramintra Technology College

LATPHRAO

Baan Suan Thon   Jusco

ajabhat Institute f Chan Kasem   Ratchada Green

Univest   RP

Thana Sup

Ratchada Ville

Exporting Promotion   Suwanaphum

Sweet Inn   Westwood

Garden Inn

AT PHRAO   Supapong

Wat Latphrao

Siam Hospital   Khet Bangkapi District Center

For You Plaza   Jusco

Benjamin College

3202   Dhanasin Market

Patthawikon

Sieng Tai Hardening Metal

3278   Wat Bang Toei

Nawa Thani Golf Course   Bang Chan Police Station

37   3278

Ratchada Trade Center   ATCHADAPHISEK

Garden Place   Ratchada Pavilion

Preecha Complex   Dragon Inn

3 Coins   Turkey

ower Hotel   Ratchada

Nikko   Nasa Garden

Thanon Latphrao   Siam 2 Market   Seiyu

Chok Chai 4 Market

Kurusapha

P. Thana   Tawan Rong Market   Porn Wattana

Driving Range

Chormuang

Imperial

Foodland Supermarket

Latphrao Hospital

Latphrao Telephone Exchange

Sky Exist

BUENG KUM

TOPS

Thanon Nawamin

Inthra Rak Market

National Housing Authority

Bueng Kum Police Station

Eastern Outer Ring Road

BANG KAPI

a-jah Palace

JAI KHWANG

Regina

Swissotel Le Concorde

Siam Beverly

WANG THONG ANG

Huai Khwang Lands Office

Wat Samakkhi Tham

Si Chan

Nakhon Thai VejThani Hospital

Rattana Bundit University Science and Technology

East Si Moom Muang Market

336

Bang Kapi Land Office

NIDA

Carrefour

Greeny Kof Golf

SAPHAN SUNG

Prom Siri Driving Range

Grand Park Town

Siam Administration Management

Eakthanee

Town in Town

Drive Inn

Tesco Lotus

Nomjit

Makro

Bang Kapi Royal Rose

3202   3278

Imperial

Thanon Ramkhamhaeng

Th. Seri Thai (Sukhaphiban 2)

Th. Seri Thai (Sukhaphiban 3)

HAILAND CULTURAL CENTER

Korea

BANGKOK MASS ral Center RAPID TRANSIT ailand   WORKSHOP

ATHWANG

Palm Street Ratchada

Pip Inn

Birlinda Resort

Engineering Institute of Thailand

My Lady Fashion Hotel

Chaleena Princess

Rajapark College

Bangkok Polytechnic

Inkham Sweet

Vaboir Lodge

The Chaleena

The Mall + IT City + Tawanna

Alexander

Plaza Dept. Store

3344   Peep Inn 1

BANG KAPI

Department of own & Country Planning

Victoria Secret

Dulya Charima

Royal Pacific Tamasorn

Expressway Control Center 3

Siam Society

The Mall 4 Dept. Store

The Mall 3 Dept. Store

Foodland Dept. Store

Thanon Ramkhamhaeng

Big C

Ramkhamhaeng University

Regent

Sports Authority of Thailand

Soi Muban Seri

Bangkok Inter Place

Assumption Business Administration University

Institute of Tourism and International Management (i-TIM)

JVK

Unilever (Warehouse)

Thanon Krung Thep Kritha

Krung Thep Kritha Golf Club

Unico Golf Course

Prawet Land Office

hisek E'way   Thanon Rama IX

Piyavate Hospital   Radisson

Benz   A-One Bangkok

Tops   Union Tower

g Carpet nt'l   Morakot

Imperial House   Camillian Hospital

eam House   SPC

Court

Yontrakit

Thonglor al Castle

Thonglor Tower

Homhuan Major 7 Mansion

Modern Love Mall

Brighten Place

ATP Industry

Lexus

Electric Station

Living Place

Klongton

Klong Tan Hospital

Chaetpanya Hospital

Chim Plee

Chin Chai Hua

Rama IX Place

Th. New Phet Buri

Th. Phet Buri

Thanon Ramkhamhaeng

Bangkok Music & The Arts Academy

2nd State Expressway

Thanon Rama IX

Kasim Bondit University

Technical Promotion Institute

North Korea

Thanon Phatthanakan

Hua Mak

Siam Jusco

Samitivej Hospital

Prasart Museum

The Flora Ville Complex

7   Bangkok - Chon Buri Motorway

to Suvarnabhumi International Airport

Ban Thap Chang Railway Station

MEA Substation

Chaiong Rai Expressway

Thanon Sukhumvit

Thanon Sri Nakarindra

Thanon Srinakarin

Vibharam Hospital

Modern Farm Tower

Regent Srinakarin

Nakarindra Honda Car

Nagara Tower

Mercedes Benz

Prawet Police Station

Suan Luang District Office

Summit Pavilion

Ricoh   A.A. Bread

World Assembly of Muslim Youth

Isuzu

Bank of Ayudya

to Thap Yao

PRAWET

VADHANA

Regent Park 2   Thong Kao

Forty Winks

EKAMAI   Chaiyapruk Place

Thailand Knitting

White Group   Jusco

Thep Tharin   Nissan

Soi Sukhumvit 71

Bay Printing House

Asian Tower

Soon Chee

Wat Mahabut

Do-It

Wat Tai

Phra Khanong Craft

Wat Thongnai

Suanluang District Center

Eiam Sombat Market

Standard Chartered

Sukhumvit 77 (On Nut)

Tot Corp.

On Nuch Waste Disposal Plant

Saeng Thong Chai Plastic

On Nut Sports Center

SUAN LUANG

SUKHUMVIT 14-15

HLONG TOEI

Wat Saphan Phra Khanong

Port Warehouse

PTT Terminal

Saint Paolo

Sin Yok Hua Kong Hak

Imm Fusion

Sinipol

Tesco Lotus

Metro Tractor

Wat On Nut

The Bedrooms Boutique

Lee Garden Inn

VP House

ON NUT Food Lion

Wool Technology

Center Point Service Apartment

Rembrandt Towers

Thanon Sukhumvit 77

Krung Thai Bank

JS Mansion

East Wood Park Condominium

Wat Ratsatthatham

FORDEC

Kasikorn Bank

The Trio Garden

Krung Thai Bank

PRAWET

RA KHANONG

PHRA ADAENG

BAN BANG KO BUA BON

BAN BANG PHEUNG NAI

ng Nai

BANG FUNG

Bua ple

Nam phhueng

g Nam dong ockyard

Naval Ordnance Department

3102   Th. Sanpha Wut

Bangkok SAMUTPRAKARN

PTT Oil Tanks

Energy Organization

2nd Oil Refinery

Swedish Motors

Thai Soluble

Glass Organization

Charoen Chai

U-Domsuk

Bang Chak Market

Diethelm

Convenient Park

Sukhumvit Tractor

Mitsubishi

Square Print'93

J.M. Mansion

Thai Toh Ah Industries

Wat Ractini Haeng Santiphap

Wat Tham Mongkhon

Lung Neng

Mahasin Market

Kluay Nam Thai 2

Nice Unity Tower

Niran Grand

Thanon Sukhumvit 103 (Udomsuk)

Nirund Residence

First State Expressway

Thanon Sri Nakarindra

Seri Center

Siam Dental Clinic

Phakhanong Land Office

Government Transportation

Suang Luang Sport Center

Wat Thung Lanna

Phra Khanong Transportation Office

Chaloem Phrakiat Ror 9

Phra Khanong Transportation Office

Chaloem Phrakiat Phirat Ratchakan Thi 9

Thanon Sri Nakarindra

King's Park Avenue

Wat Wachirathamathit

Dusit Princess Srinakarin

Kasikorn Bank

Seacon Square & Tesco Lotus

Suan Luang Animal Hospital

King Rama IX Royal Park

Patthana Kolkan

Bunyakan Apartment

Phatra Apartment

Wat Thung Lanna

Siam Micro Work Co., Ltd.

Ruam Panya Kan Chang Co., Ltd.

Siam Product Aircondition Co., Ltd.

Airdroric Supply Co., Ltd.

DOK MAI

KT Apartment

U-Dom Suk Police Station

Ram Khamhaeng Mansion

Number One Market

Ramkhamhaeng University, Bang Na Campus

NG BON

BANG NA

Forest Industry Organization

Country Tower

Siyaek Bang Na Market

Bangna Place

Like Inn

Nice Mansion

Naval Command and Staff College

Wat Yothin Pradit

Int'l Trade Center (BITEC)

Thomson

13 Coins Resort Bangna

34   Avana

to Bang Muang Mai

to Bang Bo

Big C Imperial

December

3344

Parkland

Bang Pli Revenue Office

Index

Chaleng Phrakiat Phirat Ratchakan Thi 9

Phattra Apartment

SCB

UOB

Number One

GSB

CARE Co., Ltd.

to Rose Garden
Standard Chartered
Bank of Ayudhya
Bank of Asia
Quiheng
Moobari
UK Apartment
Greater Pharma Factory
Pata Department Store
Bangkok Cooperatives Shop Co.
Pin Thip Apartment
FBCB
Tang Hua Sing
Bangkok Bank
Manorah Food Industry Co. Ltd.
to Bang Kho Laem, Samphran Elephant Ground & Zoo
Krung Thai Bank
Rattanakosin Island
Nathi Thong Mansion
Bangkok Siam City Bank
Genting
Sareerawat 2
Ammarin Printing
R.D. Hotel
Thanalongkon Building
Soi Lao Lada

ARUN AMARIN

Chao Phraya Paradise
Arun Ammarin

BANG BUMRU

Wat Noi Nang Hong
Wat Amon Khriri
Bang Chak
Chao Phraya 3
Bang Yi Khan
S. Wat Amonkiri
Bang Yi Khan Apartment
Police Residence Bang Yi Khan
Suwanin
City Apartment
Siam Rath
Suwanin

BANG YI KHAN

Kritsada Maha Nakhon
Krisdathanont 3
Sang Thai
Sri Prakob Phon 2
Soi Wat Daowadueng
Sri Ulai School
Wat Daowadueng
Wat Daowaduengsaram
Senso Corporation
Siam Flats
Bun Cheuy
Snow White
Sura Bangyikhan
Inthra Chai School
Wat Chaturamit Pradittharam
Wat Phraya Siri Aisawan School
Wat Phraya Siri Aisawan
Bangikhan Liquer Distillery Factory
Sommdet Phra Klao 7
Bang Yi Khan Police Station
Mahidol University Office
Daowadueng Pin Klao Pier

Thanon Wisut Kasat
Rama VIII Bridge
Wisut Kasat Pier

PHRA NAKHON

Rajamangala Institute of Technology
Thewet Flower Market
Rajamangala of Technology
Taewaraj
RIT Chotiwet
Department of Audit Cooperative
The Cooperative Promotion Department
Wat Noranat Sutthikaram
Thewet Pier
Rajamangala Institute of Technology

Wat Kharuehabodi
Wat Kharuehabodi School
Wat Kharuehabodi
Siam Rath

Bank of Thailand (BOT)
The Government Savings Bank
MEA
Krung Thai Bank
Bang Khun Phrom Junction

Bella Bella Riverview
Perpark Place
Wat Sam Phraya
Juldis River Mansion
Wat Sam Phraya Pier
Bang Lamphu Pier
Guesthouses
Phra Nakhon District Office
Bangkok Bank
Navalai River Resort
Rattanakosin
Buddhism Association
Office of The Constitution Court
Sawasdee
UNICEF
Office of The Maritime Promotion
New Merry V
Kin-Duem
New Siam Riverside
The Revenue Office Region 3
Sukprasath

Phra Sumen Fort
Phra Sumen
Sam Sen Junction
Bhiman Inn
May Kaidee
Nana Sugar Factory
Guesthouses
Pra Artist Guesthouse
Bang Lamphu Junction
New World Dept. Store
Bangkok Co-operative
Viengtai
Rambuttri Village Inn
Kaew
Guesthouses
Chana Songkhram

SIRIRAJ

Wat Chimthayakawat
Wat Wiset Kan School
Wat Wiset Kan
Soi Phattana Chang
Wat Singhakraison
Saeng Sueksa School
Thonburi Hospital

BANGKOK NOI

Rot Fai Market
Bangkok Noi Train Station
Thanon Nikhon
Wat Amarintharararam
Banphak Rot Fai
Wat Amarintharararam School
Thon Buri Investigation Supposition Division
Siriraj Hospital
Mahidol University
The Siam Commercial Bank
Siriraj Post Office
Siriraj Junction

Royal Barges
Royal Barges National Museum
Arun Ammarin Piers
Arun Ammarin Bridge
Khlong Bangkok Noi
Ansoral Sunnan Mosque

Thon Buri Railway Terminal
Songkran Niyosane Forensic Medicine Museum
Railway Station Pier
Phra Chan Pier
College of Fine Art
National Museum
College of Dramatic Arts
The National Theatre

Wang Ngar
Thachang
Bangkok Information Center
Office of The Council of State
Thammasat University
Maharat Market
S. Tambon Nakhon
TSCB
Wat Mahathat School
Wat Mahathat
Amulet Market
Royal Institute
Tambon Taweenbol
SCB Bangkok
Silpakorn University
Rachanawi Samsorn
Fine Art Department
Statue of Mae Thorani
Thorani Fountain

SANUM LUANG

Royal Palace

Khok Wua Junction
Phranakom Arthit Pier
Wiang Samran
Taksura
Khao San Palace
Saraban
D&D Plaza
Ranee Gh.
Buddy Boutique
Sawasdee
Talat Yot

Wat Bowonniwet
Wat Bowonniwet Sch.
Saphan Wan Chat Junction
Tatchapon 2

Maha Mongkut Ratchawitayalai Foundation
Boworn BB
Lamphu Tree House
Ban Phanthom

New World Dept. Store
Diamond House
Ban Phanthom

Th. Chakrabpongse
Th. Kraisi
Th. Ram Buttri
Th. Tanao
Th. Dinso

Th Ratchadamnoen Klang
October 14 Memorial
Rajdamnoen
Democracy Monument
RimKhobFah Bookstore
Baan Dinso

Wat Mapangpharan
Samran Rat
Arawy
New Bangkok
Administration City Hall
Wat Thep Thidaram

Ministry of Justice
Th. Bunsiri
Boonsiri
San Chao Pho Suea
Th. Mahannop
Tr. Chong Tong
Mahanop
Trok Nawa
Lak Meuang
Stone Pillar Shrine
Office of The Attorney Gen.
Th. Na Hap Phoel
Thanon Lak Luang
Th. Phraeng Nara
Th. Phraeng
The Thai Military Bank
Red Cross Health Center
Phuton
Sao Ching Cha Junction
Bangkok Bank
Sao Ching Cha (Giant Swing)
Si Kak Sao Ching Cha Junction
Dev Mar Temple

Th. Bamrung Muang

Ministry of Defence
Wat Phra Kaew (The Emerald Buddha)
Wat Phra Kaew Museum
Coine & Royal Decorations Museums
Royal Palace

PHRA BOROM MAHA RATCHAWANG

Royal Thai Survey Department
Ministry of Foreign Affairs
Thanon Saran Rom
Information Department
Saranrom Royal Garden
Wong Wian Ro Do Junction
Ministry of Interior
Labour Dept.
Wat Ratchapradit
Wat Rat Pradit
Board of Trade & Thai C of C
Johnny's Gems
Ko Phanit
Corrections Museum
Chalermkrung Royal Theatre
Old Siam Plaza

BAN CHANG LO

MILITARY ZONE
Naval Dockyard Department
The Royal Fleet Naval Suply Department
Naval Hospital
Naval Supply Department
Royal Navy Club
Ratchaworadit Pier
Ministry of Finance
National Council of Women
Public Warehouse Organization
Internal Trade Department
Rub Aroon
Bangkok Bank
Thien Pier
Tha Thian Market
Wat Arum Market
Wat Tangtrongchit
Wat Pho
Thanon Chetuphon
Wat Phra Chetuphon
Territory Defence Department
King Vajiravudh Museum
Siam City Bank
Hifi Market
Lang Krasuang
Th. Phra Phithak

WAT ARUN

Wat Yai
Bangkok Ratchadamnoen
Soi Thavon
Khlong Wat Chaeng
Wat Chinorot
Thawithaphisek School
Wat Nak Klang School
Wat Nak Klang
S. Wat Nak Klang
Saeng Duen
Thawithaphisek Primary School
Wat Arun Ratchawararam (Temple of Dawn)
Phanitchayakarn Thaphachak
Phop Suk Building
Naval Science Department
Soi Itsaraphap 29/1
Vichaiprasit
Royal Thai Navy
Wat Pho Thai Traditional Medical & Massage
Aurum The River Place
Chakrabongse Villas
Baan Pranee
Pak Khlong Talad Juction
Museum of Siam
Coconut Palm
Ministry of Culture
Wat Ratchabophit School
Land Operation Department
Saowapha School
Pho Chang Campus
Pak Kiong Market
Sri Gurusingh Sabha
Sri India
Wat Rat Burana Sch.
Royal India
Bophit Phimuk Campus
Siam City Bank
Wat Rat Burana
Electricity Authority
Chakkaphet

Thanon Arun Amarin
Thanon Somdet Phra Pin Klao
Thanon Charan Sanit Wong
Thanon Wang Doem
Thanon Itsaraphap
Thanon Phran Nok
Thanon Na Phra Lan
Thanon Mahat Thai
Thanon Na Phra That
Thanon Sanam Chai
Thanon Maharaj
Thanon Charoen Krung
Thanon Chakkraphet
Thanon Chakkaphet
Chao Phraya River

to Angthong

Bangkok Handicraft
Gems Mark
Chat Songkhro School
Baan Ratchawithi
Social Welfare Council
Silpacheep
Prasat Neurological Hospital
Phayathai Baby Aid Home
Baan Phaya Thai
Neurosis Research Found.
National Cancer Institute
Rama Thibodi Hospital

Metropolitan Waterworks Authority Water Unit
Soi Bun Chuai
Soi Ari Samphan 5
Soi Ari Samphan 4
Soi Ari Samphan 2
Abloom Exclusive Serviced Apartments
Yakult Building
Leucha Exclusive Place
SANAM PAO
Peak Tower
Phahon Yothin 2

Asoke-Rachadapisek Expressway
Khlong Samsen
Foundation for the Blind in Thailand Under the Royal Patronage of H.M. the Queen
Tuek Chai Junction
Anusawari Tower
Royal Thai Army Nursing College
Phra Mongkut Klao Hospital
The Thai Military Bank
Medical Military Department
Research Institute of Medical Science
Xavier Church

Varasupha Executive
Police Welfare Building
Samam Pao Junction
SM Tower
Phayathai II Hospital
Watthanasin School
SLK
Phahon Yothin
Bank of Asia

Royal Thai Horse Club
Social Secu Office Are
Saeng Thawi Flat
Wiphawadi Condominium Building
Ratsami Kindergarten
Pien Sun Kindergarten
Bangkok Housing
Saha Buddha Dhammic
Dek Di Ci Kindergarten
Ministry of Social Development and HumanSecurity
Puttraipidok

Blindness School
Maintenance Division
The Government Pharmaceutical Organization
War Veterans Welfare Organization
Child and Adolescent Mental Health Rajanagarindera Institute

Wat Aphaithayaram
Phatom Wai Kindergarten
Anusawari Chai
Ratsami International School
Thai-German Blind Cassette Library
Charoen Chai Building
The Thai Military Bank
Isuzu
Ministry of Labour
Muha Yiren Stil

THUNG PHAYATHAI

Thanon Rat Withi
Thanon Yothi
Science Service Department
The Thai Industrial Standards Institute
Ministry of Industry and Entrepreneur
Department of Mineral Resource
Ministry of Energy
Buddhist Monk's Hospital
11st Military Command Battalion
Department of Mineral Resources

Faculty of Tropical Disease
Queen Sirikit National Istitute of Child
Institute of Dermatology
Medical Army Department
Ratchawithi Hospital
Siam City Bank
Anusawari Chai Samoraphum (Victory Monument)
Robinson
SCB
Public Library

Thanon Rat Withi
Caltex
Dusit
Five Star Flats 2
The Government Savings Bank

Thanon Din Daeng
OP Tower
S Siam Town
OT House
OK

VICTORY MONUMENT
Faculty of Dentistry, Mahidol University
Yothi Electricity Substation
Provost Marshal General's Department
Borom Rat Chonnani Nursing College

Siam International
Nissan
Centry Theatre
Phya Thai
Phyathai Plaza + Revenue Office Area 4
Payatai Thai Plaza

Bangkok Bank
Century Park
Wat Tasanarun
Prathum Court

Faculty of Pharmacy, Mahidol University
Uni Affairs Ministry
Newton
T Building
Ratchathewi District Office
Baptist Center
Dental Center
Santi Rat Witthayalai
Santirat Education Auditorium
Intellectual Property Court

PHAYATHAI
PHAYATHAI SARL
Honda
Thanon Sri Ayutthaya
KTB
Makkasan Market
President
Interchange Tower
Piriyaphan House
Makkasan

Thanon Phetchburi
RATCHATHEWI
Ratchathewi Junction
Hollywood
Phirom Street
Phesat Hospital
Mackenna Theatre
Vanesia Residence

RATCHATHEWI
Dusit Tewee
Phitthaya
Metro Ruamprasong Theatre
Court Point
Residence Indonesia
Para Theatre

RATCHAPRAROB
Makkasan Railway Station
Makkasan Railway Yard & Workshop
MAKKA

Eastin Hotel & Spa Bangkok
Industrial Estate Authority of Thailand
Empress
Ramada D'MA
Bangkok Palace
Kasikorn Bank
The Ecotel

THANON PHETCHABURI
Jim Thompson's House
Sawan Phanit
74 Mansion
M.P. Villa
Bed & Breakfast Inn

Khlong Saen Saep
Hua Chang Pier
Bangkok Business Accounting College
Siam Inter-Continental
Bangkok Metropolitan Authority Sewerage

Thanon New Phetchburi
Kai Siew
Terng Bangkok
Withayu Complex
Daina Golf
Witthayu Court
MSD Court

PATHUM WAN
Sa Pathum Palace
Wat Pathum Wanaram School
Wat Pathum Wanaram

Isetan
Big C
Centara Grand
Central World Plaza
Chidlom
The Promenade
S Medical Spa

LUMPHINI
Bank of America
Wisanee Mansion
Caroline Court

NATIONAL STADIUM
Sport News Reporter Association
NATIONAL STADIUM
Muangphot Building

Th Rama 1
Pathumwan Junction
Lido
Scala
Tokyu
SIAM SQUARE
Siam Discovery
Siam Center
Siam Paragon
Chaloem Phao Junction
Ratchaprasong Junction
Gaysorn Plaza
Zen
Intercontinental
Golden House
Amarin Plaza

Th Ploenchit
Erawan Shrine
CHIT LOM
Maneeya Center
Suomi (Finland)
BAY (H.O)
PLOEN CHIT

Physical Education of Sri Nakharinthorawirot University
MEA
Wan Kaew
Petrochemical
Suan Luang School
Centre of Academic Resources

MBK Center
Hard Rock Cafe
British Council

Soi Siam Square
Narcotics Suppress
Scientific Division
Office of Royal Thai Police
Medical Juris Institute
Police General Hospital
Police Nursing School
Central Investigation Bureau

The Government Savings Bank
Amarin Tower
Royal Ratchadamri
Mahatlek Luang
Peninsula Plaza
Regent Royal

Northwest Airlines
Turkey
Israel

Diethelm Tower A
Chom Tower
Nguan Sri
to Suvarnabhum

(Map page — street atlas of Bangkok, Lumphini/Din Daeng/Huai Khwang/Khlong Tan Nuea area)

Major districts and labels include: DIN DAENG, HUAI KHWANG, MAKKASAN, KHLONG TAN NUEA, Thailand Cultural Center, Thanon Asoke-Din Daeng, Thanon Rama IX, Asoke-Rachadapisek Expressway, Thanon New Phetchaburi, Thanon Asok Montri, Soi Sukhumvit, Carrefour, Robinson, Jusco.

Area & District Labels

POM PRAP

CHAKKRAWAT

SAMPHAN THAWONG

SOMDET CHAO PHRAYA

TALAT NOI

HIRANRUCHI

KHLONG TON SAI

KHLONG SAN

BANG RAK

YAN NAWA

BANG LAMPHU LANG

SAPHAN TAKSIN

Selected Labels

Museum of Siam
Ministry of Culture
Wat Ratchabophit School
Song Serm Keset
Sri Gurusingh Sabha
Wat Chai Chana Songkhram
Royal Wat Mangkon Kamalawat
Phlapphla Chai Police Station
Th. Wang Chao Sai
Sai Panya School

Aurum The River Place
Baan Pranee
Chakra-bongse Villas
Pho Chang Campus
Thapthin Shrine
Royal India
Chao Mae Thaptim
Grand China Princess
Cathay D.S.
Mitphan
Wongwien 22 July

Pak Khlong Talad Juction
Pak Klong Market
Coffee Shop
Siam City Bank
KTB
GSB
Siam Commercial Bank

Rachanee Pier

Wat Kanlayamit Pier

The Marketing Organization
Pak Khlong Market (Flower Market)
Phra Buddha Yodfa Monument
Phra Buddha Yodfa Bridge

Santa Cruz Kindergarten
Santa Cruz Convent
Kudi Chin School
Santa Cruz Kindergarten

Wat Prayoon
Wat Bupparam

Khaek Market
Somdet Chao Phraya Market

PRINCESS MOTHER MEMORIAL GARDEN
Bamrong Vicha

Chao Phraya River

Chao Phraya River Park
Bangkok Riverside

Taksin Hospital

Thanon Arun Amarin Tad Mai
Thanon Itsaraphap
Thanon Prachathipok
Thanon Somdet Chao Phraya
Thanon Lat Ya
Thanon Charoen Rat
Thanon Krung Thonburi
Thanon Charoen Nakhon
Thanon Krung Thonburi
Thanon Charoen Krung

King Taksin Monument
Merry King Dept. Store
Charoen Rat Market
Robinson
Thai Rama Theatre
Wongwian Yai Market

Wongwian Yai

Wat Thong Pleng School
Wat Thong Phleng

Siam City Bank
UOB Radanasin Bank
Sinn Sathorn
Bank of Ayudhya
Krungthonburi Mansion
SK Building
SPD

Tesco Lotus Express
CM Tower
Topaz

The Peninsula Bangkok
Marriott Resort and Spa
The River Condominium
Shangri-La

Bangkok Dockyard Co. Ltd
Bangkok Fish Market
Fish Marketing Organization
Forest Industrial Organization

Wat Sutthiwararam School
The Civil Court of Southern Bangkok
Fishery Technologycal Development

Tha Saphan Taksin
Wat Yan Nawa

Soi Charoen Nakhon
Chao Phraya River

15,000 0.2km 0 0.1mile

to Angthong, Thammsat

WANG MAI

Sombun Thai · Yontrakit · Fujian Assn · Kwang Thai · MEA · Wan Kaew · Petrochemical · Suan Luang School · Model Pharmacy · Pathumwan Princess

Sitabut Bamrung Sch. · Th. Charat Muang · Thanon Banthat Thong · Soi 14 · Soi Chula 12 · Soi Chula 64 · Canteen · Department of Pharmaceutical Science · Faculty of Dentistry · Faculty of Veterinary Science · Medical Juris Institute · Grand Hyatt Erawan · Amarin Tower · Suomi (Finland) · Royal Ratchadamri

Esso · KTB · Soi 16 · Soi 18 · Pathum Wan Youth · Soi Chula 62 · Rajamangala Institute of Technology, Uthen Thawai Campus · Police General Hospital · Police Nursing College · Northwest Airlines · Peninsula Plaza · Regent Royal 1 · Mitkorn · Msn · Mahatlek Luang 1

Soi 1 · Soi Chulalongkorn 1 · Lecturer's Dorm · PHC 5 · Department of Industrial Design · Triam Udom Sueksa School · Sri Nakharin Wirot Pathumwan University · Japanese Language School · Four Seasons · Regent Royal 2 · Turkey · Mana · Courtyard · Park Lane · Baan Siri

Th. Charoen Muang · Suan Luang Market · Soi 20 · Dharma Center · Chulalongkorn Property Office · Chemical Building 3 · Baromratchakumaree · RAT DAMRI · Metro · S.Mahatlek Luang 2 · Grand Regent · Toyota

Siam City Bank · Prasert Tham Sch. · Soi Chula 22 · Soi 24 · Chula Uniresearch · Sathit Chula Elementary School · Faculty of Architecture · Faculty of Chemical Building 1 · Faculty of Fine & Applied Arts · ROYAL TURF CLUB · Baan Somtawin · S.Mahatlek Luang 3 · Thai Obayashi · Regent Royal 2 · Som 658 · SG 1&2

Thai Pu Assn · Soi 26 · Soi 28 · Sathit Chula Secondary School · Grad School · CHULALONGKORN UNIVERSITY · Faculty of Arts · Royal Bangkok Sports Club (R.B.S.C) · USA Residence · Mayfair Marriott · Samburt

TMB · Buan Hong Thai · Soi 30 · Soi 32 · Taptim · Pathum Wan District Office · Sathit Chulalongkorn Primary School · National Science Museum · Faculty of Nursing · Royal Sports Club Golf Field · A.U.A · Peng Seng · Ambassador Court

TFB · Soi Sawatdi · Central Labour Court · Phatum Wan Police Station · Soi 34 · Sathit Chula Elementary School · Faculty of Science · Memorial Center · Canteen · Faculty of Science · HIV-NAT · Metropolitan Waterworks Area 7 · Cambodia · Regent House 1&2 · Malaysia · Sahabnat · Intira · Lumpini 2

Revenue Office Area 12 · Soi 36 · Employ Service 3 · Phatum Wan School · Soi 38 · Soi 40 · Banthat Thong Fire Station · Physical Technology Museum · Faculty of Education · Chulachakrabongse · Faculty of Engineering · The Siam Commercial Bank · Bangkok Cable · UHM · The Park Place · Probike · Intacon · AS Corp · South Africa · Travex

PATHUMWAN

Thanon Phayathai · Thanon Henri Dunant · Thanon Ratchadamri · Thanon Sarasin · Lumpini 11 · South Africa, Colombia · Playground

MAHA PHRUETTHARAM

Soi Sunthonphimol · Spn Loeng · Christ Tam School · Soi Chula 42 · 7th-Day Adv · Faculty of Commercial & Accountancy · Faculty of Science · Sala Phra Keo · Language Institutions · Faculty of Economy · Faculty of Political Science · Wat Hua Lomphong School · LUMPHINI PARK · LUMPHINI

Tien Sung Church · Pramuan · Soi Rat Uthit · Thai Room Charoen · Thanon Rama IV · Soi Sawang · Soi Phraya Nakharet · SCB · KTB · Siam City Bank · Pratipok · Rumphaiphanee · The Thai Red Cross Society · Kasem Uthayanin · Wisit Prachuabmoh · Political Science Alumni · Tourist Police

Wat Kaeo Jam School · Siphraya Tower · TCI Chula · PS House · Trok Khun Nawa · Chinese Church · S. Chinda Thawin · Sam Yan Junction · Red Cross (CIG) · Soi Chula 60 · CU Hi-Tech Square · Chulalongkorn Hospital · Rama VI Statue (King Mongkutklao) · Olympia Thai Building

SI PHRAYA

Thanon Si Phraya · BBL · Buntanaphan Charatsaeng · Baan Sap Surawong · Soi 58 · Phavarolan · Soi Twilight · Charn Issara Tower · Pan Pacific · Robinson · Udom Vidhya Center · Holiday Inn Silom Plaza

New Saeng · Bang Rak District · Singer Park · Slip Tawee · Samtiphap 1 · Sathit Flat · Surawong House · FuramaXclusive · Thai Jirapat · Putthachak · Rose · Montien · Duke's · Sauna British · Rama 1 Land · Charn Issara II · SILOM · Sala Daeng Junction

SURIYA WONG

Thanon Surawong · Royal Plaza · Baan Tippawan · Metro Russia · Scoozi · Jim Thompson Factory Outlet · Montien Plaza · Panja · Wall Street · Airways · GOD · DJ Station · Fezuelig · Dusit Thani · Thai Life Insurance · SALA DAENG · Silom Complex · Holiday Inn Silom Plaza

SILOM

Thanon Si Lom · Thanon Surawong · Silpa Bharata Mandir · Mahanalamman Temple · Tower Inn · Unico · Korean Air · Silom Thai Cooking School · Sawang Watthana · KCC · Niagara · Satorn Inn · CP Tower · Silom Serene · Silom City · Silom Plaza · Saladaeng

CHONG NONSI

Thanon Narathiwat Ratchanakharin · Thanon Sathon Nua · Thanon Sathon Tai · Sathorn City Tower · Bangkok Sathorn Tower · ABN-AMRO · Empire Tower · Oriental Villa · Luxury · M.R. Kukrit Pramoj House · Suan Phlu Market · Bang Phongphang · Bangkok Immigration Office

THUNG MAHA MEK

Soi Suan Phlu · Thungmahamek · School of Deaf · Mahamek Home · Thanon Nang Linchi · Thung Mahamek Telephone Exchange · Metropolitan Waterworks, Thung Maha Mek · Aeronautical Radio of Thailand · PTT

SURASAK

Thanon Si Wiang · Thai Wivat Sweet Basil · Sathorn House · Pimarn Mansion · Th. Sathorn Nua · Bank of Asia · Robot Building · Amorn Thani · City Viva · Yellow Ribbon Hills Mansion · Charoon

Revenue Office Area 17 · Satorn Ville · King Star · Thai-Chinese the Chamber of Commerce · Fixture Maker · Assumption College Primary Sch. · Sathorn Grace · Sathorn Suite · JC Kevin Tower · Rajamangala Institute of Technology Bophit Phimuk Campus

THUNG WAT DON

Phayathai-Bangkhlo Expressway · Wat Witsanu · Wat Prok Yan Nawa · Soi Prancak Sin · Chaozhou Association · Be Lucky · Soi Wat Prok 1 · SCB · Merlin Tower · Lumpini Place · Rajanagarindra 14 · Makro · Boonchew

SATHON

to Bang Phong Phang · to Suvarnabhumi Airport

CHIT LOM

Th. Ploenchit · to Sala Thammasop

PLOEN CHIT

KHLONG TAN NUEA

LUMPHINI

Thanon Witthayu (Wireless Rd)

Th. Ratchadamri

NANA

ASOKE

SUKHUMVIT

Grand Hyatt · Erawan · Panunee · Maneeya Center · One Bangkok · Bank of Ploenchit Tower · Ton Son 2 · Grande Center Point · Casel Leather · Regent Inn · Cango · Cargo Court · La Residenz · Regent Garden · UOB Radanasin Bank · B.B. Bec

Amarin Tower · Suomi (Finland) · Meter Dei School · Ploenchit Tower · Sanguang · Bangkok Air (HQ) · Ruam Ros · KTB Plc (HQ) · Grand · Fortuna Inn · Bright City · Ambass · GP Inn

Amrin Plaza · Unico House · Chanin Court · Bliston Suan Park View H · Diethelm Holding · Q House · LPN · JW · Crystal · Poland · Sukhumvit Suites · Citadines · Villa Bajaj · Bank of Ayudhya

Peninsula Plaza · Regency One · Serge · Na Warang · Inter Design · Embassy Place · Imperial · Chom's Boutique · Nguan Sri · Ton Hom · SCB · Comedia · Vikrom's · Calypso President

LUMPHINI

Four Seasons · Park Lane · Garden View · Ratchadamri Baan · Leng Suan · Langsuan · Langsuan Soi 2 Industrial Construction Association of Thailand · Millenium Complex · Jim's Lodge · Bali

Regent · Langsuan 1 · 208 Wireless · Fraser Place · Urbana langsuan · Center Point · Bank of Asia · Gaysorn House · Conrad Bangkok · Vietnam · Virasu · Noble House · Sitthikit Mansion · Golden Palace · Nana Park · President Park · Manhattan · Comfort Inn

Natural · Lang Suan Soi 7 · Shark Fin · The Netherlands · Ukraine · New Zealand · Egypt · Amari · White Inn · Royal Dream

Sumatwin x Suan 658 · Bahai · SG 1&2 · Totah · Mitra Mansion · Ruamrudee 3 · Soi Ruam Rudi · Chateau de Bangkok · Lyon · La Mansion · Stable · Golden Plaza · SCB · Robinson

S.Mahatlek Luang 2 · Langsuan Soi 2 Center Point · Gibbins House · Jim's Lodge · Witha Center · Pattaya · Darling Square · Sheraton · Orchid Tower

Malaysia · Lumpini 2 · Langsuan Balcony · Kian Gwan + Pathumwan Revenue Office · Phanpong Mansion · Ruam Rudy House · Soi 5 · Phra Maha Thai Sueksa School · Chamberlains · Rama Mansion · Terrace Court

Regent House 1&2 · AS CorpLand · Yoe Long Kian Gwan House (European Union) · Nguan Lee · Benz · Soi Ruam Rudi · Thaire · Phra Maha Thai Cathedral · Ruam Rudi 5 · Carvary Church · Nana Tai Mansion · VNA · Chit Damrong

South Africa, Colombia · Thanon Sarasin · Sarasin Junction · Lum Phini Youth Center · Kai Thort Jay Kee · Indonesia Mosque · Prevent and Suppress Mob Control Division · Greece · Soi Sama Han · Pacific Heights · Citadines · Romania · Center Point

Playground · Lumphini School · Friends for All · Soi Polo · Polo Park · Soi Polo · Polo Residence · Baan Ardchasai · Cavalry Police Station · BENJAKITI PARK · Asia House · Rembrandt · Fairview 40

LUMPHINI PARK

Boat Rental · Chinese Pavilion · Lum Phini Police Station · Travex · Soi Phra Chen · Polo · Polo Club · Thailand Tobacco Monopoly · Lake Ratchada · Lake View · TU Court

to Sala Thammasop · Center Point · Olympia Thai Building · U Chu Liang · Royal Bangkok Sports Club · Japanese · Bangkok Vocational School · Police Flats · Division of General Administration Tobacco Monopoly · Central Mansion · Ocean Tower 1

Silom Plaza · U Chu Liang HSBC · Subway · Arch & Turnkey · Suam Lum Night Bazar · Chinese Style Clock Tower · Bangkok Metropolitan Authority Apprentice · BEC Tero Entertainment Hall · Bon Kai Flats · Kon-Im · Youth Center · MEA

LUMPHINI · Witthayu Junction · ETO Rama IV Delivery Office · PHC 16 · Bon Kai Flats · PWT Mansion · Ma Du Zi

Namphon · SLD · Silpa Thai · Suwan Tower · Cathay Trust · Guan Thai Sri Nakorn · Ireland · Thai Nakorn · Lumphini Park View · Soi Pluk Chit 1 · Bon Kai Fire Station · Suni Phitthaya Kindergarten · National Convention Center · Queen Sirikit National Convention Center

IFD Building · Mitsubishi · BKI · Jusmag Thai · Germany · Goethe Institute · Chevrolet · UB · Sunee Phitthaya · Bon Kai Flats · Samphandam Plaza · Stock Exchange of Thailand · Monterey Place

KTT · Jira Court Sukhothai · Thai Wah Bangkok Tower · Q House · YWCA · Indian-Thai Chamber of Commerce · Chanphen · The Siam Commercial Bank · Bon Kai Market · Bangkok Bank · Chao Por Sue Shrine · Krung Thai Bank · Ngam Sinsuk

Banyan Tree · Thien Prasit · Soi Goethe · Salathai · Tipamas Suites · Pinnacle Lumpini · Thai Mui · Wong Chong Sawad · Brazil · M-Bit · Lumpini Place · In For Group · Royal Lap · Metropolitan Electricity Authority · Charoensing

YMCA Collins · Satorn Garden · Sukhothai · Sujittree · Maimon · Natural Place · D. Computer · Thai Hua · Hong Sun · View Import & Export · Nissan · Thep Phrathan · Klong Toey Witthaya School · Cantra

YMCA Club · ABC · Austria · Phitak Malaysia Association · Penguin House · Ruam Chit Church · Comforta · Institut of Theology · Rama Theatre · KLONG TOEI · Thai Rugby Football Club

Aquarius House · Baptist Suksa · Siam Penthouse 2 Condominium · Palm Mera · Slovak · Baan Suan Sathorn · Thantana · GH · Soi Yim Yim 2 · Soi Prasit Suk · Lumpini Place · Ching Nam Chai · KLONG TOEI · Rama III · Thai Farmers Bank · Government Savings Bank · Thanon Rama IV

THUNG MAHA MEK

Bang Phongphang · Thung Maha Mek · Bangkok Immigration Office · Suan Plu · Naval Housing · DOA · Thammasat Association · Navy Welfare Flats · Pracha Korn · Sala Thai · Paradise Place · Sinloha Mui · Charoen Porn · Khlong Toei Post Office · Klong Toey Market · Hope of Bangkok Church · Singapore · Phra Haruethai Convent · Mang Kon Khieo

Prasat Court · Thammasat U. Dorm · Musical Division, Royal Air Force · Baan Si Thit · Sino Siamese · TTS · Silom Sauna · Khow Hah Huat · Pinang Market · Siam City Bank · Telephone Exchange · Bangkok Bank

Earn La-o Vocational College · Department of Civil Aviation · Garden International British Education in Thailand · Ngam Tawee · Suttiphan Chem · Baan Sirisathorn · Radio 88.5 & 93 · Sirikun · Pracha · Siang · Loxley · Port Authority of Thailand · Nurses Association

Thung Mahamek Telephone Exchange · Aerothai · France Cultural · Supreme Villa · Sukkamol Ratchada · Yen Akat Badminton · Rung Ruang · Nonsee Residence · Nobel House · Royal Nawin · Cherdvattanayont · TNT · Navy Flats · Metal Prods I

Metropolitan Waterworks, Thung Maha Mek · Aeronautical Radio of Thailand · PTT · Educare 2 · Kim Heng Cheng · Soi Sai Phanya · Seatran · River View Residence · Metal Prods II

The Communication Battalion 1 · Boonchew · Thong Thai Co · Thung Maha Mek Fire Station · Sri Wikorn · KC Auto · Supreme Place · New Charoen Pharmaceutical · Iceland · Wise Technology · Hang Ki Paper · Rama Foods · Thai Heng Lee · PAT Intransit Section

CHONG NONSI

Soi Ton Son · Body Fit · Lee Thai Mui · Lapha Place · Charoensin · Microtech · Nonsi Primary School · Sunny Valves · Palm Pavilion · Asia Warehouse · Post Publishing · Buay Kee · Bangkok Charoenmit

Chatern Mahanakhon Expressway · Thanon Rama IV · Thanon Ratchadaphisek · Port - Dao Kanong Expressway · Port - Bangna E/way

MYANMAR (BURMA)

MYANMAR (BURMA)

AROUND NAKHON SAWA

KAMPHAE PHET

UTHAI THAN

KANCHANABU

RATCH

KANCHANABURI PROVINCE 26

Tawku
Kada
Tawku
Hlwazingon
Naungtakho
Painggaladon
Kawsaing
Mawkhi
Khlong Lan National Park
Khlong Kha Yaeng
Thung Khuang
Khlong Khlung

Kale
Tagundaing
Tulitkon
Wettakhon
Maung E
Khao Kha Khaeng 2195m
Pang Ta Wai
Khok Lo
Khanwur Buri
Banph

Yindaung
Paungsein
Kya-in
728m
Mulayit Taung 2080m
Nong Fa
Nuay Nam Yen
Ban Daen
Bo Tham

Thanbyuzayat
Taungbauk
Meteke
Kwi-nya-a
Mae Klong Mai
Ban Lu Pu
Taling Sung
Wang San
Bang Pin Nam
Dong F

World War II Cemetery
Kyongawon
Ban Kang
Ban Palatha
AROUND NAKHON SAWA
Lat Yao
Nong

Sakangyi
Winyaw
Karesaw
Thebyu
Thung Yai Narasuan Preservation Centre
Dong Phlong
Don P

Wekame
Karesaw
Thi Ta Ro
Sawang Arom

751m
Padeik
Taungzun
Karesaw
Kariang Piya Cho
Huay Kha Khaeng Wildlife Preservation Centre
Dong Noi
Thap Salao
Thap Than

Hnitkarin
Mezali
Kyunchaung
Dong Noi
Uthai Tha

Ywathit
Lamaing
Phadaw
Phu Jue
Khao Yai 1554m
Lan Sak

Taungbon
Kyondaw
Phadaw
Sa Dai Tha
UTHAI THAN

Thingangyun
Sonmatha
3 Pagodas
1810m
Khao Lae 1495m
Khok Khwai
Ban Klang
Ban Chum

Ye
Yethanok
Phra Chedi Sam Ong
Sam Ong
Ban Thimonghta
Khao Yai 1739m
Ban Mahaeng
Pang Rai
Ban Rai

Sidaw
Manaung
Sadaik Taung 1173m
Sang Khla Buri
Sangkhlaburi
Pom Pi Nai
Khao Yai 1739m

Yinye
Khawsa
955m
Pha Phung
Thi Kai
Ban Klang

Paukpinkwin
Natkyizin
Lawthaing
64
Chalae
Ung Lu
Wang Hin Ngon
Sa Ri
Wang Kum

Myinzaung
Debyu 1290m
Le The
Khao Kala 1010m
Krasieo Reservoir
Dan Chang
Wang

Kyakhattaw
Kao Dange 1290m
Thong Pha Phum
Mae Phlu Klang
Phu Toei

Kalawni
Eindayaza
Khao Dang 1209m
Pilok
Bung Kriangkawia & Nong Namsap
Phu Toei
Khao Huat 1177m
Ban Klang
Lao Khwan

Onbingwin
Kanbauk
Kyaukshat
Plang Kasi
Kui Mang
Si Nakharin Dam
Ban Klang
Khao Chong Insi 621m
Nong Pra

Kaungma Ywa
Zadi
Pachaung
Phu Nam Ron
Si Sawat
Nong Pru
Talung

Tokkya Chaung
Nankye
1375m
Klaeng Cho
340
Tham Than Lod National Park
Lam Hoei
U Thong

1173m
Nabule
Pagawyun
Sai Yok
140
Nong Bon
Erawan National Park
Khao Mae Chae 634m

Taungminbyaung
Pagawyun
Nyaungdon
Tha Thong Mon
Bo Phloi
Tha Khamu
Ban Song

Maungmagan
Taungthonion
Myitta
Taungyhonlon
Sathani Nam Tok
Tha Manao
Thung Masang
Song Phi N
324
321

Pyingyi
Dawei (Tavoy)
Sinbyudaing
Nong Pla Lai
Lat Yot
Phanom Thuan
Talat Den Kham
50

14°
KANCHANABURI PROVINCE 26
River Kwai Bridge
Kanchanaburi
346
Kamph

Shanmaw
Peinnedaw
Taungzin
Paki Taung 1564m
Baungdaw
Chaungwa
323
Tha Rua
Tha Makat
56

Pawut
1564m
Banchaung
Myat Taung 1033m
Amya
Thung Ri
Nong Pru
Ban Pong
Na Pa

Chaungwabyin
Pyinbyugyi
Mawpabu Taung 1204m
Yebu Taung 1273m
Long Khe
Photharam
4
Bang

Zalut
Kanetthiri
Thung Krathin
Phanom

Kadwe
Munsali Taung 1163m
Suan Phung
Bo
Thung Faek
Ratchaburi
325

8
Pe
Tikawka Taung 1063m
Khao Yai 1005m
Bang Khon Thi
Son

Kyaukse
Myinmoletkat Taung 2073m
Wat Phleng
Amphawa

Aw
Minmalaw Taung 1179m
Pak Tho
24

Launglon Bok Is.
Tavoy Point
Ainshebyin
Zinchaung
Palauk
Nabalutko Kyo Taung 989m
Phu Rakam
Khlong Chong
Luang P

Mali I. (Tavoy I.)
98°

400,000
0   20km
0   10mile

Wat Pho
Pra-thap Chang
Taphan Hin
Na Rang
Tale
Nam Om
Khao Rang
1078m
Huai Na
Nam Ron
Phu Khie
Nong Bua Phak Kwian
Ban Phet
That Thong
Ban Chaeng
Nong Khan
Kaeng Khro
Sub Sombun
11
Sai Khlong Haeng
23
52 113
Chon Daen
21
Yang Lat
Nam Chan
Nan Kok
Na Nong Thum
Huai Noi
Na Fai
46
201
Huai Rai
Ban Samran
Sai Ngam
PHETCHABUN
21
Tha Daeng
Nong Pet
Pong Khlong Nua
CHAIYAPHUM
16°
Bang Mun Nak
Nng Phai
Khok Sung
Lam Kachuan
Chaiyaphum
U Thai Thong
umsaeng
68
225
Nong Bua
Nong Chaeng
Kan Chu
Ban Khwan
Tai Ton
61
Kaeng Sanam Nang
Tai
Chik Yao Tai
Prachan Khirikhet
133
Sub Samoh Tod
Na Yang Klak
Fao Rai
Hang Talat
202
n Sawan
Phaisali (Khok Dua)
Ban Khok Pu
Nam Ron
Chaturat
Non Phet
Dong Chang
Boeng Boraphet
11
Chalom Nae
Wichian Buri
Chong Samran
Nong Ya Khao Nak
Dot Tong Ton
61
Bamnet Narong
a Phluang
21
Phu Toei
225
Wa Tabaek
Pak Chap
201
Nong Lum Phuk
Non Thong lang
Nong Ya Khao
Khong
Ban Sema
NAKHON
SAWAN
Taa Than
Phu Khao Din
Si Thep
Si Thep Ruins
Khok Charoen
Ban Mai
96
Nong Bua Khok
Taluk Hin
Non Rawiang
Kham Sakae Saeng
ha Khiri
Huay Not
Kradon Yai
Na Khlong Sai
Hin Dat
205
57
anorom
Tak Fa
Nam Wing
Khok Samaesan
Khok Nong Khamoi
Dab Khun Thot
Non Thai
Wait Sing
1
11
Nong Si Ma
22
Chai Badan
Lam Narai
26
Ban Pang
Pong Kadon
201
Non Sung
Ta Khli
40
45
Khok Samrong
205
31
Si Khiu
Ban Sumthum
Nong Tho
Choho
Chaloem Phra Klat
i Nat
311
41
21
Ban Mi
1
Ban Saphan Nak
64
Nong Khon
45
Wat Phanom Wan
Nakhon Ratchasima
Buri
25
Ban Dilang
51
Phatthana Nikhom
Nong Bua
Lam Takong Reservoir
Nong Takhai
Pru Yai
Dan Kwian
Rachan
AROUND AYUTTHAYA 22
Samo Khon
2
Kaeng Hip
Mittraphap
Nong Kok Hoi
Saraphi
Rachan
Singburi
Phra Prang Sam Yod
NAKHON
RATCHASIMA
Yang Kathung
Tong Chai Nua
Suan Hom
Po Daeng
Chok Chai
Nong Hua Rat
32
Lopburi
30
1
Nong Takhian
103
Ban Pang Kae
Muaklek
Na Sok
Tha Chang
Nong Sano
Khon Buri
Sawaeng Ha
Phra Phuttabat
Khao Yai National Park
Bon Dan
Taling Chan
Si Prachan
Wat Viset Chi Chan
Phra Phuttabat (Buddha Footprint)
15
Kaeng Khoi
Khao Kaeo
4014m
110
Phak Kong Thang
Ang Thong
Khong Khanan
33
Tha Rua
Nang Rong Waterfall
Wang Nam Khiao
304
Sap Malua
anburi
Pa Mok
30
11
Nong Khae
Cha-am
Khlong Prado
Taling Chan
Pa Ma
Saraburi
22
Khao Yai
National Park
Bang Sai
Sena
Ancient Palace
Nong Khiam
Wang Takhrai
Khao Lamang
992m
Ayutthaya
Ou-Thai
AROUND BANGKOK 18-19
BuBak Kung
Bu Pram
340
Hua Khok
25
Ban Na
17
Wang Takhrai
Khao Yai National Park
95
Bang Sai
Lat Bua Luang
Bang Pa-in
Wang Noi
1
Si Yaak
15
Nakhon Nayok
Hua Khao
Wang Mut
Thung Faek
31
22
9
Sam Khok
58
Ongkharak
33
Pho Ngam
Nong Ki
Hat Makok
Ban Ma
14°
Pathum Thani
Thanya Buri
Bung Sanan
Prachinburi
Nong Hua Chang
54
Kabin Buri
304
Kut Nao
Pa Sak
33
31
1
305
Lam Luk Ka
Si Maha Phot
39
Nong Chok
46
Lam Chuat
Phai Cha
Si Mahosot
38
Pak Nam
Wan Takhian
Sa Kaew
Non Mak Kheng
Nonthaburi
9
Don Muang Airport
Min Buri
Nam Cha
Ban Thung
Ang Maha
Khao Hin Sop
359
Sra Khuan
Tha Kasem
33
Tailing Chan
BANGKOK
(Krung Thep)
304
Ko Chan
Tha Lan
Chachoengsao
Phanom Sarakham
Mai
Tha Muang
Sanam Chai Khet
Watthana Nakhon
Khao Chakan
Phra Pradaeng
Suvarnabhumi International Airport
Bang Phli
17
Tha Lat
17
Phnom
Phra Phloeng
317
Samut Prakan
Pom Phra Chunlachomkiao
Ban Pho
Talat Bang Bo
Thung Yai Chi
Nong Pru
3
Samut Sakhon
3
53
28
Thung Sadao
315
Phanat Nikhom
Trok Sakae
Wang Mai
SAMUT PRAKAN
3
7
18
23
Khok Pho
Wang Sonbun
Chonburi
Na Khuan
Khao Yai
777m
102°
Bight of Bangkok
Ban Bung
Noen Hin
Na Chik

*Bight of Bangkok
(Ao Krung Thep)*

Nakhon Pathom Town

scale 1 : 25,000

0   500m

to Suphanburi
321
S M Suan Takhrai 1
Soi Mu Suan Takhrai 2
Soi Mu Suan Takhrai 3
Sakhon Thanakom
Tawan Tok
Malaimaen
Concrete
Lom Choi
Restaurant
Malai Man Soi 4
Malai Man 5
Malai
Man 3
Malai Man 1
Thanon Sakomthanagone
Th. Suantakai
Thanon Rotfai Tawan Tok
Malai Man
Soi 2
Rotfai Tawan Tok
Thanon Nueqwang
Chan Royal
Palace
Wat Sena
Thanon Rotfai Tawan Tok
Thanon Nueqwang
Th. Banjerdjairad
Kampung
Temiang

Bakery Art
Malai
Man 3
Malai Man 1
Faculty of Engineering
and Technology
Industry
Faculty of
Science
SILPAKORN UNIVERSITY
SANAM CHAN CAMPUS
Sa-kaeo
Faculty of Art
Kasetsin
Sakae Thong
Boiled Rice
321
Mata Suki
Buffet
Au Ji
Potchana
On Aree
Coconut Jelly
Chom Thong
Korean Bar-B-Q
4
Songphol
Soi 2
to Ratchaburi
Lam Phaya
Chinta Suksa
Nakhon Pathom
School
Luxor
Lam
Phaya
Songphol Soi 7
Tai Sia Hod
Jow Shrine
Sanam
Chan
Songphol Soi 3
Th. Songphol
Rim Rua
Pharmaceutical
Community
Office
Telecommuni-
cation Center
Th. Ratchawithi
Th. Sanamchan
Chantharakham Phithak
Chantharakham 6
Chantharakham 5
Sanam Chan 4
Soi Suea Du
Tantawan
Red Cross Child
Development
Center
J & J
Supermarket
IDEO
Rebaming Art
Baan Thai
Ying Pao
Ying Pao 4
Sinlapakorn
University
Demonstration
School
Krungthai
Bank
Thanon Ratchawithi
Ratchawithi
Soi 15
Ratchawithi 6
Soi Ya Suk 1
Soi Ya Suk
Soi Ya Suk 3
Phetchakasem Soi 1
Rachada
Academic
Rose Inn
O'Neill Yo Bar &
Restaurant
Phra Pathom Golf Course
& Country Club
golf course
The Pizza
Nakhon
Pathom
Phaya Pan
Pra-Ngam
Temple
Th. Phayapan
Dusita
Th. Ratchadamri
Th. Ratchadamri
Khun Yai Fueang
Buiding Tutor
Chinese Church
Christ Catholic
Church
Serm Panya
Kindergarten
Th. Ratchadamnoe
Thewasathan
Thao Mahaprom
Nakhon Prathom
Sanam Chan
Kindergarten
Ban Dek
Whale
Soi Ya Suk 1
Soi Chawang Sak
Songkhram
Ratchawithi Soi 11
Soi Chum Sai Thorasap
Soi Araya
Ratchawithi
Soi 21
Nakhon
Inn
City Inn
Ratchawithi Soi 3
Suites Inn
Siriwan
Kindergarten
O'Neill Yo Bar
& Restaurant
Nakhon Pathom's
Market
Nakhon Pathom
Municipal Children
Development Center
Tha Prince
Th. Ratchawithi
Rachinee
Burana School
Youth Tutor
Nakhon Pathom
Ta Pae Shrine
Sanam Chan
Kin Duem
Nakhon
Pathom Tutor
Kiatnakin
Ton Silp
School
Nakhon Pathom
Train Station
3095
Thahan
Bok Soi 4
Th. Phya Kong
Th. Sai Pra
Th. Langra
Th.o.p Bhudharucksa
Th. Phaya Ngam
Th. Phra Pathom Ngam
Nakhon Pathom's
Market
Ban Mai
Noodle
Krungtep
KhrtianNakhon
Pathom Hospital
3095
Nakorn Pathom
Christian Hospital
Bamrung
Tham Church
Krung Thai
Thanon 25 Makara
Wat Phra
Pathom Chedi
Phra Pathom Chedi
National Museum
3036
Th. Thawin Phatthan
Phluang
Samli Soi 5
Thawirat Burana
Phluang
Samli Soi 1
Soi Chaowana Pricha
Wijitpanichakarn
Soi 5
Soi 3
Soi Sai
Mani
Good Health
Company
Limited
Wat Huai Chorakh
Children
Development Cente
25 Makkara
Soi 5/1
25 Ma-
kkara 3
Thanon Pipitprasat
Thephakon Hospital
Thanon Tesa
Phra Pathom Chedi
National Museum
Th. Kotgrich
Tesa Soi 9
Matum
Ban Kottakrit
Community Public
Health Center
Thanon Naphra
Thanon Wat Pho
Suthathip
Shopping
Center
Nakhon
Pathom Hope
of Church
Wat Phra Men
Ratchamakkha Nok
Na Phra
Thanon Tawarawadee
Nakhon
Prathom
Market
Huai
Cholakhe
Thanon Phaitoey
Soi Phaitoey 2
Soi Phaitoey 5
Soi
Phaitoey 4
Wat Philom
Mae To
Jang Sik
Good Health
Company
Limited
Wat Udonwitee
Soi Saunlamwit
Phra Pa
Wittayalai 1
Eazy Cente
Mo
Khomth
Da
Th. Phetkasem
4

Ratchaburi (Ratburi) Town

scale 1 : 25,000

0   500m

to Khao Ngu
3291
to Khao Ngu
3087
to
Th. Phetkasem
Chao Mae
Tubtim Shrine
Mae Klong
Bridge
Krua Four Flavors
4
Big C
Pan Restaurant
Raft
Lak Muang Sub
District Municipal
Children Development
Wat
Amarintharam
330
Ratchaburi Chao
Por Lak Muang
Shrine
Wat
Muang 1
Wat Sattanat
Pariwarat
Municipal 1 School
3291
Wat Chetiyaram
School
A.I. Technology
and Service
Co.,Ltd.
3087
Muangraj
Hospital
Phra Prang
Wat Mahathat
Municipal
4 School
Haiphong
Restaurants
Thanon Phetchakasem
San Khu
Wat Rong
Chang
Kaow Ngu 3
Kaow Ngu
Chedi Hak
Thanon Chedi Hak
Ratchaburi
Christian
Church
Chedi
Hak 3
Chao Din
Chao Din 2
Chao Din 1
Western
Grand
Sirichai 4
Sirichai 3
Sirichai 2
Sirichai 1
Sirichai
Wat Sri
Siriyawong
Krai Phet
Thanon Si Suriyawong
Soi Si Suriyawong 3
Soi Si Suriyawong 2
Chedi Hak
Ban Prok
Khaw Ngu 1
Wat Chong
Lom
Ratchaburi
National
Museum
Prachomkao
Ratchaburi
University
Thai Comm.
Banks
Woradet
Woradet
Woradet
Maenam Maekhlong
Thai Military
Bank
Sanam
Atom
Happhoei
Sattanart
Sattant
Police station of
Maung Ratchaburi
Suriyawong
School
Th. Kraipetch
Th. Ammarin
Surasn Soi
Lotus
Supermarket
Ratsadon Yindi 1
Royal Park
Ratsadon Yindi 2
Ratsadon
Yindi 3
Ratsadon
Yindi 4
Naree
Wittaya
School
Ratsadon
Yindi
Hang Song
Noodles
Electric Factory
Gymnasium
Montri
Suriyawong
Thano
A.I. Technology
Kaow Ngu
Siri Seafood
Restaurant
Prom Phatthana 1
Chao Din 4
Chao Din 3
Chao Din 2
Chao Din 1
Kim Heng
Restaurant
Somboon Kun 3
Municipal
2 School
Ratchaburi
Municipal Office
Robinsons
Children and
Mom Hospital
Ratchaburi
Technical College
Thanon Si Suriyawong
Suda
Weerapong
Condotel
Somboon Kun 2
Somboon Kun
Ratchaburi
Somboon Kun 4
Darunaratchaburi
School
Charoensuk
Apartment
Na Mueang
Pop Korean
Grilled Shrimp
Sai Fon Club Mate
The Augusta Pub
Tulip Inn
Sweet Home and Bakery
Prom Phatthana 3
Yutitham
Somboon Kun 2
Ratchaburi
Stadium
Ratchaburi
Hospital
Ruampaet
Hospital
Round Crushed
Restaurants
Wat Thung Tan
Phetkasem 3
Phetchakasem
Junction Restaurant
Sueapa
Sueapa 1
Sueapa 2
Sueapa 3
Sueapa 5
Ratchaburi
Law Court
Lang Saka Klang
City Hall
Amphoe
Udom Siri
Ratchaburi
Saifon
Maen Ramluk 1
Ratchaburi 1
Udomsiri
Maen Ramluk 2
Thao Uthong
Maen Ramluk 3
Ratchaburi
Railway Station
Wat Khao Wang
Ratchaburi
Muang Thai Life
Assurance Ratchaburi
Thanon Phetchakasem
4
to Ban Namphu
3208
Chedi Hak
Khao Wang
Phetkasem 7
Phet:
kasem 6
Don Kratai
Noodle Mae
Kfong
Bangkok Bank
Witsawa Senanikhom
Kam Koon Pork
Korea
Maen
Ramluk 4
Maen
Ramluk 5/1
Maen
Ramluk 6
Champion Chicken
& Rice 88
Maen Ramluk
Thao Uthong
Thanon Maen Ramluk
Thanon Somboon Kun
Thanon Khatha Thom
Mam Ba In
Koyrot Mosque
3339
to Phetchaburi
to Don Tako
to Ban Kubua

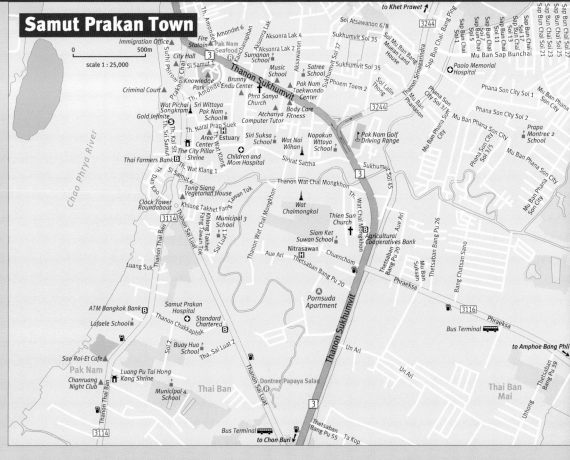

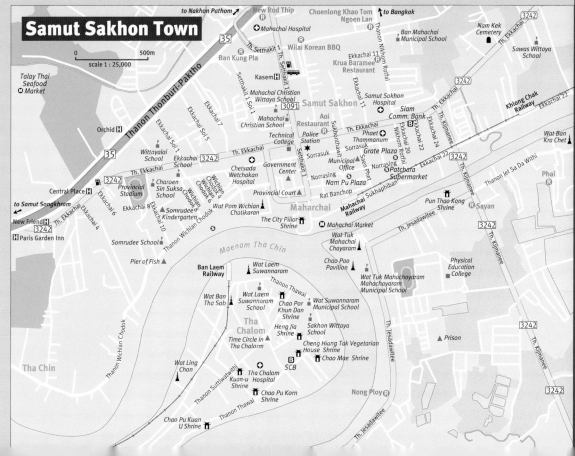

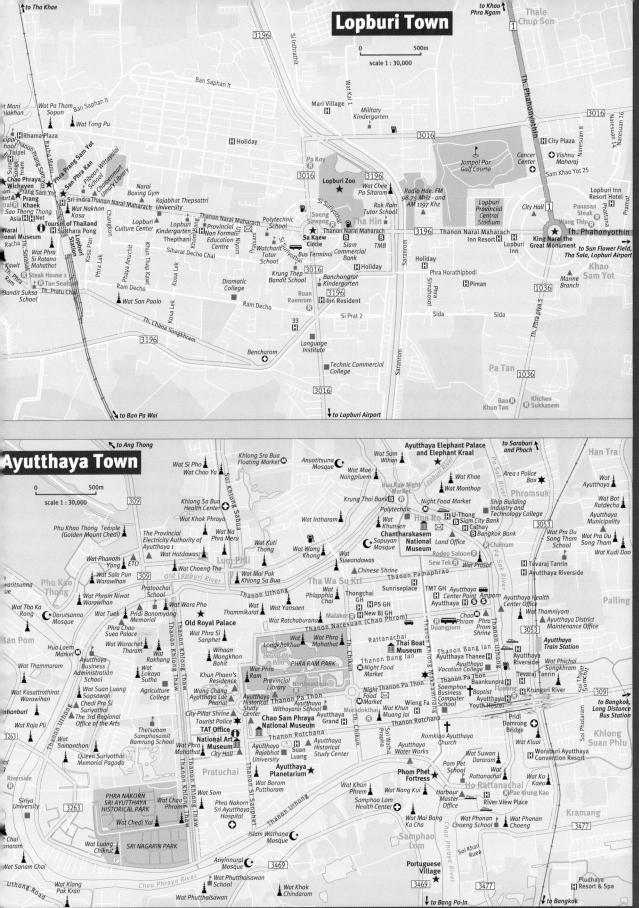

Lopburi Town

scale 1 : 30,000

0   500m

to Tha Khae

to Khao
Phra Ngam

Thale
Chup Son

3196

Si Inthrathit

Th. Phahonyothin

Ban Saphan It

3016

Wat Kai 1

Mari Village

Military
Kindergarten

City Plaza

3016
Naresuan 14

Wat Mani
nlakhan

Wat Pa Tham
Sopon

Ban Saphan It

Holiday

Pa Koy

Cancer
Center

Vishnu
Maharaj

Naresuan 8

Wat Tong Pu

Rhama Plaza

Jompol Por
Golf Course

Sam Khao Yot 25

Taipei

hoo!

Thanon Prang Sam Yot

Racha Manu

3016

Lopburi Zoo

3196

Wat Chee
Pa Sitaram

Radio Hde. FM
98.75 MHz - and
AM 1197 Khz

Lopburi Inn
Resort Hotel

Phra Prang Sam Yot

Chao Phraya
Wichayen

San Phra Kan

Piboon
Wittayaloi
School

Chaoemort
Umary Library

Si Suriyothai

Rak Rain
Tutor School

Lopburi
Provincial
Central
Stadium

City Hall

1

Panasan
Steak

Phatana

Pramot

Prang Sam Yot

Sri Indra

Thanon Narai Maharach
University

Narai
Boxing Gym

Rajabhat Thepsattri

Polytechnic
School

Tha Hin

Wang Thip

Th. Phahonyothin

Prang
Khaek

Lopburi
Culture Center

Lopburi
Kindergarten
Thepthani

Thanon Narai Maharach
Provincial
Non Formal
Education
Centre

Saeng
Sawang

Thanon Narai Maharach

Inn Resort

Lopburi
Inn

King Narai the
Great Monument

Sao Thong Thong
Asia

Net

Tourism of Thailand

Sutthara Pong

Watcharit
Tutor
School

Sa Kaew
Circle

Bus Terminal

Siam
Commercial
Bank

TMB

Thanon Narai Maharach

to Sun Flower Field,
Tha Sala, Lopburi Airport

Narai
onal Museum

Racha

Lopburi
Station

Wat Nakhon
Kosa

Changkon

Khun Thap Kawi

Siharat Decho Chai

Krung Thep
Bandit School

Holiday

Holiday

Phra Horathipbodi

Piman

Khao
Sam Yot

1036

Marine
Branch

Wat Phra
Si Ratana
Mahathat

Kawit

Steak House 1

Tue Seafood

Kosa Pan

Phra Lak

Phaya Anuchit

Kosa Lek

Dramatic
College

Banchongrat
Kindergarten

Phra
Simahosot

Sida

Sida

Th. Phra
Ram

Th. Pratu Chai

Ram Decho

Ram Decho

Ruan
Ruenrom

3196

Inn Resident

Si Prat 2

1036

Bandit Suksa
School

Wat San Paolo

Kosa Lek

33

Language
Institute

Pa Tan

3196

Th. Chana Songkhram

Bencharom

Technic Commercial
College

Ban
Khun Tan

Kitchen
Sukkasem

to Ban Pa Wai

3016

to Lopburi Airport

Ayutthaya Town

scale 1 : 30,000

0   500m

309

to Ang Thong

to Saraburi
and Phach

Han Tra

Khlong Sra Bua
Floating Market

Ayutthaya Elephant Palace
and Elephant Kraal

Wat Si Pho

Soi Khlong Sabua

Ansotitsuna
Mosque

Wat Sam
Wihan

Area 1 Police
Box

Wat
Ayutthaya

Wat Chao Ya

Wat Mae
Nangpluem

Wat Khae

Wat Monthop

Phromsuk

Wat Bot
Ratdecha

Khlong Sa Bua
Health Center

Hua Raw Night
Market

Krung Thai Bank

Night Food Market

Lopburi River

Pa Sak River

Ship Building
Industry and
Technology College

Ayutthaya
Municipality

3053

Phu Khao Thong Temple
(Golden Mount Chedi)

Wat Khok Phraya

Wat Intharam

Polytechnic

Hua Ro

U-Thong

Siam City Bank

Cathay

Wat Pra Du
Song Tham School

Wat Pra Du
Song Tham

The Provincial
Electricity Authority of
Ayutthaya 1

Wat Na
Phra Meru

Wat Kuti
Thong

Wat Khunsen

Sapuyan
Mosque

Chantharakasem
National
Museum

Land Office

Bangkok Bank

Chainam

Wat Kudi Dao

Wat Phanom
Yong

Wat Hatdawas

Wat Choeng Tha

Lum Phli

Wat Mai Pak
Khlong Sa Bua

Wat Wong
Khong

Wat
Suwandawas

Chinese Shrine

Rodeo Saloon

Wat Prasat

Sew Tek

Tevaraj Tanrin

Ayutthaya Riverside

ETO

309

Pratoochai
School

Old Lapburi River

Tha Wa Su Kri

Wat
Phlapphla
Chai

Thanon Pamaphrao

Sunriseplace

Wat Thamniyom

Ayutthaya District
Maintenance Office

Wat Tha Ka
Rong

Darutsanna
Mosque

Wat Sala Pun
Warawihan

Wat Phrom Niwat
Warawihan

Wat Wora Pho

Wat
Thammikarat

Wat Yansaen

Thongchai
GH

PS GH

Center Point
Ayutthaya

Ampom

Ayutthaya Health
Center Office

3053

Phu Kao
Thong

Wat Tuek

Pridi Banomyong
Memorial

Old Royal Palace

Wat Phra Si
Sanphet

Wat Ratchaburana

Malakor

New BJ GH

TMT GH

Ayutthaya

Duangporn

Ayutthaya
Train Station

Ban Pom

Phra Chao
Suea Palace

Wat Worachet
Tharam

Wat
Rakhang

Wihaan
Mongkhon
Bohit

Belung Phra
Ram

Wat Phra
Mahathat

Rattanachai

Chao
Phrom

Chao
Phrom Plaza

Ayutthaya
Riverside

Wat Phichai
Songkhram

Hua Laem
Market

Ayutthaya
Business
Administration
School

Khun Phaen's
Residence

PHRA RAM PARK

Thanon Naresuan (Chao Phrom)

Thanon Bang Ian

Thanon Uthong

Tevaraj Tanrin

Wat Thammaram

Wat Suan Luang
Sopsawan

Agriculture
College

Wang Chang
Ayutthaya Lae
Phariat

Wat
Phra
Ram

Provincial
Library

Thai Boat
Museum

Night Food
Market

Ayutthaya Thanee

Ayutthaya
Vocation College

Soemphon
Business
Computer
School

Baptist
Ayutthaya
Youth Hostel

Baankunpra

Krungsri River

Wat Kasatrathirat
Worawihan

Chedi Pra Si
Suriyothai

The 3rd Regional
Office of the Arts

Northeastern

Ayutthaya
Historical
Study Center

Thanon Pa Thon

Night Thanon Pa Thon
Food
Market

Wieng Fa

Floting

309

to Bangkok,
Long Distance
Bus Station

ohanburi

Wat Raja Pli

Thanon Khlong Thaw

City Pillar Shrine

Tourist Police

TAT Office

Ayutthaya
Withayarai School

Ayutthaya
Grand

Thanon Makhamriang

Moradokthai

Wat Khun
Muang Jai

Thanon Rotchana

Pridi
Damrong
Bridge

Wat Kluai

Khlong
Suan Phlu

Riverside

Thetsaban
Samphasamit
Bamrung School

National Art
Museum

City Hall

Thanon Pa Thon

Chao Sam Phraya
National Museum

Thanon Rotchana

Ayutthaya
Rajabhat
University

Suan
Luang

Ayutthaya
Historical Study Center

Soi Watha
Prapha

Ayutthaya
Water Works

Romklao Ayutthaya
Church

Ayutthaya
Convention Resort

Siriya
University

3263

Queen Suriyothai
Memorial Pagoda

Wat
Samonthon

Thanon Uthong

Wat Phra
Mahathat

Ayutthaya
Planetarium

Pom Pet
School

Wat Suwan
Dararam

Woraburi Ayutthaya
Convention Resort

Wat Ko
Kaeo

Kramang

3477

Chai
anaram

Wat Chao
Phrom

Wat Som

Phra Nakorn
Sri Ayutthaya
Hospital

Wat Borom
Phuttharam

Wat Khun
Phrem

Samphao Lom
Health Center

Phom Phet
Fortress

Wat Nang Kui

Harbour
Master
Office

River View Place

Ho Rattanachai

Pae Krung Kao

PHRA NAKORN
SRI AYUTTHAYA
HISTORICAL PARK

Thanon Khlong Thaw

Thanon Uthong

Wat Mai Bang
Ka Cha

Wat Phanan
Choeng School

Wat Phanan
Choeng

Wat Chedi Yai

SRI NAGARIN PARK

Samphao
Lom

Chao Phraya River

Pludhaya

Resort & Spa

Wat Luang
Chikrut

Islam Wathana
Mosque

Soi Khu
Ruea

Soi Photaram

Wat Klang
Pak Kran

Ariyinnural
Mosque

3469

Portuguese
Village

Uthong Road

Chao Phraya River

Wat Phutthaisawan
School

Wat Khok
Chindaram

3469

to Bang Pa-In

3477

to Bangkok

Wat Sanam Chai

Wat Phutthaisawan

CENTRAL THAILAND

Around Nakhon Sawan

to Mai Sot
Banphot Phisai
to Chiang Mai
1118
Tha Mai
Chumsaeng
Goddess Shrine
Chumsaeng
Nong Krachao

117
Bang Khian
Ban Nong Sang
Dong Prathun
225

Scale 1 : 500,000
0   10km
Hua Dong
1084
Kao Liao
Khok Mo
Phan Lan
Chum Saeng
Phai Sing
Huai Yai

Ang Thong
1182
Huai Thua Tai

Ban Rai
1001
Nong Kradon
Maha Pho
Bang Pra
Luang

Noen Khi Lek
Sala Chao
Kai To
1046
Kham Tai
Wang Yai

Lat Yao
Nong
Nom Wua
1
1072
Nong Kradon
Bang Muang
Wang Na
3475
Sai Lamphong

1072
Nong Yao
225
Phanom Sat
3475

Lat Yao
3013
Nong Krot
NAKHON SAWAN TOWN 25
Sawan Park
Bungboraped
Buong
Boraphot
Wang
Mahakon
Chalom Nae

Wang Ma
1
Nakhon Sawan
Nakhon Sawan
Airport
3004
Phra Non
Hua Phluang

Map Kae
NAKHON SAWAN
UTHAI THANI
122
3004
Hua Thanon

Phai Khiao
3456
Nang Klang
Bang Pra
Mong
40
Khao Thong
Khao Kala

Sawang
Arom
Sala Daeng
1
Yan Matsi
Nong Luang

Sawang Arom
3456
Khok Mo
3070
Krok Phra
Noen Kwao
Phayuha
Khiri
Tao Than
Tin Dong
1145

Phluang
Song Nang
3013
Hat Sung
Nikhom Kao
Bo Kaeo
Udom Thanya

Khao Patthawi
4035
Nong Yai Da
3319
3220
Nam Song
3329

4022
Thap Than
Non Lek
Phayuha Khir
Ban Udom
Thanya

Nong
Krathum
3013
Thap Than
Muang Uthai
Thani
3328
1145
Tak Fa

4003
Nong Sra
4003
Ban Kao
3221
Dong
Khwang
333
1
Tha Nam Oi
4047
Nong Pho

Taluk Do
Nong Kae
Khao Sakae Krong
Nong Phikun
3331

5006
Thung
Phung
Don Kloy
3220
UTHAI THANI TOWN 25
NAKHON SAWAN
CHAI NAT
Hua Wai
Kao Chai
Thong

Thung Pho
3438
Nong Chang
Thung Pho
333
Uthai Thani
1014

2114
Nong Khayang
19
Hang Nam
Sekhon
Rai Patthanai
3329
1145

Non Bua
3025
Nong Chang
Nong Yang
Dong
Khwang
Lum Khao
32
1

UTHAI THANI
CHAI NAT
5017
Manorom
Takhli Airport
Takhli

4003
3133
Nong Bua
1
U Taphao
Nong Me

Nong Mamong
4006
Bo Rae
3213
22
8

4010
Makham Thao
Nong Mamong
Wat Sing
Hat Tha Sao
CHAI NAT TOWN 25
3196
Chong Khae

Saphan Hih
Wang Man
Nong Noi
Chai Nat
Chai Nat Muni
National Museum
311

4010
5020
5016
340
Sanphaya
Khao Kaeo
Soi Thong
3196

3033
CHAI NAT
UTHAI THANI
5016
Nang Lu
NAKHON SAWAN
SINGBURI
Phai Yai

Nong Bom Klui
Phri Nok
Huai Ngu
Pho Nang
Dam Ok
22
2001

3033
5016
Sam Ngam
Tha Bot
Thiang Thae
Huai Krot
Pattanan
11
Dong
Yang

4028
Den Yai
Sankhaburi
Bang Khut
CHAI NAT
SINGBURI
Phochai

Kaboktia
340
Dong Khon
Sankhaburi
Pho Ngam
311
2010

Noen Kham
Hankha
3184
Dan Kam
Huai Chan
Hua Phai

3211
3039
3251
Choeng Kiat
32
Ngio Rai

Ban Chian
Pak Nam
Khok
Chang
Pak Than
Bang Krabue

CHAI NAT
SUPHANBURI
Mai Dat
3028

Nong Krathum
4014
3350
Hua Na
Doem Bang
Nang Buat
340
Khao Phra
Thung Khli
Sra Chaeng
Bang Phutsa

Pa Sakae
Wang Si Rat
Yang Non
Pho Tale
Chak Si
309
to
Bangkok

Om Khar
Pha
Om Khao Krok pha
Wat Suw
to Kamphae
Phet
Klong
M
Th. Sawav
S. 64
Soi Sawanvitee
11

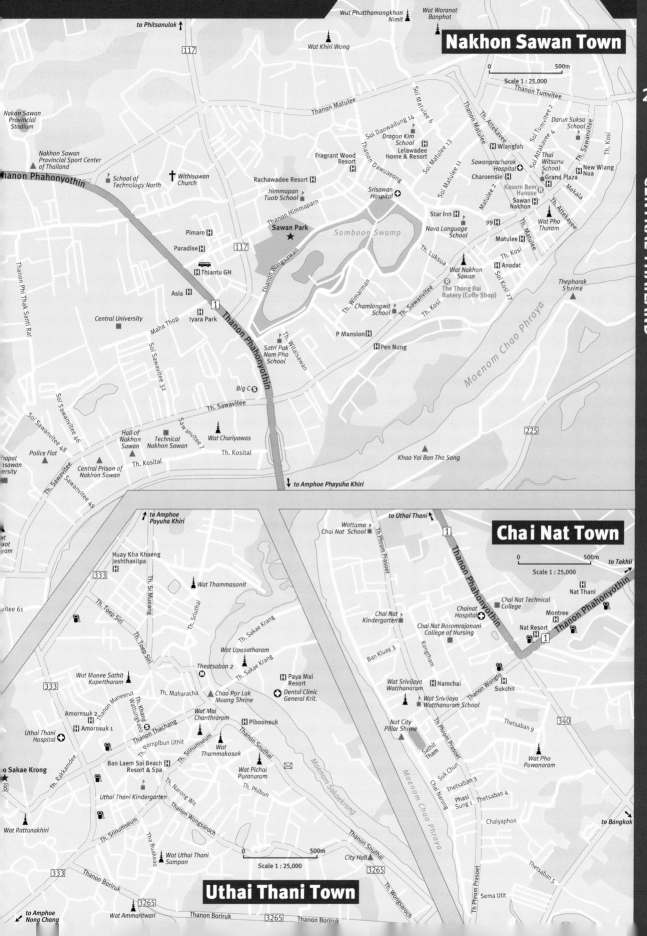

Nakhon Sawan Town

Scale 1 : 25,000
0   500m

to Phitsanulok ↑

117

Wat Phutthamongkhon Nimit
Wat Woranat Banphot
Wat Khiri Wong

Thanon Matulee
Soi Matulee 6
Thanon Matulee
Thanon Tumvitee

Soi Daowadung 14
Dragon Kim School
Lelawadee Home & Resort
Soi Matulee 13
Soi Attekavee 4
Darun Suksa School
Soi Tumvitee 2
Th. Sawanvitee

Fragrant Wood Resort
Thanon Dawuaeong
Soi Matulee 11
Sawanpracharak Hospital
Wiangfah
Thai Witsanu School
New Wiang Nua
Th. Kosi

Nakon Sawan Provincial Stadium

Rachawadee Resort
Srisawan Hospital
Charoensin
Grand Plaza
Mekala

Nakhon Sawan Provincial Sport Center of Thailand

Thanon Phahonyothin

School of Technology North
Withisawan Church

Himmapan Tuob School
Thanon Himmaparn

Matulee 2
Kasorn Beer Haouse
Sawan Nakhon

Star Inn
Nava Language School
99
Wat Pho Tharam
Th. Attekavee

Pimarn
Sawan Park
Somboon Swamp
Matulee
Th. Matulee

Paradise
117
Th. Luksua
Anodat
Th. Kosi

Thiantu GH
Thanon Wongsawan
Wat Nakhon Sawan
Soi Kosi 27

Asia
The Thong Bai Bakery (Coffe Shop)
Thepharak Shrine

Central University
1
Thanon Phahonyothin
Iyara Park
Maha Thop
Th. Winarman
Th. Chamlongwit School
Th. Sawanvitee
Th. Kosi

Soi Sawavitee 32
Saw anvitee 7
Satri Pak Nam Pho School
Th. Witaisawan
P Mansion
Pen Nung
Moenom Chao Phraya

Thanon Phi Thak Santi Rat
Big C

Th. Sawavitee

Soi Sawanvitee 46
Hall of Nakhon Sawan
Technical Nakhon Sawan
Wat Chariyawas
225

Soi Sawanvitee 48
Police Flat
Th. Kosital
Th. Kosital

...hapat ...sawan ...ersity
Central Prison of Nakhon Sawan
Khao Yai Ban Tha Song

Th. Sawanvitee 49
↓ to Amphoe Phayuha Khiri

Chai Nat Town

to Uthai Thani
Chai Nat Town
Scale 1 : 25,000
0   500m
to Takhli

↑ to Amphoe Payuha Khiri

Wattama Chai Nat School
Th. Phrom Prasoet
1
Thanon Phahonyothin

Huay Kha Khaeng Jeshthasilpa
Th. Si Mueang
Chai Nat Technical College
Nat Thani

333
Wat Thammasonit
Chainat Hospital
Chai Nat Kindergarten
Montree
to Bangkok

...vitee 61
Th. Toep Siri
Th. Sakae Krang
Chai Nat Boromrajonani College of Nursing
Nat Resort
1

Th. Toep Siri
Wat Uposatharam
Ban Kluay 3
Kongtham

Wat Manee Sathit Kapettharam
Theatsaban 2
Th. Sakae Krang
Wat Srivijaya Watthanaram
Namchai
Thanon Wongto
Sukchit

Amornsuk 2
Thanon Maneerut
Th. Khang Wattungkaeo
Th. Maharacha
Paya Mai Resort
Wat Srivijaya Watthanaram School
340

Amornsuk 1
Wat Mai Chanthraram
Chao Por Lak Muang Shrine
Dental Clinic General Krit.
Thetsaban 9

Uthai Thani Hospital
Thanon Thachang
Piboonsuk
Nat City Pillar Shrine
Sathit Tham
Wat Pho Pawanaram

to Sakae Krong
Th. Rakamdee
Th. Pornplbun Uthit
Thanon Snuthai
Suk Chun
Thetsaban 3

8
Ban Laem Sai Beach Resort & Spa
Wat Thammakosok
Thanon Snuthai
Chai Narong
Phasi Sung 1
Thetsaban 4

Th. Srinumseum
Wat Pichai Puranaram
Th. Phibun
Suk Chun
Chaiyaphon
to Bangkok

Uthai Thani Kindergarten
Thanon Wongsaroch
Thetsaban 5

Th. Srinumseum
Tha Buakeao
Maenom Sakaekrang
Thanon Snuthai

Wat Rattanakhiri
Wat Uthai Thani Sampan
City Hall
3265
Moenom Chao Phraya

500m
Scale 1 : 25,000

333
Thanon Boriruk
Thanon Snuthai
Th. Wongsaroch
Th. Phrom Prasoet
Sema Utit

Uthai Thani Town

to Amphoe Nong Chang
Wat Ammaritwari
Thanon Boriruk
3265
Thanon Boriruk

Sangkhlaburi

Kanchanaburi Province

0   500m

scale 1 : 30,000

to Tha Ma Kham

323

to Tong Pha Phum

onal Park

500m

to Phra Cave

Kanchanaburi Technology School

Thanon Charoen Samakkhi

Wat Khao Lanthammaram

Wat Hua Na

Pak Phraek Sub District Administration Organization

Krung Thai Bank

Ploythai Jewelry

Chian Chuanchim

The River Kwai Bridge

Nai Kuem

Fut Fit For Five Inn

Ban San Fan

Sabai@kan Resort

Pavilion Rim Kwai Resort

Ead Raft

Apple's Retreat & Guest House

Sam's House

T & T Guest House

Blue Star

Sugar Cane Guest House

Amelia Resort

Guesthouse

Je Roon Kang Pa

Tequando Boozoo

Kwai River

Thanon Sangchuto

Phurang Nimit Soi 12

Thanon Phurang Nimit 1

Hua Na Bon Soi 1

Hua Na Bon Soi 1/5

Hua Na Bon Soi 2

Th. Phurang Nimit 1

Th. Phatthanakan

Thanon Uthong 9-Liang Mueang

Hua Na Lang Soi 8-Wang Saraphi Soi 12

Ban Hua Na School

Hua Na Lang Soi 6

Hua Na Lang Soi 4

Wang Saraphi Soi 2

Pak Phraek

Wang Saraphi Soi 1

Wat Udom Mongkol

to Nong Khao

Kanchanaburi Technical Collage

Bavom Wittaya Kindergarten

Sam Anong

Wang Saraphi Intersection

Nai Rueang Larb Ped Sriwara 2

323

Thanon U-Thong

Khao Tong View

Talay Pao Khao Thong

to Tha Lo

Allied War Cemetery

Souvenir

Thavorn Wararam School

Thepmongkol Rangsee School

Wat Thewa Sangkharam

Municipal 3 School

River Kwai Resotel

Discovery Nightclub

60th Anniversary Hall

Man Tim

Lisery

Ban Rao

Sabai Chit

River Kwai

Thanon Uthong 9-Liang Mueang

Gems Cutting Vocation Training Center

Hua Na Boiled Rice

Monday Lotus

Kanchanaburi Vocational Education College Saeng Chuto

Municipal 2 School

Chan Pattana Suksa Tutor School

Maitri Chit

Mueang Kanchanaburi Municipal Children Development

Monday Lotus

324

Ban Tai

Cha Wang Bo Wom

Sitthi Suksa School

Th. Songkwie

Th. Pakpak

Chao Mae Kuan Im Shrine

Smart English Kanchanaburi Branch

Kanakan Mall

Kanchanaburi Bus Station

Ban Nua 1 Library

Kanchana Nukro School

Kanchanaburi Kindergarten

Th. Tauwpoon

Ko-Sak Boat Noodle

Ban Nua

Kanchanaburi Suksa Special School

Pat Tharaburi

Night Market

City Pillar Shrine

Kanchanaburi Church

Th. Sanam Pao

Si Charoen Bungalow

Kan

Pong

Daughter

Suksan

Suphatkan Kindergarten

to Tha Lo

Kanchanaburi

Pramae Kuan Im Maha Phrotisat

Jeath War Museum

Wat Chaichumphon Chanasongkhram

Wat Chanosongkram Kindergarten

Thiam Ter

Th. Chaichumpol

P.S.

Wisutarangsa

Municipal 5 School

Thai Seree

Kanchanaburi Boriban School

Mahachulalongkornrajavidyalaya University

Thanakan

Kanchanaburi Church

Sathanee Rodfai 3

Thanon Thung Na-Liang Mueang

Wat Sai Yok Yai

Sai Yok Yai School

Park Enterance

Thanon Sangchuto

323

Chaichit Wittaya School

323

Th. Cuk Don

Government Housing Bank

Sangchuto Soi 36

Huai Pool

Tanawasri

Krua Chukdon

Ton Mae Krong

Korean Kanchana Chiangkong

Ko Kard

Ko Au Noodle Boat

Sangchuto Soi 28

Sangchuto Soi 20

Sangchuto Soi 18

Municipal 3 School

Pahonpol Payuha Sena

Luk Sao Nongkai

Ko Kae

to Tha Ruea

Maneeyakhet King Piya School

Kasem Island Resort

Tesco Lotus

Je Noo 2

Kanchanaburi City Hall

San Chick

China Town

Bungalow Wang Thong

Jasmin

Lok Home Resort

Soi Phueng Luang

3429

Smile Ice Cream

Chao Pho Khao Uai Shrine

323

Visuttharangi School

to Tha Sao

Kanchanaburi Provincial Employment Office

Kanchanaburi Provincial Court

Sor. Poonphol

to Tha Lo

Food Vendors

Japanese Cookstoves

Springs

Kaeo Cave

Sai Yok Yai Waterfall

Viewpoint

Bat Cave

Alisa Raft

Kwai River

Krua Siang Phai

3429

Sai Yok Cave

Wat Ban Tham

Wat Nang No

scale 1 : 1,400,000
0   20km

Senap Thuen
309
Bo Ta Lo
Wang Noi
1 Wihan Daeng
Khao Phoem
Khao Phuang
Nang Rong Waterfall
Wang Takhai
Ban Na
33
Nakhon Nayok
Khlong Yai
Prachinburi
Ongkharak
Na Mueang
3051
3076
Phai Cha
Si Maha Phot
Pho Ngam
Ban Tham
Kabin Buri
33
Bo Thong
Kut Nao
Ban Na
Sa Kaew
Tha Kasem
33
Nong Sai
Aranyaprathet
Phumī Preav
Khao Phoem
Taling Chan
Sap Malua
Ban Prakham
Som Poi
Khao Lamang 992m
Song Phi Nong
Sae O
348
San Ro Cha
Khok Phek
Non Mak Kheng
Han Sai
Ban Mai
57
Watthana Nakhon
Khao Samsip
Phra Phloeng
Khao Chakan
THAILAND
CAMBODIA
Khlong hat
Wang Mai
Thai U Dom
Wang Sonbun
317
3259
Roneam Daun Sam Wildlife Sanctuary
Phumī Kung K
Ampil Pram
Phumī Sop
Phumī Sie
Phumī Kung K

305
Thanya Buri
Bung Sanan
Don Muang Airport
Lam Luk Ka
Nong Chok
304
Nong Chok
Suvarnabhumi International Airport
Bang Phli Yai
Bang Phnang
Khlong Dan
7
33
SAMUT PRAKAN
CHONBURI TOWN 30
Chonburi
No Ri
315
331
3284
Ban Bueng
3340
Nong Irun
344
Nong Phai Kaeo
3245
Bo Thong
3245
Thung Sadao
Thung Yai Chi
Khlong Takrao
Tha Takiap
Khao Yai 777m
Thap Chang
317
Sai Khao
Takhian Thong
Thep Nimit
Phumī Ta Krei
Phumī Khohcey
Phumī Phnu Damrei
Phumī Chr

SI RACHA 29
Si Racha
3
Ko Si Chang
KO SI CHANG 29
Ko Phai
Thung Sukhla Bang Lamung
Bang Lamung
Nong Pla Lai
Pong
Ko Lan
Pattaya
PATTAYA 29
Bang Sare
Hat Noi
332
Phlu
Ta Luang
Sattahip
Samaesan
U-Tapao Intol Airport
Ko Khram Yai
Ko Samaesan
Ko Raet
Ban Chang
Mao Ta Phut
Mao Ta Phut Industrial Port
36
Choeng Noen
Rayong
RAYONG TOWN 31
Ban Phe
BAN PHE 28
Ko Samet
Khao Laem Ya-Mu Ko Samet
KO SAMET 28

Sun Ta Then Waterfall
Khao Khansong
331
Ta Sit
3245
Khao Sok
Khao Noi
Pa Yup Nai
344
Khao Chamao
3377
Chum Saeng
Khao Chamao 1028m
Krasae Bon
Klaeng
48
3
Song Salueng
Thung Khwai Kin
55
Na Yai Am
San Muang
Nam Tok Krating
Khao Baisi
Chanthanimit
Chanthaburi
CHANTHABURI (CHANBURI) TOWN 31
Khlong Khut
Sanam Chai
Nong Chim
Bang Chan
Phlio
Tapon
Khlung
Saen Tung
3157
3159
3157
Wan Takhian
3271
Chang Klua
3194
Bo Rai
Khao Saming
3157
Nong Samat
KO CHANG 31
TRAT TOWN 31
Trat
Laem Klat
318
Chamrak
Phu
CAMBODIA THAILAND
3299
Map Khla
Ban Khamen
Wild Life Preservation Center
Khlong Yai
Thap Sai
Samnak Tin Lao
Makham
Phumī Chr
Pallin
Phum Balaing

Khao Chamun 739m
Khun Song
Thung Phraya
359
Sra Khuan
Wang Takhian
Wang Thai Chang
Ta Lang Nai
Sai Thong
359
Phanom Sarakham
304
Khao Hin Son
Khu Yai Mi
Nam Cha
3347
Si Mahosot
Lam Chuat
319
3200
Ko Chan
Tha Lan
304
Chachoengsao
3304
Tha Lat
Plaeng Yao
3259
Nong Mai Kaeo
Talat Bang Bo
Phanat Nikhom
Phanat Nikhom
Na Pa
Ban Pho

 Trat Airport
Tha Som
Reservoir
Klong Son
Ban Kwan Chang
Ko Chang
Ko Chang National
Ban Chamrung
Ao Yai
Ko Chang
Ban bang Bao
Koh Mai Si Ya
Ko Wai
Ko Khlum
Ko Kra Dad
Ko Mak
Ko Rang
Ko Kut
12°

Nai Rai Soi/13
Nai Rai Soi 2
Nai Rai Soi 1
3140
Lame Pra Du Soi 11
Khoad Kliang
Khoad Kliang Soi 2
Lame Pra Soi 7/3
Soi 12
Lame Pra Du Soi 7
Chao Por Samruai Nava Shrine
Lame Pra Soi 7/1
Soi 7/2
Lame Pra Du Soi 5
Thanon Naichak-Nairai
Sukhaphiban 2/6
Bon Ban
Bon Ban Soi 2
Sukhaphiban 2/8
Wat Phetra Sukharom School
Wat Suan Komoniaram Dhara
Soi 7/4
Wilaiwan Kindergarten
Anan Sueksa School
to Klaeng
Phe
Nhong Yai In Soi 1/4
Nhong Yai In Soi 9/3
Kon Ao Soi 2/3
Mab Kha Soi 5
Mab Kha Soi 7
Nhong Yai In Soi 9/2
Kon Ao Soi 2/2
Soi 1/5
Soi 1/3
Soi 1/1
Nhong Yai In Soi 9/1
Kon Ao Soi 2/1
Thanon Watthana
Kon Ao Soi 1/2
Rayong Aquarium
Mountain Beach Resort
Krom Luang Chumpom
Khet Udomsak Shrine
Ban Phe
Ban Phe Pre
to Rayong
Sea Side Resort
Hat Mae Rumphueng
Wat Chedi Pak Nam
Nice Beach
White@ Sea House
Laemya Inn
Mae Ram Phueng Beach
3142
Ban Lim Talae
Rayong Resort

Ko Samet

to Klaeng
Wilaiwan Kindergarten
to Ban Phe
to Ban Phe
Mooban Talay Resort
Samet Hut
Samet Club
Cliff Resort
Baan Ploy Samed
Ao Pa Cha Beach
Ban Samet Hill
Le Blanc Samet Resort
Lima Bella Resort
Ao Kham Beach
Beach House
Sai Kaew Beach Resort
Ao Prao Resort
Paradise Beach
Le Vimarn
Sai Kaew Beach
Laem Rua Taek
Phutsa Beach
Ko Samet
Tubtlin Bangalows
Tub Tim Beach
Samet Grand View Resort
Ao Nuan Bangalows
Ao Nuan Beach
Malibu Garden Resort
Ao Cho Beach
Samet Cabana Resort
Ao Cho Grand View Resort
Vongdeuan Resort
Vongdeuan Villa
Ao Wong Deuan Beach
Talebure Bed & Bar
Vimarn Samed
Ao Thian Beach
Sunset View
Lung Dum Resort
Samet Ville Resort
Ao Wai Beach
Vongdeum Villa
scale 1 : 90,000
0   2km
Ao Klo Coral Beach
Ko Hinkao
Ao Kiew Na Nai Beach
Paradee
Nimmanoradee
Ao Kiu Na Nok Beach
View Point
Ao Karang Beach

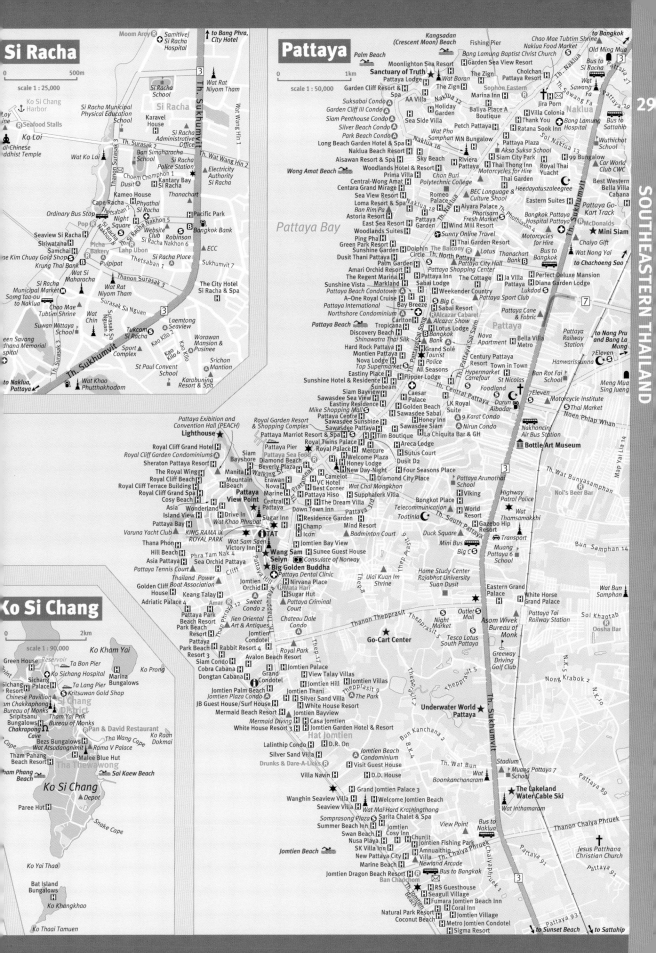

SOUTHEASTERN THAILAND

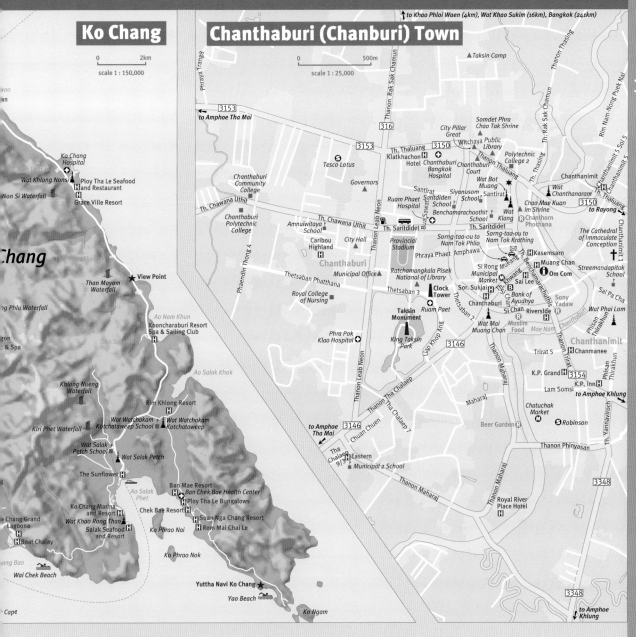

Ko Chang

0   2km
scale 1 : 150,000

Ko Chang Hospital
Wat Khlong Nonsi
Ploy Tha Le Seafood and Restaurant
Non Si Waterfall
Grace Ville Resort

Chang

★ View Point
Than Mayom Waterfall

ng Phlu Waterfall

on & Spa

Ao Nam Khun

Khlong Nueng Waterfall
Kooncharaburi Resort Spa & Sailing Club

Ban Si

Ao Salak Khok

Rim Khlong Resort
Klri Phet Waterfall
Wat Watchakam Kotchataweep School
Wat Watchakam Kotchataweep

Wat Salak Petch School
▲ Wat Salak Petch

The Sunflower

Ao Salak Phet

Ban Mae Resort
Ban Chek Bae Health Center
Ploy Tha Le Bungalows

Ko Chang Marina and Resort
Chek Bae Resort
Wat Khao Rong Than
Suan Nga Chang Resort
Salak Seafood and Resort
Rom Mai Chai Le

Ko Phrao Nai

Chang Grand Lagoona
Boat Chalay

Ko Phrao Nok

ang Bao

Wai Chek Beach

Yuttha Navi Ko Chang ★

Cape

Yao Beach

Ko Ngam

Chanthaburi (Chanburi) Town

↑ to Khao Phloi Waen (4km), Wat Khao Sukim (16km), Bangkok (241km)

0   500m
scale 1 : 25,000

3153
to Amphoe Tha Mai ←
316
3153

● Taksin Camp

Thanon Rak Sak Chamun
Thanon Thasing
Rim Nam-Nong Puek Hai
Thanon Thasing
Rim Nam-Nong Puek Hai

Somdet Phra Chao Tak Shrine
City Pillar Great
Witchaya Public Library
Th. Thaluang
Klatkhachon
Th. Thaluang
Polytechnic College 2
Chanthanimit
Chanthanimit 5 Sol 5
Th. Thaluang

Tesco Lotus
Chanthaburi Community College
Governors
Chanthaburi Bangkok Hospital
Chanthaburi Court
Thanon Thaluang
Wat Chanthanaram
Wat Bot Muang
Chao Mae Kuan Im Shrine
3150
to Rayong →

Chanthaburi Polytechnic College
Th. Chawana Utith
Amnuiwitaya School
Th. Chawana Uthit
Santirat
Siyanusom School
Santirat
Saritdiden School
Benchamarachoothit School
Wat Klang
Chanthorn Phochana
The Cathedral of Immaculate Conception

Caribou Highland
City Hall
Th. Saritdidet
Th. Saritdidet
Sorng-taa-ou to Nam Tok Phlio
Amphawa
Sorng-taa-ou to Nam Tok Krathing
Kasemsarn
Muang Chan
Om Com
Streemandapitak School
Chanthaburi

Provincial Stadium
Chanthaburi Municipal Office
Ratchamangkala Pisek National of Library
Phraya Phaet
Si Rong Muang
Municipal Market
Sai Lee
Sony Yadaw
Sai Pa Cha

Thetsaban Phatthana
Thetsaban 3
Royal College of Nursing
Clock Tower
Ruam Paet
Sor. Sukjai
Bank of Ayudhya
Riverside
Wat Phai Lom

Taksin Monument
Phra Pok Klao Hospital
King Taksin Park
Wat Mai Muang Chan
Muslim Food
Si Chan
Mae Nam Chanthaburi
Chanthanimit

3146
Thanon Maharaj
Trirat 5
Chanmanee
Phisan Thirakhun

Thanon Leab Neon
Thanon Tha Chalaep
Maharaj
K.P. Grand
3154
Phisan Thirakhun
Lam Somsi
K.P. Inn
to Amphoe Khlung

Thanon Tha Chalaep 7
Chuan Chuen
Chatuchak Market
Thanon Yannaviroch

to Amphoe Tha Mai ←
3146
Tha Chalaep 9
Eastern
Municipal 2 School
Thanon Phinyasan
Beer Garden
Robinson

Thanon Maharaj
3348

Royal River Place Hotel

3348

to Amphoe Khlung ↓

Rayong Town

to Bang Lamung ↗

0   500m
scale 1 : 25,000

Phatthana

36
IRPC Public Company Limited
to Buppharam →

3139

Bua Khao Restaurant
Soi Rungrueang

Sukhumvit
Soi Ploenta 3
Soi Ploenta 2
Soi Ploenta 1

3139
Thanon Sukhumvit
Nakornrayong 75

Lang Thang Luang
Saensuk
Very Happy Bungalows
Rose Inn
Poonchai 2
Suksomjai Bungalow

to Klaeng ↓

ong Kha 2
Soi Kokhabkk
Rayong Parkview

3
to Klaeng

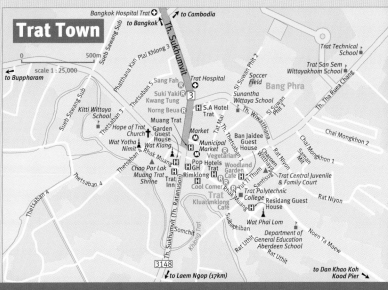

Trat Town

Bangkok Hospital Trat ✚
to Bangkok ←
Th. Sukhumvit
to Cambodia →

0   500m
scale 1 : 25,000

Sueb Sawang Sub
Sueb Sawang Sub
Patthana Kan Phai Khlong 3
Sueb Sawang Sub
Sang Fah
Suki Yaki
Kwang Tung
Kitti Wittaya School
Thetsaban 3
Thetsaban 5

Trat Hospital
3
Si Suwan Phit 2
Si Suwan Phit 2
Soccer Field
Trat Technical School
Trat San Sem Wittayakhom School
Bang Phra

Norng Beua
S.A Hotel Trat
Sunantha Wittaya School
Si Suwan Phit 1
Th. Wiwathana
Th. Tha Ruea Chang

Hope of Trat Church
Muang Trat
Garden Guest House
Market
Ban Jaidee Guest House
Chai Mongkhon 2

Wat Yotha Nimit
Wat Klang
Municipal Market
Woodland Garden Cafe
Charoen Withaya
Chai Mongkhon 1
Saman Wittaya

Chao Por Lak Muang Trat Shrine
Thetsaban 4
Pop Hotels
Rimklong
Cool Comer Cafe
Vegetarian
Rat Niyon
Trat Central Juvenile & Family Court

Trat Inn
GH
Trat
Santisuk
Wut Thi Thum
Residang Guest House

Thetsaban 4
Thetsaban 3
Thetsaban 2
Trat Polytechnic College

Thetsaban 4
Somchit
Kluaimklong Cafe
Trat
Rat Niyon

Th. Sukhumvit (Th. Ratanuson)
Khlong Trat
Anan Muang
Suk Phiban
Wat Phai Lom
Rat Uthit

3148
to Laem Ngop (17km) ↓
Department of General Education Aberdeen School
Noen Ta Maew
to Dan Khao Koh Kood Pier
Rat Uthit

31

SOUTHEASTERN THAILAND

CHIANG RAI PROVINCE 40

CHIANG MAI, MAE HONG SON & LAMPHUN PROVINCES 33

MYANMAR (BURMA)

LAOS

Mae Hong Son

Chiang Rai

Chiang Mai

Lamphun

Lampang

Phrae

Nan

LAMPANG, NAN, PRAE & UTTARADIT PROVINCES 43

Uttaradit

Phetchabun

Mae Sot

Tak

Sukhothai

Phitsanulok

Phichit

PHITSANULOK, SUKHOTHAI & PHICHIT PROVINCES 44

KAMPHAENG PHET & TAK PROVINCES 46

Kamphaeng Phet

Nakhon Sawan

Uthai Thani

Chai Nat

NORTHERN THAILAND

Dong La Khon
Doi San Klang
Pang Kwao
Doi San Chon 1281m
Thung Waen
Mae Aen
Wat Walu Karam
Huay Sai
Mae Tung Ting
Phra Kha Wan
Tin Dong
Na Fan
Huay Pu
Prem Tinsulanda International School
Thong P
Mae Tom
Wat Pong Pa
Mae Khi
Pang Hai
Bang Pa Khai
Wat Sawang Phet
Nong
Oi
Thung Pong
Mae Pa
Wat Pang Toem
Thung Pa Haew
Pang Haew
Wat Tamnak Tham Nimit
Mae Sa Golf Course
Doi Kiu Tao Pun
Nga Maeng Nua
Nga Maeng Tai
Wat Ban Phok
Pok
Thung
Nong Hoi Maew
Mai
Hai
Mae Raeu
Nong Hoi Mai Na Hi
Na Hi
Kong Khak Nua
Wat Kong Khak
Tin Doi
Doi Khom Rong 1459m
Doi Mae Luat
Thung Pong
Thung Do
Doi Liam
Kong Khak Luang
Doi Son Kiu Sung
Pong Khrai
Doi Luang
1096
Mae Mae
Thung Pa Muang
Thung
Doi Huay Miang
Doi Pha Ta
Pa Miang Pang Ton Lung
Doi Pha Chang Mup
Mae Sa Elephant Camp
Mae Nai
Huay Wai
Doi Khun Huay Mai Tong
Wat Pong Yaeng
Pong Yaeng Nok
Queen Sirikit Botanic Garden
Kong Khak Noi
Doi Sang
Pa Miang Pang Thong Daeng
Pong Yaeng Nai
Kong Khan
Wat Thepharam
Hua Thung
Luang
Dong Nok
Dong
Nam Rin
1096
Montakrai Resort
Kong Hae
Doi Pha Dam
Doi Mae Sa Noi
Maen Huay Mae Nai
Doi Pa Kha
Mae Sap Mai
Hua Dong
Pa Kluai
Tha Sala
Wat Pheri Phichai
Doi Daen
Maew Chang Khian
Wat Mae Sap Nua
Mae Sap Tai
Dong Chang Kaeo
Lao
Sai Mun
Doi Pui 1685m
Maew Chang Khian
Maew Doi Pui
Doi Pha Chedi
Pang Yang
Mae Na Sai
Doi Suthep
Phuping Rajanivet Palace
Wat P Doi
Doi Ma Nai
Doi Kaeo
Mae Khanin Nua
Wat Pracha Kasem
Mae Ha
Chiang Mai University (CMU) Suan Sak Campus
Phak Madoe
Doi Tham Pa Len
Suanbua
Kao Dua
Man
Doi Huay Hia
961m
Yang Mae Lan Ngoen
Yang Pu La
Huay Kaeo Waterfall
Huay Rai
Thung Pong
Wat Khirikhet
Hua Dong
Chiang Universi Hia/Doi Cam
Doi Pha Yang
Thung Kong
Dong
Pong Nua
Mae Hia Nai
Wat Phra That Doi Kham
Maew Pha Chino
Wat Nin Prapha
Pong Tai
Wat Doi Kaeo
Klang
Mae Khanin Tai
Doi Son Luang
Royal Flora Ratchapruek
Nong Pla
Doi Mon Pha Sing 1005m
Doi Pha Phung
Klang
1269
Huay Siaw
Doi Siaw
Night Safari
Fon
Phae Na Kham
Phan
Huay Chaek Tai
Kong Khing
Wang Dong
Home
Wat Luang
Bua Khao
Sop Huay Yao
Yang Huay Yao
Doi Tham
Khong Kh
Tha Sala
Phae Khwang
1105m
Huay Thong
676m
Nam Phrae
Thung Pa Tong
Wat Eran Khwang
Huay Kho
Wat Huay Thong
Hua Fai
Nam Phrae
Thung Nang Laeng
Rong Wuai
Huay Yuak
Nong Wai
Huay Kaeo
Wat Si Udom
Nong Ha
Mai
to San Pa Tong

1 : 150,000

2.5km   1mile

to Khilek

Phae Huay
Bong
Don
Den   Soi Hok
Tiu   Mai   Hong Hae
Tiu   1001
Wat Nantharam
That   Huay Bong
eng   Wang Mun   Lum
Pradit   Chedi Mae
hm   Nikhom Sahakon   Khrua
Chang   Nong Hai   Mae Tao Hai
a Chang   Nam Ton
ng   Khoh Tan   Pa Bong
Kaset Sin   Phae
Mae Sa Laung   Don Tan   Makham Yai   Phae
Nong Fan   Wat Wiwek
Bo Pu   Hua Rua   Waharam
Wat Dawn   Wang Pong
Gaew   Thung Rok Fa
107   Thung Yao
Don Kaeo   Wat Nong Kieo   Mai Lamphup   Mae Jo
Pa Khoi Tai   Golf Course
phanaram   Sala   Wat Pa Koi Nua   Si Bun Ruang
Pa Ngae   Tha Kwian   Si Bun Ruang
Wat Piyaram Nong Pom   Fa Mui   Nong Pu
Hua Rin   San Pa   Mae Jo Mae Jo University
             Thung   Sak Noi
Nong Khrai   Mun Noi
RTA Lanna   Luang   San Sai Kom
Sports Center Tha Luk   Fa Mui
Mae Yuak   Nong Khrai   Muang Ha
Klang   Nang Liaw   Lak Pan
Chiangmai   Rai Nong Ho   Chiang Mai   Mae Yoi
Lanna   Garden Land San Sai
Golf Course Muang Lang   San Phi Sua 1006
Chang Phuak Patan   Langka   118
Si So Da   Khuang   Mae Khao
Mai Zoo   National   Sing
quarium   Museum   Fa Ham   San Sai Noi
eng Doi   Chet Yot   San Phra Net
Doi Suthep   Wat Ku Tao   Klang
Mai   Si Phum   Chang Moi   Thung
sity   Wat Pa Pao   San Phra Net
Suan Dok   CHIANG MAI   Wat Ket
ng Ha   Phra Sing   Mon
Phra Sing   1006
U Mong   Pimonthip   Buak Khrok Noi
Chiang Mai   Golf Club   CAT Telecom
Airport   Chiangmai   Handicrafts
Suthep Haiya   Rong Khun
CENTRAL CHIANG MAI 36-37   Wat Hua Fai   Si Pan Khrua
Mae Kho   Tha Sala   Pa Daet
108   1141   Dok Chan
Ton Du   Pa Daet   Montfort College   San Klang
             Nong Hoi   School   Tai
Chedi Liam   Rong Wua   11
Pa Pao   Tha Wang Tai   Mae Ping   Aware
Tamnak   Police Station Corporation
onville 5,6,7   Klang   Chai Sa Than   Limited
Pin   Rong   Gassan Driving
Khua Deng   San Khu   Range Golf Club
Ko Sai   Wat Yang Yoi   Ton
121   Pa Kluai   Kong Sua   Yang   San Pa
Noi   Buak   Luang Na Ho Kha
Boe   Khrok   Tha Mai   Thepharam
Phak   Nua   Ton Chok
n Noi   Hang Khwae   Thung
Wat Wang   Tamnak   Phaya Chomphu
Sing Kham   Christliche Deutsche
Phai Lom   Nong Khi   Schule Chiang Mai   Si Photharam
Nam Lom   Kwai   Wat Si Don
Don Kaeo   Buak Khrok Tai   106   Mun   Thung
Nam Thong   Wat Phra That   Khi Sua
Tawai   Pak Muang   Hariphunchai
Minmin Cargo II   Wat Pro Bath   San Pa Sak Nong Si Mai
on Kaeo   Kao   Tak Pha   Ku Daeng   Chaeng
             Pa Dua   Hua Lim   Wat Chang
                                         Khoeng
                      to Muang Noi to Muang Lamphun

121
107
1004
11
1005
1185
1141
1108
108

Tambon Chet Yot
Tambon Chiang Mai
Tambon Si Phum
Tambon Phra Sing
Tambon Suan Dok
Tambon Haiya

Chiang Mai National Museum
Petronas
Lanna Commercial College
Chiang Mai Rast Hospital
St Peter Eye Hospital
Anuban 2
Thai-Lar Church
Lanna Kindergarten
Super Highway
to Mae Sa Valley, Mae Rim, Don Kaeo, Chiang Dao
Sirithon
Khuang Sing
Ling Kok
Ling Kok
Ling Kok
Anantasiri Tennis Court
Wat Chet Yot
Chedi Plong
Chiang Mai Rajabhat University
Pracha Utid
B.K.
Sirithon
Wat Chiang Chom
Chiang Mai Rajabhat University Demonstration School
Spirit House
Iyara
Phattana Chang Phueak
Chang Khian Yu Yen
Chang Khian Yu Yen
Chang Khian- Ched Yot
Sukhaphiban 24
Thewan
Than Tawan
Than Tawan
Chedi Plong
Wiang Bua
Siri Watthana
Muen Dam Pra Kot
Soi 11
Wiwang Kaeo
Northern Palace
Holiday Garden
Nice Nails
Tarin
Thorakhammanakhom
Thewan
Thewarit
The Guest
Thong Kwao
Thong Kwao
Wiang Bua
Sod Sueksa
Foreign Language and Computer Institute (North)
Ku Tao 2
Chomdoi House
Chiang Mai Phucome
Chiang Mai Hill 2000
Bualuang
Chiang Mai Administrative Court
Chiang Mai Grand View
Thep Rak
Thewarit
Santi Suk
Anusan Sunthorn Deaf School
Hassadisawee 6
Wipanan Mansion
Ku Tao
Wat Ku Tao
Round Building
Chomdoi Condotel
Kat Rin Kham Night Bazaar
Chiang Mai Polytechnic College
Lanna Villa
Lanna Villa
Charoen Suk
Santi Suk
Ratchadamri
Hassadisawee 6
Sri Santitham
S&P
Tops
Thep Bodindecha School
Chiang Mai Stadium
Muthita Pracharak School
U-Thong
Hillside Condotel
Sanit Rak
Sanit Rak
Morakot
Morakot
Pong Suwan
Mercure
Chang Phueak
White Elephant Monument
Chiang Mai Provincial Physical College
The Pub
Living Space
Antique Textile
Amari Rincome Hotel
Mu Ban Nanthawan
Kholand
Fa Thani
The Dome Residance
Huay Kaeo Polyclinic
Pub Plueng
Consulate of Sweden
Sudsanan Samsuk
Nakorn Ping
Wat Santitham
Inthanin Sa-Nga
Choeng Doi
Chiang Mai Fire Station
Chang Phueak
Erawan
Chiang Mai Phu Viang
Chiang Phueak Bus Station
Nantawan Arcade
Mike's Burger
Lots of Arty
Ginger
Srisan-3 panmai
Pasta Cafe
Lanna
Srithana Commercial College
YMCA
Mengrai Ratsami
Vista 12 Huay Kaeo
Chang Phueak
Worachet Anusson School
Chiang Mai Pacific Mansion
Kowit Thamrong Chiang School
Velocity
Wat Chiang Yeun
Wat Chiang Yuen Municipal School
Suk Kasem
Nimmana Haeminda 4
Chabaa Thai
Baan Say La
At Niman
Shinawatra
Shell
Orchid
Discovery
Computer Plaza
Northern Inn
S&P
Wat Chiang Yeun
Nimmana Haeminda 6
Baan
Nimmana Haeminda 7
Kad Suan Kaeo/Central & IT City
Kad Suan Kaeo
Dae Jang Kum
Wat Lokmoli
Chiang Mai Mosque
Smoothie Blues
Yesterday
Nimmana Haeminda 94
Starbucks
Green Palace
Siri Mangkhalachan
Siri Mangkhalachan 5
Lotus Pang Suan Kaeo
Public Library
Thanon Manee Noppharat
Kantary Hills
Nimmana Haeminda 11
Nimmana Haeminda 13
Consulate of Australia
The Nest
Central Duangtawan
Thanon Manee Noppharat
Pratu Chang Pheuak
North Gate
Peter
Charcoal
Chiang Rai 2
Khun Chum
Nimmana Haeminda 12
Siri Mangkhalachan 7
Pang Suan Kaeo
Sri Tokyo
Hua Lin
Arak 1
Red Hibiscus Guest House
Wat Kuan Kama
Ratchaphakhinai 5
Paneeda
Vista
Supreme
Pignakorn
Nim Mhan
Doi Chang
Siri Mangkhalachan 9
Maze Cafe
Ratchawithi
Wat Pa Phrao Nai
Lanna
Wat Hua Khwang
RCN
Court Lamchan
Warm Up
Sai Nam Phueng
Oasis Spa
Siri Mangkhalachan 11
Arak 2
Thanon Wiang Kaeo
Chiang Mai Vocational College
Thai Inter Airways
Malak
Jonadda GH
I berry
Pann Malee
International Center
Sai 28
Ratchawithi
Wat Dab Phai
Ho Phra Nai
Chiang Mai Technical College
Chiang Mai Woman School
Phra Pok Klao 13
Yuparaj Wittayalai School
Summit
On the Road Books
Irrigated Experiment Station of CMU
Srinakarin Health Park
Chiang Mai University
CMU Art Culture Hall
Sai 26
Arak 3
Singharat 1
Soi 1
Anusawari Sam Kasat
Th. Ratchawithi
Chiang Mai Provincial Court
Nayok Fa
Safe House
Moon Muar
to Chiang Mai Zoo
Chiang Mai University Art Museum
Convention Center
Sai 25
Sai 23
Malaria Center
Arak 4 Ko
Wat Pha Pong
Grand Warorot
Wat Thung Yu
Pak Do
Buri
Wat Chai Phrakiat
Chiang Mai City Arts & Cultural Center
Montri
Wat Duang Di
Moon Muar
Rendezvous
Public Health Center
Sai 22
Hill Tribe Products Foundation
Chiang Mai Neurological Hospital
Maharat Nakhon Chiang Mai Hospital
Sujinno Building
Pratu Suan Dok
Th. Inthawarorot
Camp Fitness
Th. Inthawarorot
Wat Phra Sing Waramahawihan
Th. Ratchadamnoen
Tamarind Village
Wat Pan An
Gap House
Sanambin Kao 2
Sanambin Kao 4
Sanambin Kao 6
Thanon Suthep
Thanon Suthep
Suandok Vegetarian
Wat Suan Dok School
Bangkok
Chiang Come
Chiang Mai Provincial Ratchamangklaphisek National Library
Arak 6 Rachamankha
Mountain Biking
Wanasit GH
Oasis Spa
Dor Dek
Paper
Maker
Wat Phra Tao
Wat Chedi Luang Worawihan
Lanna Architecture Center
Sis Putthisopon School
Yoga Sala
Top North
Top Pan
Mu Ban Dao Dueng
Wat Suan Dok
Darunrak Kindergarten
Mali Son
Sirorot
Arak 7
Ban Poem Panya
Evening Vendors
Thanon Ratchamankha
Wat
Heuan Phen
Garden GH
New Collection
Anodard
Nat
Julie
Bodhi Serene
Tambon Suan Dok
Pai Yuai-Ma Ruai
Suan Dok 5
Suan Dok 7
Sirorot
Sirorot 5
Wattanothai Payap School
Pimanthip Golf Course
Thanon Ratchamankha
Koto
Th. Ratchamankha
Wat Muen Ngoen Kong
Wat Phra Jao Mengrai
Wat Chang Taem
Wat Chedlin
Banana GH
Blue Moon
Thapae Gate
Kata
Mu Ban Suthep
Mu Ban Suthep
Wat Methang
Yoga Studio
Mengrai Kilns
Khru Thep Arts School
Wat Phra Singh
Wat Pan Waen
Tambon Phra Sing
Wat Pan Tao
Wat Fon
Wat Muen Tum
Phra Pok Klao
Phra Phai GH
Mu Ban Khumkhon Phing 1-4
Buak Hat Public Park
Wat Phuak Hong
Ku Huang
Pratu Suan Dok
Th. Bumrung Buri
Wat Phuak Taem
Soi 1
Wat Phuak Hong
Th. Bumrung Buri
Pratu Chiang Mai
Rat Chiang Sean
Mu Ban Ping Phayom
Technic Center
Kad Suan Kaeo
Suan Prung Psychiatric Hospital
Consulate of China
Intellectual Development Institute
Serenity
Ruam Phaet Hospital
Wat Muang Mang
Thanon Chiang Lo
Wat Phuak Pia
Wua Lai
Consulate of Japan
Chiida Spa
Kad Suan Kaeo
Nanthana
Wat Sisuphan
Silver Shops
Hai Ya
Chiang Mai Gate
Wat Muen Sai
Siam Silver
Chatree
Wat That Kham
Rat Chiang Sean
Air Force Unit 41
New Krua Thai
Wing 41 Hospital
Suthep
Sala Mangsavirat
Thippanet Market
Thippanet
Tri Yaan Na Ros Colonial House
Thanon Wua Lai
Chiang Mai College of Dramatic Arts
Wat Yang Kuang
Suriyawong 5
Chiang Mai Airport
Thanin Club
Technic Center
Niyom Panich
Toyota
Chiang Mai Plant Market
Sala Daeng Public Library
Rin Kaeo Povech
Si Ping Mueang 1
Thong Pan Chang Sauna and Fitness
Mahidol
Passenger Terminal Building
Plant Quarantine Station
Consulate of Japan
Airport Business Park
Old Medicine
Rimping Supermarket
Si Ping Mueang
Mu Ban Inthranurak
Airport Hotel
Airport Road
Immigration Office
Amari
The Far Eastern University
Chiang Mai Cultural Center and Sbun-Nga Textile Museum
Uang Phan Park
Air Observation Station
Regional Custom
Chez John
Central Airport Plaza
Wine Connection
Old Chiang Mai Cultural Center
to Sankamphaeng, Mae Om
Tawee Koon

1 : 20,000

0.5km 0.2mile

Super Highway 11

to Tambon Patan
to Don Kaeo
to Muang Kaeo
to Nong Chom, San Sai, Phrao
to Nong Chom, San Sai, Phrao

118
to San Na Moeng, Doi Saket & Chiang Rai

Esso
Goodyear Eagle Tires

Lotus
Wat Pa Tan
Wat Pa Tan School
Mazda
Thep Panya Hospital

to Chai Sa Than

Mahanaga
Mo Wach Clinic
Chiang Mai Church
Goodyear
Truck Center
Mercedes
118
Isuzu
Green Bus Company
Thetsaban 2 Soi 3
Thetsaban 2 Soi 4
Thetsaban 2 Soi 5

Wat Kam 3
Mahanaga
Charoen Rat 4
Charoen Rat 2
Trat Wong 1
Trat Wong 3
Trat Wong 5
Chiang Mai District Court
Residential Complex

Ban Im Boon
Khao Soi Sampe Jai
Wat Fah Ham
Khao Soi Lam Duan
Trinity Gospel Church
Rattana kosin 1
Chiang Mai Provincial Juvenile Court
Arcade Inn
Arcade Bus Station

Si Mongkhon
Huan Soontaree
Chiang Mai Chinese Church
Consulate of Peru
Rattana Kosin 1

Tambon Chang Moi
Wat Pa Phaeng
Wat Pa Phaeng municipal School
Chalerm Prakiat Rama IX Bridge
Consulate of India
AKA Spa

Wat Koo kam Municipal School
Wat Koo kam
Thung Hotel

Rattanakosin
Rattanakosin
Lanna Him Ping
Pun Pun Guest House
Payap University (Kaeo Nawarat Campus)
Dara Wittayalai School
Bann Mao Dek
Thung Hotel 4
Thung Hotel 5
Thung Hotel 3

Wang Sing Kham 3
Suan Samoonprai
Oshion Resort
Chetuphon Suksa School
McCormick Hospital
Thung Hotel 1/1

Muang Mai
Wang Kham
Je t'Aime
Wat Chetuphon
Thanon Chetuphon
Thai Tribal Crafts

Zahaheng

Muang Fa
The Prince Royal's College
Caltex
Nakorn Ping Yamaha Music Academy 2
Tambon Nong Pa Krang
Bann Tazala

Khao Soi Lam Duan, Ban Faham
Wat Sikong
Surin Clinic
Imm Eco
Education Park School
Esso

Chang Moi Fresh Market
Rimping Condominium
Taraburi
Dalaabaa
Consulate of United Kingdom
Wat Nong Pa Krang School
Wat Nong Pa Krang

Consulate of USA
SCB
Duangkamon
Wat Nong Pa Krang 4
Wat Nong Pa Krang 3
Wat Nong Pa Krang 2

Nakorn Ping
Nakhon Ping Bridge
Baan Orapin
Sop Moei Arts
Attakawa Mosque
Ban Si Suk
Ban Si Suk
SR Complex

Prince
New Mittraphap
The Brasserie
Foot Bridge
Baan Rai 2
Flora
Jitt Phakdee School
Phingharat School
FedEx

Chinatown Arch
Aomngam
Good View
Miss Chocolate
The Gallery
Vilacini
Rarin Jinda Wellness Spa & Resort
Sayuri
Shell

Wat Saen Fang
Namdari
Lam Chang
Baan Rai 2
Bamrungraj 4

Top Gear Bike Shop
Philatelic Museum
Le Pont
First Church of Christ
C&C Teak House
Puripunn

Tha Phae Inn
Finland
Chiang Mai Municipal Hospital
Wawee Coffee
Bossotel Inn

Ruang Tha Phae
Dusit
Chedi
TAT
Galare
San Pa Khoi Bus Station (to Bor Sang & San Kampaeng)
BBL
SCIB
Palm Garden

Wat Bupparam
Banthai
Chiang Inn
Wat Uppakhut
Nawarat Bridge
Sri Prakard
Wat San Pa Khoi
Thanon Charoen Mueang

Phae 4 Ko
D2
River View Lodge
Love at First Bite
Tea Vana
San Pa Khoi
CC Kiatwong
Pattana Language School
Shewe Wana
Chiang Mai Technology School

Manathai
Wat Chang Kong
Kalare Night Bazaar
Antique House
Diamond Riverside
Iron Bridge
Downtown Inn
TAT
Rimping Village
Osathaphan
Kawila Boxing Stadium
Dr. Wong Hospital
Oasis

Wat Loi Khro
Le Meridien
Royal Lanna
Thanon Loi Khro
Thanon Charoen Mueang

Suriwongse
Gecko Books
Mike's Burger
The Imperial Mae Ping
Star Royal Princess
CM Pavillion
Just Khao Soy
Rimping
Spa de Siam
Thanon Kong Sai
Chiang Mai

Lanna
Yaang Come Village
Wat Si Don Chai
Park Inn
Chedi
Wat Tha Satoi
Wat Tha Satoi Municipal School
Wat Khet
Kawila Anukul School
Anu Withi

Nakorn Ping Hospital
Anusarn Night Market
Thanon Anusan Sunthon
Piccola Roma
The Restaurant
Mandarin Oriental Dhara Dhevi
Maitreejit Christian Chiang Mai School

Suriwong Book Center
Good Health
Lanna Earth Come Spa
Whole
Wat Chai Mongkhon
Kawila Military Barracks
Kawila Hospital

Chao Mae Tubtim Shrine
Siam Plaza
Shangri-La
Vihara Liangsan
Baan Kaew GH
Consulate of France
Chez Daniel
Mae Ping River Cruise

Santi Suksa School
Chabad House of Chiang Mai
Regina Coeli College
Peaks Town
Yaang Come
Chairot Wittaya School
Phra Chao Kawila Monument

Lanna Palace Paradise
Central Chiang Mai Memorial Hospital
Empress
Wild Flower Inn
TFB
Sacred Heart Cathedral
Sacred Heart College
Electric Administration Area 1(North)
Bus Station to Lamphun
Rat Uthit 3
Wat Muang Kai
Jitra Wittaya School
Nestle

Golden Inn
Khantoke Palace
The Park
Buarawong Residence
Aruntara
Montfort College Primary School
Gymkhana Club
Lanna International Church
Northern Heritage Resort

Chang Khlan Mosque
Mo Wimol Clinic
Al Farooq
Den Damrongtham Church
Den Damrongtham Church Cemetery
Gymcana Golf Course

to Sop Mae Kha, Pa Daet
to Lamphun, Pa Sang, Saraphi
Pangviman Place
Soi 6
Mueang Sat
to Saraphi
to Lampang, Bangkok

Ping River
Super Highway 11

Tambon Chang Moi
Tambon Chang Khlan
Tambon Wat Ket
Tambon Nong Pa Krang
Tambon Tha Sala

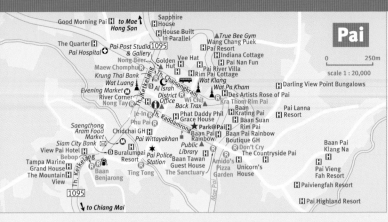

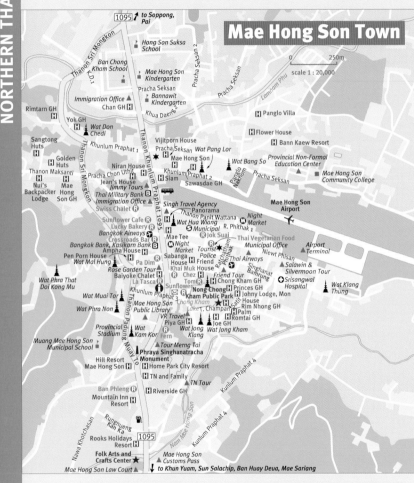

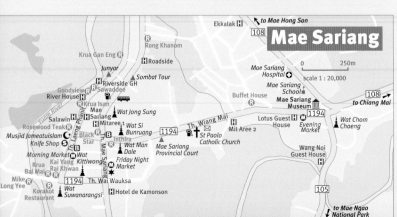

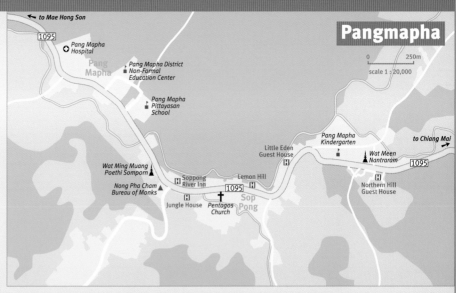

Pangmapha

to Mae Hong Son ←

1095

Pang Mapha Hospital

Pang Mapha District Non-Formal Education Center

Pang Mapha Pittayasan School

0   250m
scale 1 : 20,000

Pang Mapha Kindergarten

to Chiang Mai →

Wat Meen Nantraram

Little Eden Guest House

1095

Wat Ming Muang Poethi Somporn

Nong Pha Cham Bureau of Monks

Soppong River Inn

Lemon Hill

1095

Sop Pong

Northern Hill Guest House

Jungle House

Pentagos Church

ONG SON TOWN 38

ng Son

e Hong Son Airport

Wat Pa Ban Mai

Ruan Noppakao Resort
k City Resort
Family

Mae Surin
Waterfall
tional Park

Mae Sakud Waterfall

erng Tai
ang

Fern Resort
View Point

n Mae Sakud
Jpatham
of Monks

Pha Bong

Wat Pha Bong South

108

to Amphoe Khun Yuam, Mae Sariang

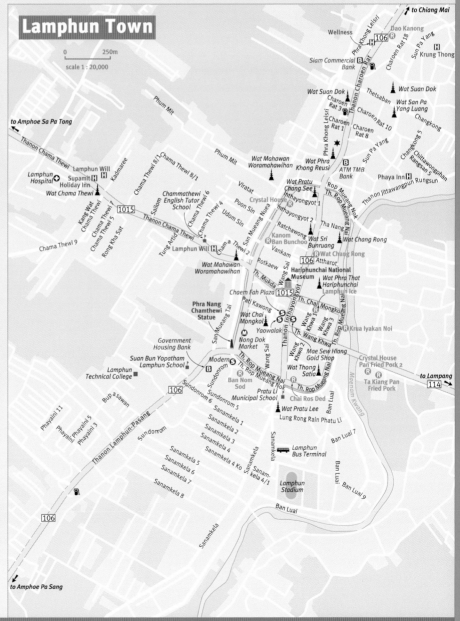

Lamphun Town

0   250m
scale 1 : 20,000

to Chiang Mai ↗

Wellness

106

Dao Kanong

Phra Khong Leisri

Charoen Rat 18

Sun Pa Yang

Krung Thong

Siam Commercial Bank

Thanon Charoen Rat

Thetsaban

Wat Suan Dok

Wat Suan Dok

Charoen Rat 3

Charoen Rat 10

Wat San Pa Yang Luang

Changkong

Phum Mit

Charoen Rat 1

Charoen Rat 8

Sun Pa Yang

Chamnongsuk Chittawongphan Rangsan 5

to Amphoe Sa Pa Tong ←

Thanon Chama Thewi

Phum Mit

Wat Mahawan Woramahawihan

Wat Phra Khong Reusi

Phaya Inn

Lamphun Will

Kadmaree

Lamphun Hospital

Supamit Holiday Inn

Chama Thewi 8/1

Chama Thewi 8/1

ATM TMB Bank

Thanon Jittawangpun Rungsun

Wat Chama Thewi

Chama Thewi 7

Chama Thewi 6

Viratat

Wat Pratu Chang See

Rop Mueang Nok

Inthayongyot 1

Kang Wat Chama Thewi

1015

Sailom

Poon Sin

Crystal House

Inthayongyot 2

Th. Rop Mueang Mai

Chama Thewi 5

Chama Thewi 4

Udom Sin

Ratchawong

Wat Sri Bunruang

Wat Chang Rong

Chama Thewi 9

Rong Kha Sat

Thanon Chama Thewi

San Mueang Nuea

Kanom Ban Bunchoo

Wat Chang Rong

Tung Lamphun Will

Chama Thewi 2

Vankam

106

Atharot

Wat Mahawan Woramahawihan

Rotkaew

Hariphunchai National Museum

Wat Phra That Hariphunchai

Lamphun Ice

Th. Mukda

1015

Chaem Fah Plaza

Pati Kawong

Th. Chai Mongkon

Phra Nang Chamthewi Statue

Wang Khwa

Wat Chai Mongkol

Th. Inthayongyot

Wang Khwa 1

Th. Wang Khwa

Krua Iyakan Noi

San Mueang Tai

Yaowalak

Wang Khwa 2

Wang Khwa 3

Mae Sew Hlang Gold Shop

Crystal House Pan Fried Pork 2

Government Housing Bank

Nong Dok Market

Th. Rop Mueang Nai

Th. Wang Khwa

Ta Kiang Pan Fried Pork

to Lampang →

Suan Bun Yopatham Lamphun School

Modern

Th. Rop Mueang Nok

Wat Thong Satia

Th. Rop Mueang Nai

114

Lamphun Technical College

Sundonrom

Ban Nom Sod

Pratu Li

Chai Ros Ded

Menom Kwang

Phayaini 11

Sundonrom 6

Sundonrom 5

Municipal School

Wat Pratu Lee

Ban Luai

Phayaini 5

Phayaini 3

Phayaini

Bup asawan

Sundonrom

Sanamkela 1

Lung Rong Rain Phatu Li

Ban Luai 7

Sanamkela 2

Sanamkela 3

Sanamkela 4

106

Sanamkela

Lamphun Bus Terminal

Sanamkela 5

Sanamkela 4 Ko

Sanamkela 4/1

Ban Luai 9

Sanamkela 6

Thanon Lamphun-Pasang

Sanamkela 7

Sanam-kela 4/1

Lamphun Stadium

Sanamkela 8

Sanamkela

Ban Luai

106

Th. Khunlumprabat

to Amphoe Pa Sang ←

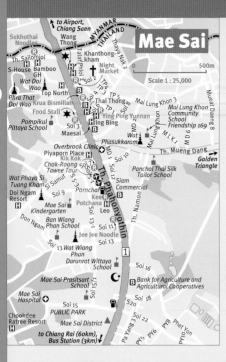

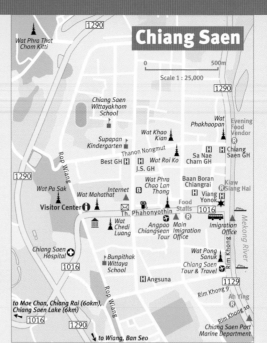

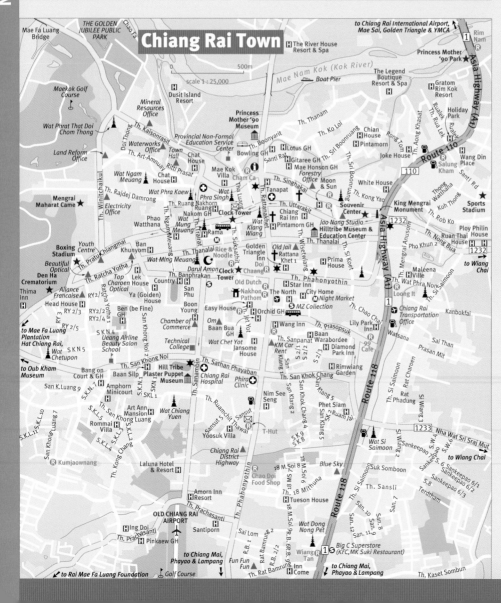

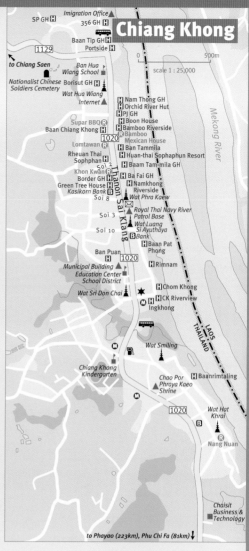

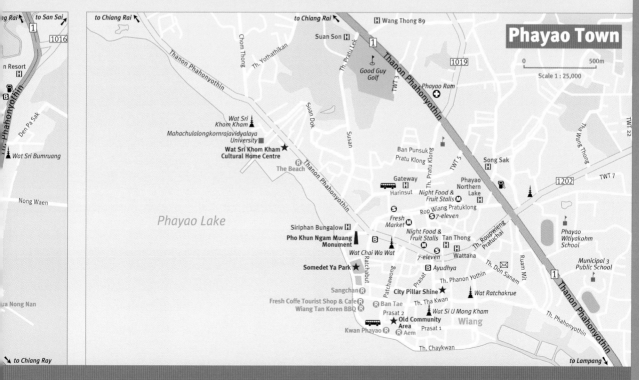

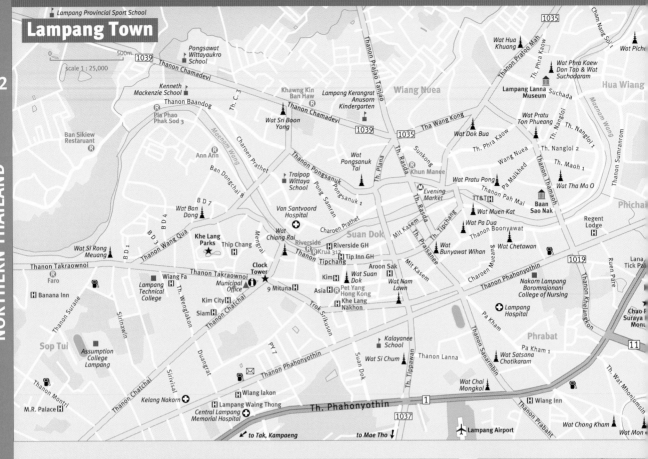

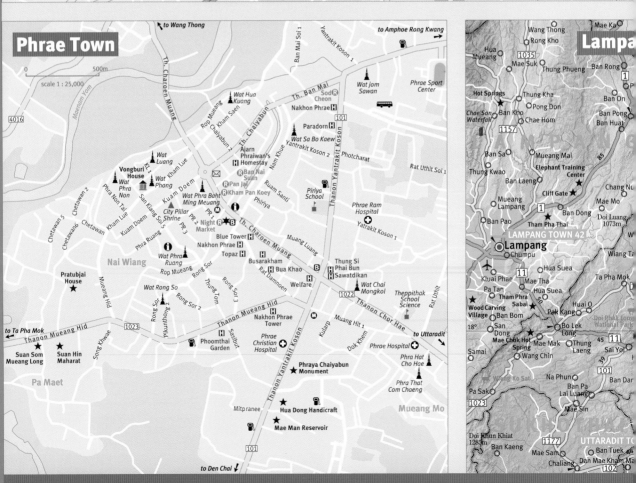

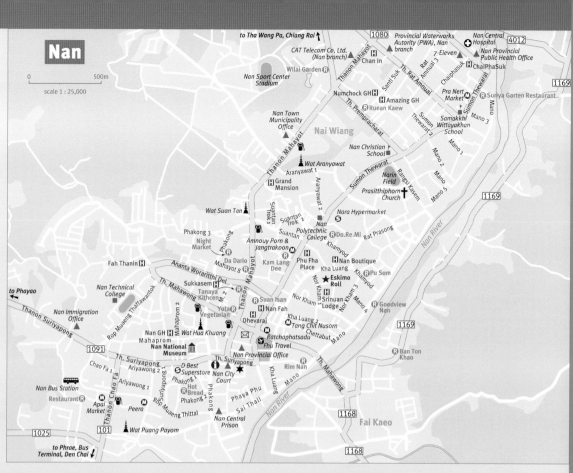

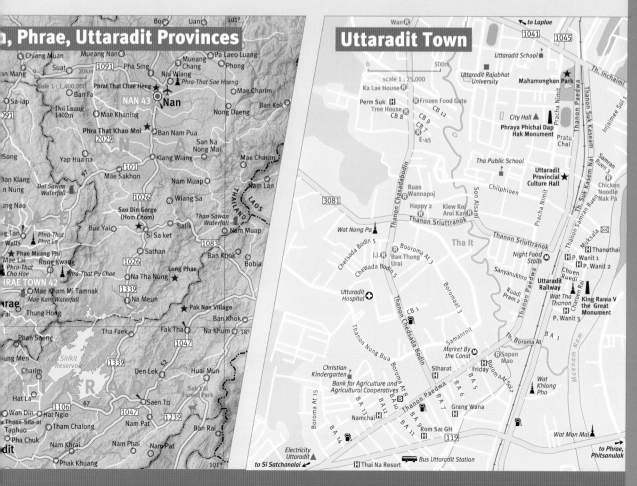

44

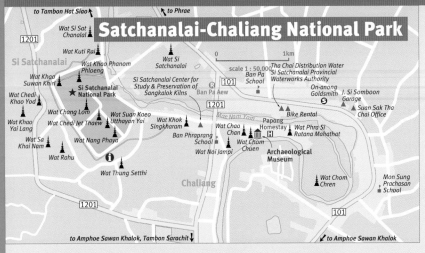

Satchanalai-Chaliang National Park

scale 1 : 50,000

to Tambon Hat Siao • to Phrae

Si Satchanalai

Wat Si Sat Chanalal
Wat Kuti Rai
1201
Wat Khao Phanom Phloeng
Wat Si Satchanalai
Si Satchanalai Center for Study & Preservation of Sangkalok Kilns
Tha Chai Distribution Water
Si Satchanalai Provincial Waterworks Authority
Ban Pa School
Wat Khao Suwan Khiri
Si Satchanalai National Park
101
Ban Pa Aew
On-anong Goldsmith
J. Si Somboon Garage
Wat Chedi Khao Yod
Wat Khao Yai Lang
Wat Chang Lom
Wat Chedi Jet Thaew
Wat Suan Kaeo Utthayan Yai
Wat Khok Singkharam
Bike Rental
Papong Homestay
Wat Phra Si Ratana Mahathat
Suan Sak Tha Chai Office
1201
Ban Phraprang School
Wat Chao Chan
Wat Sa Khai Nam
Wat Nang Phaya
Wat Noi Jampi
Wat Chom Chuen
Wat Rahu
Wat Thung Setthi
Archaeological Museum
Chaliang
Wat Chom Chren
Mon Sung Prachasan School
1201
101
to Amphoe Sawan Khalok, Tambon Sarachit
to Amphoe Sawan Khalok

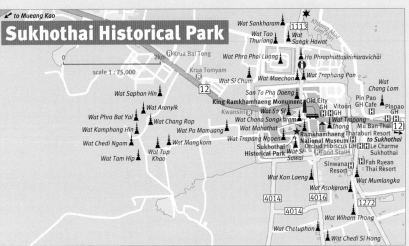

Sukhothai Historical Park

scale 1 : 75,000

to Mueang Kao

Wat Sankharam
1113
Wat Tao Thuriang
Wat Sangk Hawat
Krua Bai Tong
Wat Phra Phai Luang
Ho Phraphuttasirimaravichai
Krua Tomyam
Wat Maechon
Wat Traphang Pan
Wat Chang Lom
12
Wat Si Chum
Wat Saphan Hin
San Ta Pha Daeng
Old City
Pin Pao GH
Pinpao GH
Pinpao GH Cafe
Wat Phra Bat Yai
Wat Aranyik
King Ramkhamhaeng Monument
Wat Sa Si
Wat Trapang Thong
Mu Ban Thai
Wat Chang Rop
Kwansiri
Wat Chana Songkram
Wat Mahathat
Wat Kamphang Hin
Wat Pa Mamuang
Ramkhamhaeng Tharaburi Resort
12
Wat Chedi Ngam
Wat Mangkorn
Wat Trapang Ngoen
National Museum
to Sukhothai
Wat Tup Khao
Sukhothai Historical Park
Orchid Hibiscus GH
Le Charme Sukhothai
Wat Tam Hip
Wat Si Sawai
Food Stalls
Sinwana Resort
Fah Ruean Thai Resort
Wat Kon Laeng
Wat Asokaram
Wat Mumlangka
4014
4016
1272
4014
Wat Wiharn Thong
Wat Chetuphon
Wat Chedi Si Hong

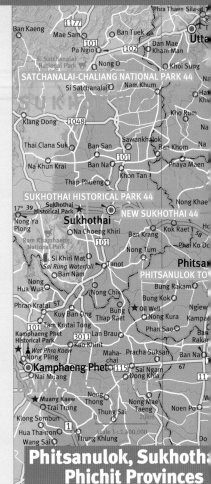

SATCHANALAI-CHALIANG NATIONAL PARK 44

SUKHOTHAI HISTORICAL PARK 44

NEW SUKHOTHAI 44

Phitsanulok, Sukhothai, Phichit Provinces

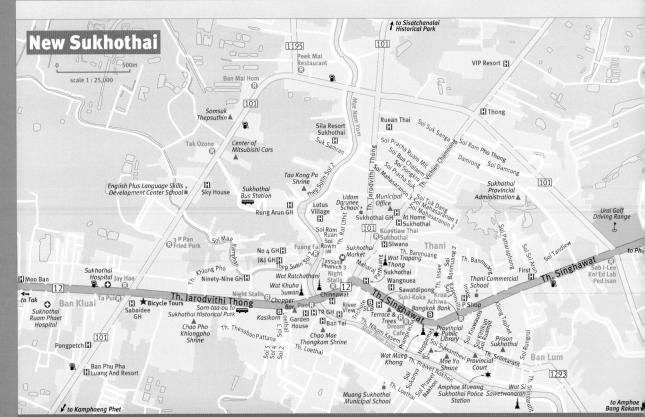

New Sukhothai

scale 1 : 25,000

to Sisatchanalai Historical Park

1195
Peek Mai Restaurant
101
VIP Resort
Ban Mai Hom
101
Somsak Thepsuthin
Sila Resort Sukhothai
Suk Samran
Ruean Thai
Thong
Tak Ozone
Center of Mitsubishi Cars
Tao Kong Pa Shrine
Sukhothai Provincial Administration
Urai Golf Driving Range
English Plus Language Skills Development Center School
Sky House
Sukhothai Bus Station
Lotus Village
Udom Darunee School
Municipal Office
Rung Arun GH
Sukhothai GH
At Home
101
3 P Pan Fried Pork
No 4 GH
J&J GH
Fuang Fa Bar
Kuaytiaw Thai
Sukhothai Market
Slwana
Thani
Sukhothai Hospital
Tassani Phanich 3
Wat Trapang Thong
Th. Banmuang
Thani Commercial School
Jay Hae
Ninety-Nine GH
Wat Ratchathani
Night Stalls
Wangnuea
Moo Ban
12
Wat Khuha Suwan
Sawatdipong
Suki-Koka
Achiwa
Sab I-Lee Roi Ed Lab Ped Isan
to Tak
Ban Kluai
Ta Pui
Bicycle Tours
Night Stalls
Chopper Bar
Chinnawat
12
P Shop
Sukhothai Ruam Phaet Hospital
Sabaidee GH
Sorn-taa-ou to Sukhothai Historical Park
Kasikorn
River View
Bangkok Bank
Provincial Public Library
Pongpetch
Chao Pho Khlongpho Shrine
Garden House
Ban Tai
Terrace & Trees
Dream Cafe
Provincial Court
Prison Sukhothai
101
Chao Mae Thongkam Shrine
Th. Loethai
Wat Maeg Khong
Wat Si Ruamit
Ban Phu Pha Luang And Resort
Wat Ya Shrine
Amphoe Mueang Sukhothai Police Station
Sawetwanaran
1293
Muang Sukhothai Municipal School
to Kamphaeng Phet
Ban Lum
to Amphoe Bang Rakam

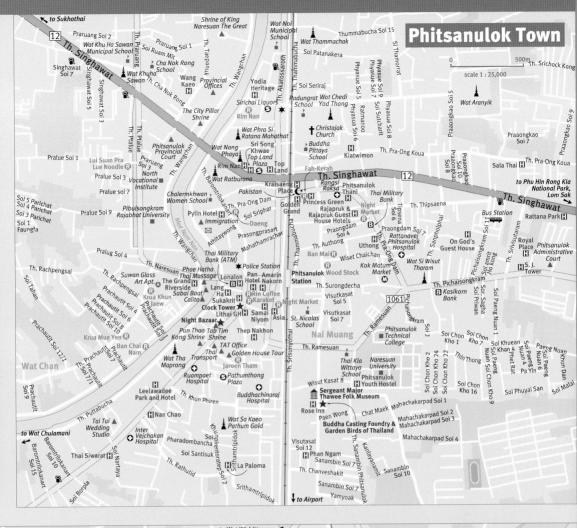

Phitsanulok Town

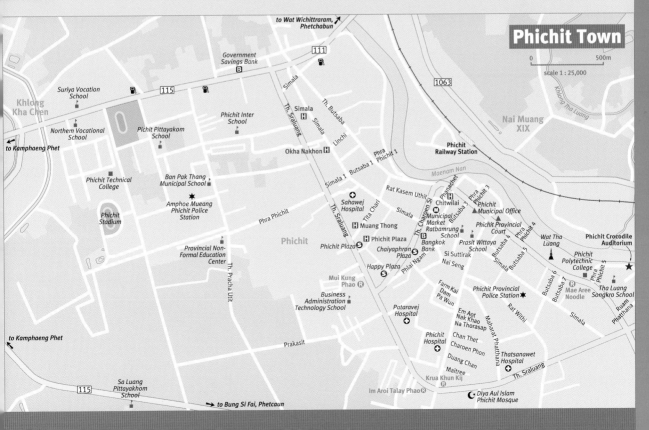

Phichit Town

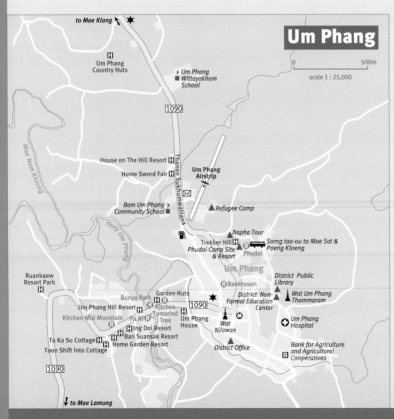

Tak Town

Kamphaeng Phet Town

Northeastern Thailand

scale 1 : 2,000,000

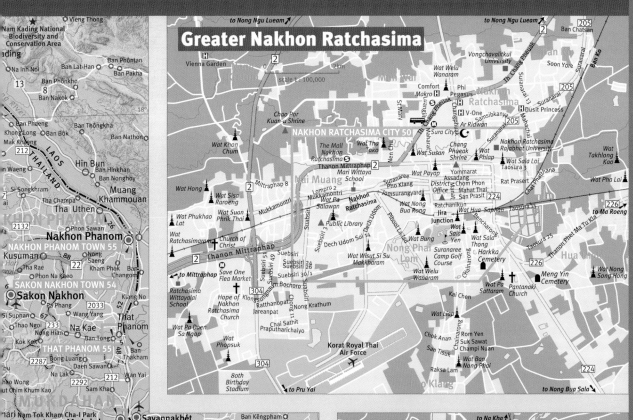

Greater Nakhon Ratchasima

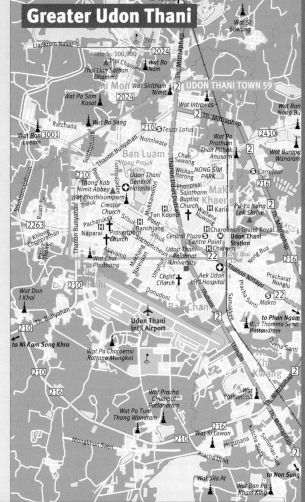

Greater Udon Thani

Nakhon Ratchasima City

scale 1 : 25,000

0   500m

to Cho Ho   Sura City
St. Mary's Hospital
Ratchasima Avenue Building
Sima City Condominium Maharat
Maharat   Star GH
College of Nursing Borommaratchachonnani
Thai Immigration
Maharat
VIP 12   VIP 4   VIP 4   St. Mary
VIP 11   VIP 3   VIP 9
VIP 10   VIP 3
VIP 2
VIP 1/2
VIP 1
Wat Tha Tako
Trong Somrongian
Moe Nam Mun
Bumaka 4
Bumaka 2   Bumaka 1
Chaya Dakar Garden House & Resort
Municipal 4 School
Phopan Wittaya School
Korat Noodle Carts
Nen Chu
Prapa
Charat Pradit Driving School
Vocational College
Arisadang Lake
Wat Susan
Sur
Wittaya School
Sch
Municipal 3 School   Junior

Water Gardens Fantasia Lagoon
Bangkok Hospital   Crystal Place Mansion   The Mall   Somrongian 1
Mae Nam Mun   Boiled Indian Almond   SCB Bank
Dairy Queen
Top Huat
224
Thanon Mittraphap   Wat Rat Bamrung   Cathay   Wat Payap   Big Chili
Clumphon
Pon Sean
Thanon Mittraphap
IT Plaza Mall
Good House Prapa
A-Match Tutor School
Big C
Rachaphruk Grand
Thanon Mittraphap
Ratchadamnern
Thao Suranari Museum
Korat
Maharat
Assada
Ratchasima
Klang Plaza A
Chom Phon University
Bangkok
Wat Phra

Pidaso
King   2
Nai Muang
Chevrolet   Tesco Lotus
Wat Khok Phrom
Sawai Riang
Samorai
Lompru 2/8
Zap Corner
City Park   KS Pavillion
Yamo   Yamo Apts
Thai Commercial Bank
Baan Thai Desserts
Technical College
Korat Memorial Hospital
Chan
Wat Pho
Burin
Tokyo
Th. Suranaree
Sansabai House
Srivijaya
Mae Gimhaeng
Wat Sakae
Potong
Trolley Tour
Southern Blue City
Net Guru

Mary Technology School
Taj Mahal
Crab Seafood
Lompru 2/8   Lompru 2/2
Wat Nong Chabok
Lompru 2   Wat Samo Rai
Five Star Makro
Lompru 2
Thanon Mukkamontri
Nong Cream Grilled Korean
Cowboy Roast Beef Korean
Mari Wittaya School
Community Basic Public HealTh. Center
Provincial Electricity Authority
Thanon Suranaree
Municipal Office
Sunrise
Siri
Thanon Pho Klang
Wat Chaeng Nai
Wat Chaeng Nok
Thanon Jomsurangyard
Red Pepper
Trok Kaset
Trok Teetok
Chao Mae Tubtim Shrine
Chaophaya Inn
Kitchen Survey
Anego
Bangkok Bank
Th. Mahat Thai
Maha Wirawong National Museum
Yotha
Fah Thai
Tim Bum
Chomsurang
City Hall
Chez Andy
Rice Shop
Provincial Hall

Lompru 2/8
Lompru 2
Suebsiri 1
Suebsiri
Mukkamontri 5
Table Tennis Korat Center
NONG WILL LAND
Sort Sawat
Zap Corner
Nong Hua Lao
Nakhon Ratchasima
Samakee Rot Fai School
Phukaew Apartment
MILITARY LODGING NONG BUA RONG
Wat Nong Bua Rong
Wat Suttha Jinda Worawihan
Ratchadamnern
District Office
Th. Ratchanikun
Ratchanikun
District Cou
Provincial Court
Jira Junction

TAT
Sima Thani
Suebsiri 1
Doctor's House
Church Garage
Cabbages & Condoms
Suebsiri 3/3
You Little Chicken
Suebsiri 3/9
Wat Pa Salawan
Suebsiri 3/11
Maree Business Administration School
MILITARY LODGING PHAI LOM
Dech Udom
Udomsuk
Phu Nong Ko Deng Noodle
MILITARY LODGING NONG BUA RONG
Je Noodle Nut
Rim Bung
Grilled Korean Emperor
Suranari Central Stadium
Sunaree Badminton

White Rabbit
Ubonrat School
Cherdchai Bus Garage
to Mittraphap
Suebsiri 3
Nakhon Ratchasima Japanese School
Suebsiri 3/36
Suebsiri 3/34
Public Library
Suebsiri 7
Non-Formal Education Center
Supaporn
Suebsiri 3/26
Suebsiri 3/24
Sukree
Satween Day
Suebsiri 11
Suebsiri 3/22
NONG KAE CHANG PARK
Curry House
Suebsiri 3/19
Dech Udom 6
Dech Udom 6/14
Dech Udom Soi 6
Dech Udom 6/8
Dech Udom 6/9
Dech Udom 6/11
Dech Udom Soi 6
Dech Udom Soi 6
Phu Nong Ko
Nakhon Sukprasert
Fort Suranari Hospital
Terrace Marsh
Wat Bung
Horse Suranaree Camp Stadium
Suranaree Camp Golf Course
Yothinnukun School
Ban Pradu Khok Phrai School

Suebsiri 10
Suebsiri 12
Suebsiri 14
Suebsiri 16
Suebsiri 18
Suebsiri 20
Suebsiri Ray Grand
Suebsiri 22
Suebsiri 24
Suebsiri 26
Suebsiri 28
Suebsiri 30/1
Suebsiri 30
Suebsiri 32/1
Thanon Suebsiri
Suebsiri 17
Suebsiri 19
Suebsiri 25
Suebsiri 27
Suebsiri 33
Bencharong
Three Cities Stick
Cholprathan Songkhro School
Dech Udom Soi 14/21
Dech Udom Soi 14/9
Dech Udom Soi 14/15
Dech Udom 14/11
Dech Udom Soi 14
Dech Udom 14/7
Dech Udom 14/9
Dech Udom 22/2
Dech Udom Soi 14
Dech Udom Soi 14
Dech Udom 18
Dech Udom Soi 22
Dech Udom 24
Dech Udom Soi 15
Dech Udom Soi 13
The Airport
Wat Wisut Si Su Makkharam
Wat Nong Phai Lom
Kitchen Blockhouse
Marsh Along the Korean Grilled Beef
Sun Terrace House
Bung Ta Lua
Nong Phai Lom
Bung Ta Lua Monument
BUNG TA LUA PARK
Wat Welu Wanaram

Army Airport
Army Corps Driving Range
2nd Army Support Command Nursery
Thanon Dech Udom

Around Phanom Rung

scale 1 : 500,000

0   10km

to Nakhon Ratchasima   Hua Thanon   to Lam Plai Mat   Bee Resort   to Buriram   to Buriram
Thanon 218   Suun Kaew Resort   Wat Khok Tabak   Wat Ban Khok Klang   Khok Ma   2208   Wat Ban Khok   Phai San
24   Ta Ni   Pru
Krok Kaeo   Tako Ta Phi   24   Rainbow City Hotels   Wiangchai Resort   Wat Pa Kok   24
2016   Wat Suwannaram   Wat Pho Tharam   E-san Khet   Wat Champa   Prakhon Chai   Wat Nong Male   2375   Chok Na Sam
Non Suwan   Wat Neem   Wat Nong Sakae   Pratatbhu   Wat Ban Pratatbhu   Wat Khawoo
King Rama Ram Forest Bureau   Sadao   Ta Pek   Wat Ban Chot   Khok Yang   Wat Ban Hin Kong   219   Kok Makham   Lawia   Wat Pathum   Chok S
2016   Non Suwan Hospital   Chaloem Phra Kiat   Wat Ban Charoen Suk   Wat Ban Pang Ku   Pang Ku   Wat Ban Nong Bon   Wat Ban Yang   Wat Suk
Chum Saeng   Wat Khok Yang   Wat Ban Charoen Suk   Phanom Rung Resort   Wat Sahamit   Wat Huai Po   Nong Bon   Wat Ban Lak
Wat Phai Photharam Khlung   Wat Pha Daeng   Sup Phraya   Nong Sai   Wat Khao Angkhan   Phanom Rung Historical Park   2221   Chorakhe Mak   219   Wat Ban Nong Bon   Khok Klang
Thai Charoen   Wat Khok Samran   Thawon   4013   Yai Yam Wattana   Wat Lam Duan Khok Sa   Wat Sophon Buraporam   Kao Din Nua   2375
Prasat Ban Khok Ngio   Wat Mai Phai   Kok Wan   Wat Ban Yang   4013   Wat Bon   219   2165   Wat Si Ram   Chik Daek
Khok Mamuang   Pakham   348   Lahan Sai   Wat Kok Wan   Khao Khok   Wat Ban Nong Tako   Hin Lat   2165   Non Charoen   Wat Ban Nong   2375
Nong Bua   224   Lahan Sai Bungalow   Wat Chumphon   Ta Chong   Wat Pho Thong   Wat Ban Lahan Sai   Muang Tam   Tao Sawai   Wat Ta Mang   2407
Lodging View Star Resort   224   Thai Charoen   Nong Takrong   2120   Ban Kruat King Resort   Tao Nai Chian   224   Ta Mang   Ta Mang
Wat Khok Muang   348   Wat Samrong   Samrong Mae   Nong Mai Ngam   Wat Nong Prue   Lang Hin Dtat   219   224   Wat Sai Ta Ku   Phanom Dong Rak
Wat Sai Thong   2120   Hu Thamnop   Wat Pa Nong Prue   Wat Nong Kok   Wat Chong   Wat Sri Mongkol   Bung Charoen   Wat Ban Sai   Chan Thop Phet   Wat Prasat Thong   2407   Prasat Ta Meuan
to Aranya Prathet   348   Som Poi   Wat Sophon Wanaram   Purple Top Bungalows   Wat Tham Pa Sila Ram   THA   CAM

Yasothon Town

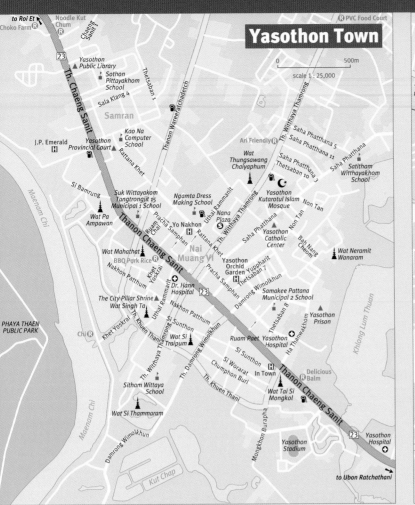

Si Saket Town

Surin Town

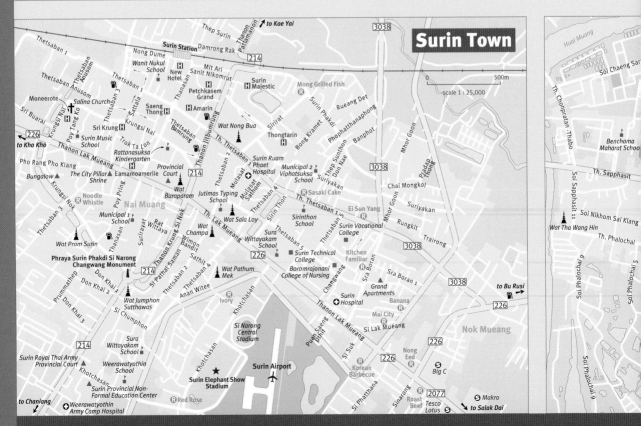

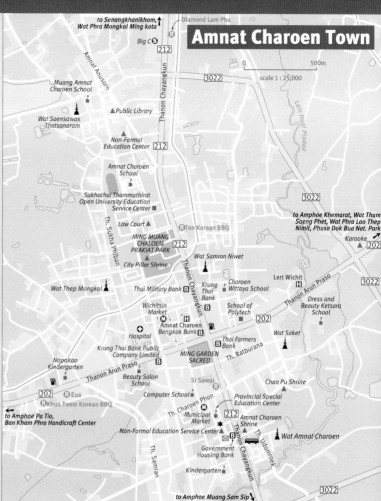

Amnat Charoen Town

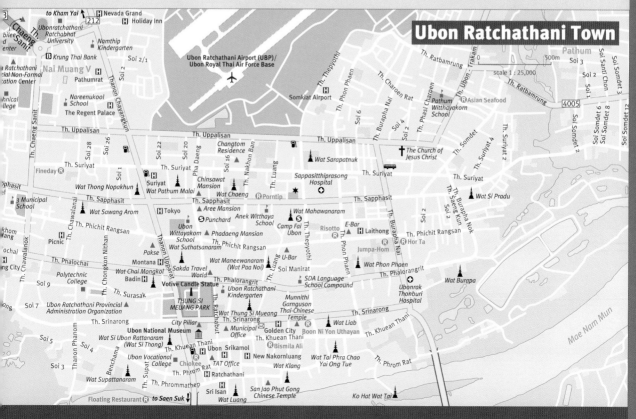

Ubon Ratchathani Town

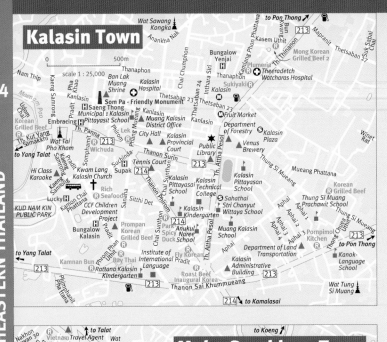

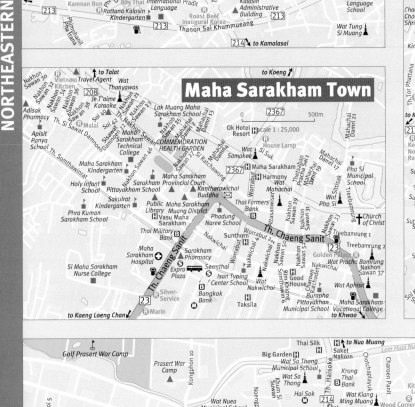

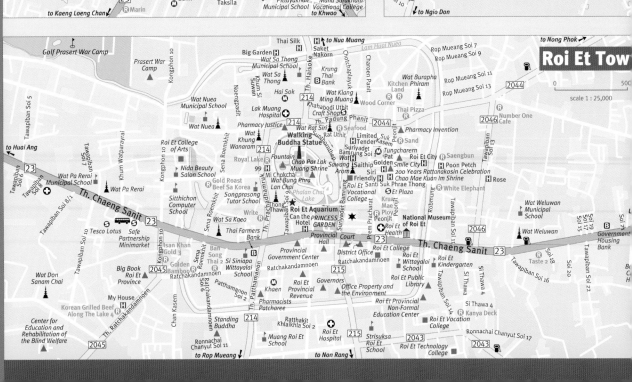

Phetchabun Town

Chaiyaphum Town

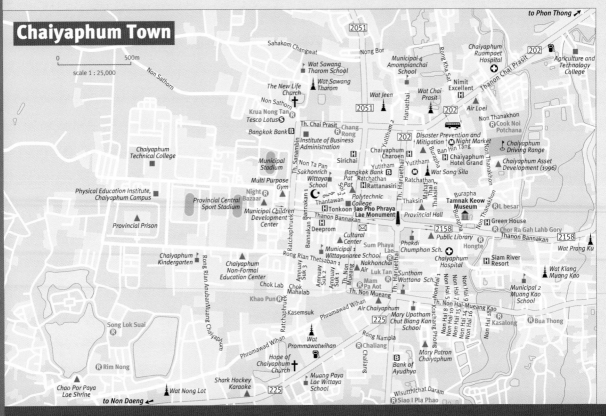

scale 1 : 25,000
0   500m

to Samran

Pa Adunlayaram
Adunlayaram Soi 6
Adunlayaram

Ruam Pattana
Santi Suk
Si Patcharin
Camp Golf

Rat Khanueng 8
Rat Khanueng 10

The Charm
Boutique Resort
Songpon
Siri Pom
Suan Thong
U Udom Suk
Seri
Camp Sri Patcharin
Rat Khanueng Si
Son Thong
Wat Non Chai
Wanaram

Thawan Mai
Je Tui
Mae Bua
Soi Mittraphap
Kasikom Tungsang 7
Rat Khanueng 7
Ban Non Chai
Municipal School
Son Thong
Kindergarten

Arkom Special School
Saiyud Srimarat
School of Technology
Suan Hansa
Vocational and Business
Administration College
Thurakit 13
Rat Khanueng 4
Rat Khanueng
Trail Mit

Soi Mittraphap 8/5
Por Sanan
Royal 77
Pracha Phatthana
Rat Khanueng 3
Technology
Thurakit
Archewa School
(T-TECH)

Soi Mittraphap 8/1
Pizza & Bake
Wat Mak Cruise
Chom Phon
Tham Chang

Soi Mittraphap 6
Soi Lang Soon Rachakam 14
Pong Pinyo
Kindergarten
Soi 5
Soi 4
Soi 3
Soi 2
Soi 1

Thepnimit
Soi Mittraphap 16
Mo Chan Uthit
BB-Foot Corner
Th. Lang Soon Rachakam
Tawantong
Golden Sun
Vegetarian Food
BEUNG TOONG
SAANG PARK

Municipal Home Triangle
Ban Sam Liam
Municipal School
Gau Yang Rabeab
Gai Yang Rabeab
Song Sab
Sakunsi
Khon Kaen
National Museum
Aomjai Coffee
Kasikom
Thungsang 25
Soon Rachakam

Pa Noi Aroi Dee
Thapphasuk
Som Tam Kai Yang Tung
Soi Mittraphap 14
Krua Mae Si
CAT Customer
Service Northeast
GOVERNMENT
CENTER
Soon Rachakam
City Hall
Lang Muang
The Election
Commission Office
Beung Thung
Sang

Sai Fon 16
Prasanmit
Khon Kaen
Provincial Court
Depatment
of Forestry
Na Soon Rachakam

Soi Srimarat 3
Mae Noi
Chok Sathit
Schools Airport
Khon Kaen Province

Oho New Nai Bai
Fishballs
Th. Maliwan
Uthai
Pharmacy
Khon Kaen
Kindergarten
District Office
Kiatnakin
Bank

Signed Tony
Lisa Mansion
Th. Pracha Samosoh
Tourism Authority of
Thailand
Centara
Isan Buri
Supa Tree
Hia Lee

Soi Maliwan
Aroi Ded
Chatuchak
Piman
Garden
Trajit
Sueb
San
Vocational
College
Pimpasut
Sirlwadi
Thanon Pracha Samoson
Coffee
House
Khao Soi
Chiang Mai
College
of Asian
Scholars

Orchid Hospital
Jira
Bussarakam
First
Choise
Sila
Pimpasut 2
Sri Mongkol
Industrial Finance
Corporation
Soi Pracha Samoson 13
Pimantan 2
Place Pine
Corner
Chata Phadung
Jesus Christ
Church

Central Plaza
Khon Kaen
Mr. Lee
Khon Kaen
Thai Ruang Fah
Na Mai
Ammat
Saen Samran
Chokdee
Tampai
Marine
Home
Municipal Value
Nong Khu
Krua Suwanan
Soi Chata Phadung
Consulate
of Vietnam
Mueang
Ubon
AB Computer
School

Weza
Chai Pat
City Inn
Roma
Khon
Dee
Soi Padungsit
Ammat
Snooker
Party House
Central
Prison
Khon Kaen
Hospital
Center
for Maternal and
Child Health
Tamarind
Pharmacy

5 Star
Noi Nimced Duck
Thanon Sri Chant
Seven's
Corner Bar
Krom Ulu
Soi Na Mueang 27
Mae Sai
Manoch
Hair Cut
Kuk Noi Kaen
Kham
Krung Thai Bank
Rajamangala
Northeastern
University

Kosa Bowl
Bank of Thailand
Northeast
Phu Inn
Wat Si Chan
Khon Kaen
Provincial Health
Office
Thanon Sri Chant
Amphawa
Coffee
Khon Kaen
Commercial
School
to Bung Niem

Chao Por Lak
Muang Khon
Kaen Shrine
Grand Leo
Pomodoro
Tukcom
Charoen
Thani
OTOP Center
Bang
Lamphu
Gurdwara Sri Guru
Singh Sabha
Thanon Sri Chant
Kaen Nakorn
Poonphol
Technical
College
Ice Cream
Smile
Redeemer
School
Nonthaburi
Thanon Sri Chant
to Bung Niem

Khon Kaen Rotfai
Golf Court
Didine
Kosa
Pullman
Kaen Raja Orchid
U-Bar
Princess
Pian Pen
Cheethakhon
Kanlayanawat
school
Turm Rom
DMA
Cheethakhon
Sirindhorn
College of
Public Health
Chittavech Khon Kaen
Ratchanakharin
Hospital
Infant Jesus
School
Duck
Lek Pao
Tao Yang

Khon Kaen
Station
Railway
Phi Phi Kaen
Soi Na Mueang 25
Rin
Thai Silk
Bo Bae
Comp for
Chuanchun Kids
Unity Foundation
Amarin Plaza
Wat Pa
Wiwek Tham
Redeemer School
Education Northeast
Khon Kaen
Wutthichai

Khon Kaen Yamaha
Music Academy
Khon Kaen
Pleasant
Phai Lom
Prathamakhan
Municipal
Market 1
Wat Si
Nuan
Charoenchit
House
Living
Room
Chuanchun
Piyaporn
Natthapon
Chata Phadung
Soi Chaiyaphruek 8
Soi Pinthawin

Marina
Manmat
Soi Wuttharam 9
S-Force
Wetcha Yan
Anamai 6
Sirin
Pom Papaya
Salad
Thip Maruay
Chaiyaphruek
Soi Suk Sabai

Wat
Wutharam
Kanokporn
Dental Clinic
Plus Sport Club
Klang Muang
Mansion
Hong Moon Mung
Khon Kaen City
Museum
Anamai
Herb
Chrysoberyl
Anamai
Soi Anamai 2
Soi Nam Thip 2
N-Joy
Chaiyaphruek 4
Soi Chaiyaphruek
Soi Saengthawan

Kow
Ltd
Pla Chum
Fairy Plaza
Municipal Ban
Non Wat Nong
Municipal
Parks
Children
Development
Center
Plapayai
Pu Khru
Yen Shrine
Soi Anamai 4
Soi Nam Thip 1
Nai Pan
Phonthisan
Chata Phadung
Soi Suk Sabai
Phet

Beautiful
Bondin
Na Mueang 9
Wat
Wutharam
Ong Ard Paradee
Tutor School
Wat
That
Nikorn Samran
LAN KHON PARK
District 4 Public
Relations Department
Wat Jeen
Beung
Plapanoy
Phothisan
Chim Phli 5
Phonthisan 19
Little Green
Papaya Salad
Phonthisan
Soi 15
Phonthisan
Khon Kaen
Soi Mitseri

Library
Na Mueang 9
Kaen Nakhon
Wittayalai School
My House
Khon Kaen
Condo
Mud
Rop Beung
Lakeside
Market
Kuan Yin
Chim Phli
Ja Tui
Phonthisan
Chim Phli 9
Phothisan

Deaf School
Na Mueang 7
Je Ped
Pai Quan
Potchana 1
Plapanoy
Wat Pho
Non Than
Chim Phli 5
Nongnot
Mae Prasong

Soi Lao Nadi 10
Soi Lao Nadi 8
Nandi Karam
Th. Lao Nadi
Sitrak School
Mahesak Shrine
Kaen Nakorn
Lake
Kuan Yin
Bua Luang
Nonthong
Chim Phli
Soi Pattaya 1
Soi Pattaya 2
Luk Luang
Kindergarten

Soi Lao Nadi 6
Soi Lao Nadi 4/6
Na Mueang
Khon Kaen
Stadium
Soi Wuttharam 12/1
Wat Klang
Khon Kaen
Tea Pharmacy
Sam Yan Seafood
Soi Rop Beung 2
Rim Bung
Riam Rim Bueng
Krua Ban Rai
Chim Phli 9
Soi Pattaya 4
Soi Pattaya 5
Soi Misuk
Soi Sirathon
Chim Phli
Church of City
Northeast

Nai Wan Resort
Soi Bulan
Soi Lao Nadi 4/3
Nong Nueng
Wat Nong
Waeng
Muang Kao
to Tha Phra
At Love
Chaluay Seafood
Poramutsuksa
Khon Kaen
School
Non Than
Wat Si Light

Chiang Khan

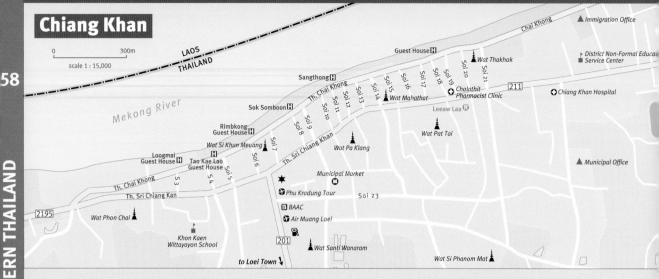

0   300m
scale 1 : 15,000

LAOS
THAILAND

Mekong River

Chai Khong

▲ Immigration Office

Guest House 🏨

Sangthong 🏨

Th. Chai Khong

Soi 13
Soi 14
Soi 15
Soi 16
Soi 17
Soi 18
Soi 19
Soi 20
Soi 21

▲ Wat Thakhok

▸ District Non-Formal Educa...
■ Service Center

Sok Somboon 🏨

Soi 11
Soi 12

Wat Mahathat ▲

Cholathit
Pharmacist Clinic

211

✚ Chiang Khan Hospital

Rimbkong
Guest House 🏨

Soi 9
Soi 10

Leeaw Laa Ⓡ

Wat Si Khun Meuang 🏨

Soi 8

Th. Sri Chiang Khan

Soi 7

Wat Pat Tai ▲

Loogmai
Guest House 🏨

Soi 6

Wat Pa Klang ▲

Tao Kae Lao
Guest House 🏨

S 3

Th. Chai Khong

S 4

Soi 5

Municipal Market Ⓜ

▲ Municipal Office

Th. Sri Chiang Kan

★

Soi 23

2195

Phu Kradung Tour Ⓡ

Wat Phon Chai ▲

Ⓑ BAAC

Khon Kaen
Wittayayon School ■

Ⓑ Air Muang Loei

201

Wat Santi Wanaram ▲

to Loei Town ↓

Wat Si Phanom Mat ▲

Loei Town

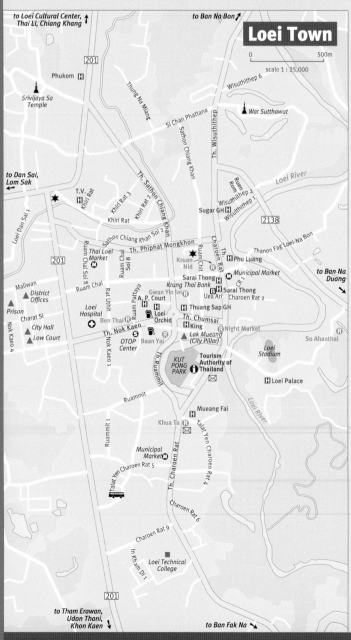

to Loei Cultural Center, ↑
Thai Li, Chiang Khang

to Ban Na Bon ↗

0   500m
scale 1 : 25,000

201

Phukom 🏨

Wisuthithep 6

Srivijaya Sa
Temple ▲

Si Chan Phattana

Wat Sutthawat ▲

Thung Na Miang

Sathon Chiang Khan

Th. Wisuthithep

to Dan Sai, ←
Lom Sak

T.V. ▲

Khiri Rat

Khiri Rat 3

Ruen
Rom

Wisuthithep 1

Loei River

Th. Sathon Chiang Khan

Khiri Rat

Sathon Chiang Khan Soi 2

Sugar GH 🏨

2138

Loei Dan Sai 1

Khiri Rat

Sathon Chiang Khan Soi 3

Charoen Rat

Thanon Fag Loei-Na Bon

201

Thai Loei
Market Ⓜ

Th. Phiphat Mongkhon

Ⓡ Phu Luang

to Ban Na
Duang →

Ruam Chai Soi 8

Ruam Chai Soi 6

Kruan-
Nid ★

CR 1

Municipal Market Ⓜ

Ruam Chai Soi 8

Krung Thai Bank Ⓑ

Sarai Thong 🏨

Maliwan

Rat Uthit

Ruam Chai

Gwan Yin Jai Ⓡ

Uea Ari Ⓡ

Sarai Thong
Charoen Rat 2

District
Offices ▲

A. P. Court 🏨

Thuang Sap GH 🏨

Prison ■

Ruam Pattaya

Ben Thai Ⓡ

Ⓡ Loei
Orchid 🏨

Th. Chumsai

Loei
Hospital ✚

Th. Nok Kaeo

Baan Yai 🏨

🏨 King

Charat Si

Ⓡ Night Market

So Ahanthai Ⓡ

City Hall ▲

Th. Nok Kaeo

Lak Mueang ▲
(City Pillar)

Nok Kaeo 4

Low Court ▲

OTOP
Center

Loei
Stadium

Th. Ruammit

KUT
PONG
PARK

Tourism
Authority of
ⓘ Thailand
✉

Loei Palace 🏨

Ruammit 1

Ruammit

Mueang Fai

Talat Yen Charoen Rat 4

Loei River

Khua Ta 🏨

Th. Charoen Rat

Municipal
Market Ⓜ

Talat Yen Charoen Rat 5

Charoen Rat 6

Charoen Rat 9

Th Kham Di 1

Loei Technical
College ■

201

to Tham Erawan, ↓
Udon Thani,
Khon Kaen

to Ban Fak Na ↘

Nong Bua Lam Phu Town

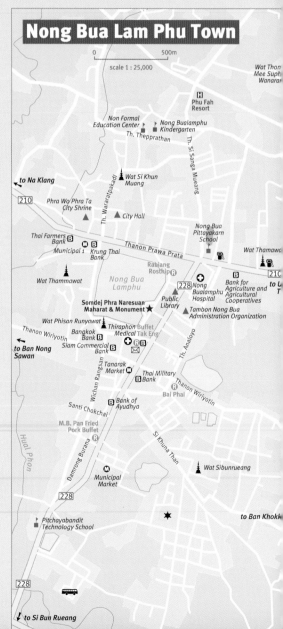

0   500m
scale 1 : 25,000

Wat Thon
Mee Suph...
Wanarar

🏨 Phu Fah
Resort

Non Formal
Education Center ■

■ Nong Bualamphu
Kindergarten

Th. Thepprathan

Th. Si Sanga Mueang

Wat Si Khun ▲
Muang

to Na Klang ←

Th. Wararatpakadi

210

Phra Wo Phra Ta ▲
City Shrine

▲ City Hall

Nong Bua
Pittayakarn
School ■

Thai Farmers
Bank Ⓑ

Municipal 1 Ⓜ

Ⓑ

Wat Thamawo... ▲

210

Krung Thai
Bank Ⓑ

Thanon Prawa Prata

Rabiang
Rosthip Ⓡ

228

Nong
Bualamphu
Hospital ✚

Bank for
Agriculture and
Agricultural
Cooperatives Ⓑ

to L...
T...

Wat Thammawat ▲

Nong Bua
Lamphu

Public
Library

Somdej Phra Naresuan
Maharat & Monument ★

Tambon Nong Bua
Administration Organization ▲

Wat Phisan Runyawat ▲

Thiraphon Buffet
Medical Tak Eng ✚

Thanon Wiriyotin

Bangkok
Bank Ⓑ

Wichan Rangsan

Siam Commercial
Bank Ⓑ

✉ Ⓡ Ⓑ

Thai Military
Bank Ⓑ

to Ban Nong ←
Sawan

Tanarak
Market Ⓜ

Thanon Wiriyotin

Th. Analoyo

Bai Phai

Santi Chokchai

Ⓑ Bank of
Ayudhya

M.B. Pan Fried
Pork Buffet ■

Si Khuna Than

Damrong Burana

★

to Ban Khokk...

228

Ⓜ Municipal
Market

Wat Sibunrueang ▲

Huoi Phon

Pitchayabandit ■
Technology School

228

to Si Bun Rueang ↙

to Ban Khokk...

Upper Gulf Coasts

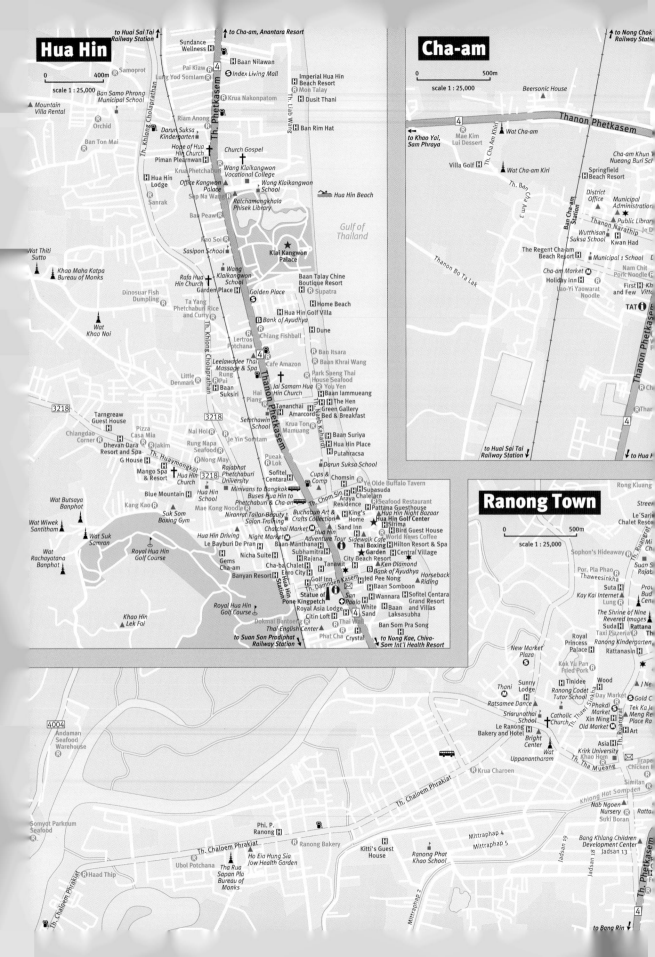

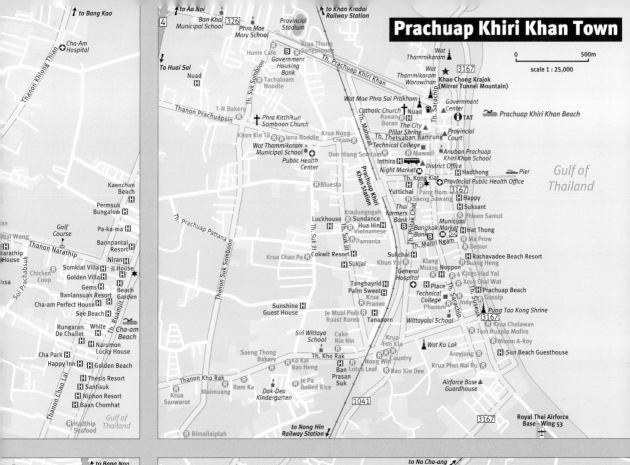

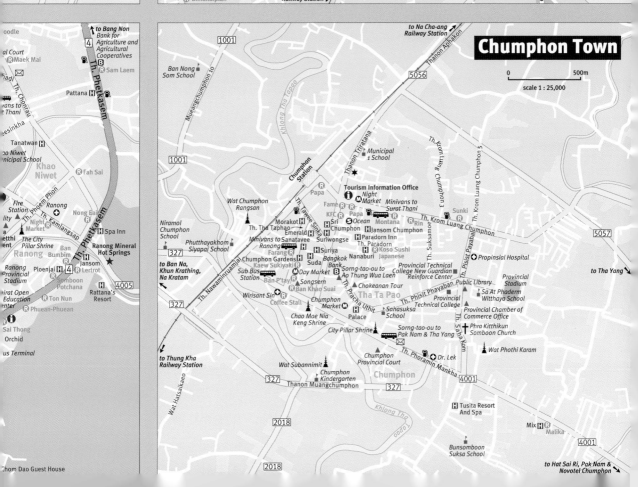

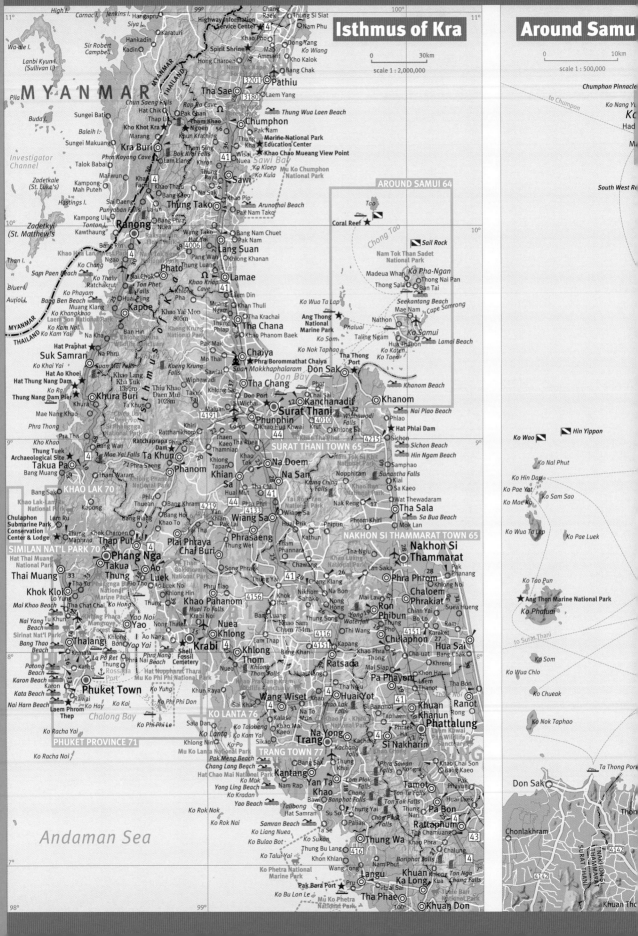

Surat Thani Town

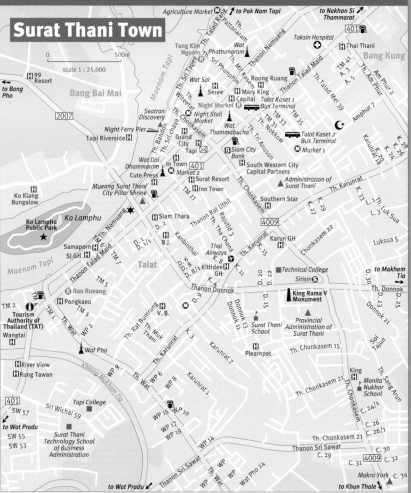

scale 1 : 25,000

Nakhon Si Thammarat Town

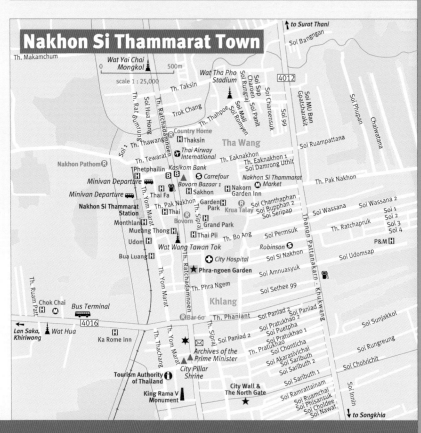

scale 1 : 25,000

KO PHA-NGAN 68

Ko Pha-Ngan

KO SAMUI 66

Ko Samui

Gulf of Thailand

Sail Rock

Ko Samui

Chong Pha-Ngan

0   1km
scale 1 : 100,000

Ferry to Tongsala
Ferry to Ao Tong (50km)
Ferry to Had Rin
Ferry to Had Rin (13km)

Express Boat to Ko Pha-Ngan (9km)

Cape Na Hin Dong
Cape Yai
Samui Amanda Resort & Spa
Ban Bai Fern
The Emerald Residence
Santisook Villas
Monkey at Work (Coconut-picking)
Chalet
Wine de Samui
Garden Home
Big Jiew Seafood
Samui Shell Museum
T.A.T.
Full Gospel Church
Grand Seaview Tourist Police
Bus Station
Samui Hospital
Ko Samui Church
Sawai Home Bungalow
Temple Samui Tararam
The Siam Residence
Santi Bay
Ban Suriya
Kanok Buri Resort
Lipa Lodge Beach Resort
Rajapruek Samui Resort
Chon Khram Bay
The Lipa Lovely Resort
Big John Beach Resort
Little Pearl Family Resort
Ko Samui Naval Base
In Foo Palace
A.R. An Resort
Cape Chon Khram
Thong Yang Bay
Cococabana
Cape Yai Krai
Nasai Bay
Ban Sabai Sunset Beach Resort & Spa
Wiesenthal Resort
Vastervik
Cape Lingload
Talingngam Beach
Taling Ngam Bay
Five Island Restaurant
Yao Beach
Al Lacosta Seaview Villa & Private Spa
Sea Gull
Pearl Bay
Cape Phang Ka
Phangka Bay
Pangkha Beach
Emerald Cove
Simple Life
Hinta Beach Bungalow
Coconut Villa
Thongkrut Bay
Cape Hinkhom

Dara Arrium Petit
Jartiya Bungalow
Royal Starlight Villa & Apartment
Royal Living Residence
Coconut land & House
Axolotl Village
The Terrace
Bang Po Beach
Samui Hill Resort
Natural Wing Resort & Restaurant
Villa Ban Waan
Ban Laem Hoi School
JP Supermarket
Temple Si Suwanna Ram
Santi Buri Samui Country Club
Santiburi Samui Country Club
Hope of Church
Bird Garden
Buffalo Fighting Stadium
Wat Sietavib
St Anna
District Office
Samui Medical Clinic
Wat Chaeng
Temple Khong Kharam
Immigration Office
Lizard Garden
Fire Department
Temple Khong Samui
Elephant Trekking
Wanorn
Wat ara Charoensuk
Temple Ko Samui
Buffalo Fighting Stadium
Baan Taling Ngam Resort & Spa
Top Cats Fresh Water Fishing Resort
Wat Khiri Wongkaram
Veneto
Elephant Gate
Khao Khwang 410m
Wild Life Park
Sundowner Horse Ranch
Triple Coconut Tree
Gems House Bungalows
Snake Farm
Bang Kao Tropical Boutique Residence
Wat Santi Karam
Thong Krut
Naga Pearl Farm
Kung Kaew
Waikiki
Wat Khao Chrdi
Wat Laem Saw
Cape Saw

Ban Suan Siriwan
Ban Thai Resort
Manasai Samui Island
Pinnacle Resort Samui
Home Bay Coco Palm Resort
Phlam Inn Napharn Revilla
Samui's Buri Napharn Revilla
Asian Village Shangri-La Sunrise
Point Golden Beach Hut
The Florist Resort
Wat Na Phra Lam

Mae Nam Pier
Lolita Bungalow Samui / S.S. villa
Lolita Resort / Lolita Bungalow Samui
Santi Buri Resort Samui
Phlam Point Resort
Mae Nam Beach
Bo Phut Resort

MAE NAM 67

Buffalo Fighting Stadium
Mae Mai Home
Ban Shadis Samui
Wat Phukhao Thong
Ruen Thip Homes
Health Centre
Family Zoo
Wazzah Resort & Bungalow
Kirikayan Luxury Pool Villas & Spa
Mountain Viewpoint
Triple Coconut Tree
Song Rua
Samui Everest Viewpoint
Thaan Rua
465m
Phaengkhanoon
Lookout
467m
322m
MAE NAM ANG THONG
464m

ANG THONG LIPA NOI
350m

Wat Hin Lat
Hin Lad River Stone
Hin Lad Waterfall
Hew Khwaay Tok

Khao Pom 630m
Samui Gallery Hill
Woodland Park View
Yan Khao Viewpoint

Ko Samui

545m
LIPA NOI NA MUEANG
Samui Highlands
Khao Phlu 635m
Uncle Nim's Waterfall & Magic Garden
630m
Secret Statuary Garden
416m
Mountain Viewpoint
Mountain Viewpoint
Mountain View Paradise Resort
Insila Retreat / Charity Towers B&B
Wat Lamai & Cultural Hall

LIPA NOI TALING NGAM

Elephant Trekking
Na Muang Waterfall 2
Wangsaotong
573m
Namuang Waterfall 1
465m
Elephant Trekking
Baan Chang Elephant Trekking
Coral Buddha Image
Overlap Stone
467m

TALING NGAM NA MUEANG
168m
Buffalo Fighting Stadium
Wat Khunaram (Mummified Monk)
4173
Coral Buddha
4169
Old Buddha Image
Buddha Statue
Tropical Zoo
4173
Living Thailand Cultural Center
Wat Samret
Wat Praderm
Nagalaya
River Garden
Wat Klong
River Garden
Diamond Villa
Easy Time Resort
River Garden
Oriental Lodge Resort & Spa
Banburee Resort & Spa
Kamalaya
Laem Set
Bang Kao Bay
Cape Na Thian
Cape Set

NA MUANG MARKET

Samui Garden Home
Thai Clinic
Buffalo Fighting Stadium
LAMAI 67
Samui Sport Stadium
Hi-He's Resort
Beach Village house
Samui Marina Cottage
Wanna Samui Resort
Samui Aquarium & Tiger Zoo
Samui Orchid Resort
Butterfly Garden
Central Samui Village
Shasa

Health Centre
Save House
Fisherman Village
Go Kart
Buffalo Fighting Stadium
Nature House
Samui Monkey Theatre
Ban Phu Pha Resort
Ban Khao
Island Safari & Elephant Trek
Big C
Samui Frisbee Golf
Maya Buri Boutique Resort & Spa
Tesco Lotus Supercenter
Makro
Shooting Ranch
Samui Shooting Sports
Thai International Hospital
Tesco Lotus
383m
Wat Chaweng
Chaweng Pattana Home
BB Chaweng Beach / Chaweng Bury Resort
The Library / Beachcomber
Horseback Riding
Chaweng PR Guesthouse
Chaweng Residence / Samui Plaza
Bangkok Samui Int'l Hospital
Superpobo Samui
First Bungalow Beach Resort / Samui First House
423m
Elephant Trekking
Chaweng Noy Resort
Marcopolo Resort & Spa
Soleil d'Asie Residence
Ban Sukreep Resort
Jungle Club
BW Samui Bayview Resort & Spa
Ban Hin ai Chaweng Noi Boutique Resort / Ban Laem Sila
Hi Coral Cove / Coral Cover Resort
350m
Samui Mountain Village / Eden Rock Villa
Best View Bungalow
Golden Cliff Resort / Big Re
332m
Samui Cliff View Resort
Viewpoint
Crystal Bay Resort
Thongtakian Resort
Promjit
Rocky Boutique Resort (Mango Village)
Hin-Ta & Hin-Yai (Grandfather & Grandmother Rocks)
Lamai

Ban Lo
The Tongsai Bay
Wat Plai
Cape San
Six Senses Hideaway
Som
The Coleridge Institute
Idyllic Samui Dream Villas Beach Re
Araya Buri Boutique Res
Keymati
Sunris
Anthong
Samui Honey Co
Papillon Reside
Destination Beach Villa
Samui Puresho
Big Buddha Beach Resort
Wat Laem Suwan
Ban Phuttaksa
Villa Medici
Big
Big Buddha Pier

Bang Rak Bay
Bo Phut
Samui Garden
Samui Escape
Charlie's
Samui Airport
Eranda Resort
Chaweng Bay
Samui Driving Range
The Briza Beach Re
Samui International Hos
Corto Malese / Amari Pal
Chaweng Bea
The Island Res
Iyara Beach / Muang Samui R
Bungy Jump
Samui Coral Resort / Als Resort
Laem Din
Wat Jee Kong
Seascape
Samui Bea
Sans Se
Fair House
New Star Be
The Imperial
Santa Lucia
Victorian Re
Impiana Sam
Tropicara
4169
View

Chaweng
Wot Bo Phuttharam
Beach House Samui
Palm View
Wat Bang H

Bangsabai
Waterfront / Ban Fang Talay
Bang Rak Beach
Bo Phut Beach
Hacienda / Cape Diem
Chalee Bungalow
Beach Front
Red Snail
Smile House
Full Moon Res
Blue Diam
Secret
Full Moon Bu

Raja Car Ferry to Donsak (30km) Khanom (55km)
Surat Thani (76km)
Seatran Car Ferry to Suratthani (Ban Don) (80km)

4169 4172 4174 4170 4173

Long Tail Boat to Ko Taen (3km), Ko Matsum (6km), Ko Mot Daeng (7km), Ko Rap (13km)

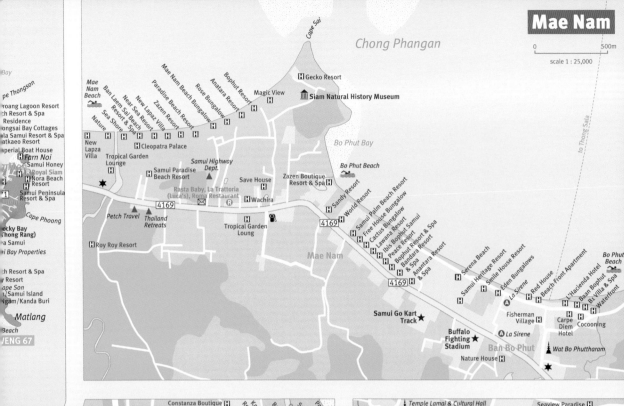

LOWER GULF & ANDAMAN COASTS

0   1km
scale 1 : 100,000

*Gulf o
Thaila*

Ko Pha-Ngan

Thong Lang Beach
Kong Nui
Kong Yai
Cape Lia
Ma
Khom Beach
Coconut/Haad Khom/Ocean View Resort
Hat Kuat Bay
Cape Son
Koh Ma Dive Resort
Pha-Ngan Coral Tree
Chai/Royal Orchid Resort
Viewpoint
Pim
Coral Bay
O.D.
Bottle Beach
Mae Haad Bay Resort/Island View Cabana
Hin Ngam View
Niramon Villas
Rock Beach
Bottle Beach II&III
Mae Had Bay Resort/Mae Haad Cove
Wong Sai Garden
Wattana Resort
Smile Resort
Cape Pak Chong
Green Papaya Resort/Haadlad
Chaloklum Bay Resort
Chalok Lum Try Thong/Fantasea
Thai Life Waterfall
Bottle Beach I
Prestige Resort & Spa
View Point
Nanthawan/Sarisa Place/Rose Villa
Viewpoint
Tapan Noi Bay
Salad Beach
Reggae Village
Mandalai
Wang Sai Waterfall
Thong Ta Pong/Thong Ta Pan Resort
Santhiya/Ayurvana Spa
Salad Beach Resort/Asia Bungalows
Smile Beach Resort
Wat Chalok Lum
Health Centre
438m
Thong Nai Pan Noi Beach
Kruad Beach   Cape Naay
My Way/Asia Bungalow
Trai Thong Resort
Raiwin/Rasananda Resort
Lucky/Dragon Hut Resort
Haad Tian Beach Resort/Benjawan
Phuwadee Resort & Spa/Baan Panburi Village
Dream Hill/Blue Coral/Graceland
Salad Hut/Cookies Salad Resort
Paradise Waterfall
Panviman Resort
Haad Yao Bay View/Long Bay Resort
Khao Kin Non 440m
Wat Thong Nai Pan
Tapan Yai Bay
Thong Nai Pan Yai Beach
Haad Yao Villa/Long Beach
Pha-Ngan Safari & Elephant Trekking
Than Prawet Waterfall
Candle Bungalow
Ibiza/Haad Yao See Through
Haad Yao Resort/Haad Yao Over Bay
Dreamland Resort/Dreamland Divers
White Winds/White Sand
Seaboard Bungalows/Sandy Bay
Baan Haad Yao Villas & Guest House
Khao Ra 627m
Pop Bungalow/White Sand
Haad Son Resort
Tantawan
Khao Ta Luang 476m
Wat Paa Sang Tham
Dolphin/Havana Beach Resort
Starlight Resort/Nice Beach
Son Beach
Khao Khaew
250m
Wat Srithanu
Wangthong Waterfall
Than Sadet
Rock Garden/Green View
Hut Sun/Sunset Cove
Khao Ra Viewpoint
Sun View/Jinda Resort
Haad Chao Phao/Pha-Ngan
Chinese Temple
378m
Hat Kruat Bay
Thian Beach
Cabana Resort/Jungle Hut
498m
Cape Tham Gangkao
Pha-Ngan Cabana/Seaflower
Rasta Side Garden
Seethanu Bungalows
Village Green/Pha-Ngan Paragon
Saampan Waterfall
Sadet Beach
Blue Ocean Garden
Nid's Bungalow/Silver Cliff
Bovy/Laem Son 2
Laem Son
Lada
Wat Srithanu
100-year old Jade Buddha Image
S Hut Resort/Mai Pen Rai
Golden Rock
Daeng Waterfall
Thansadet Seaview/Thong
Sea View Rainbow/The Beach
Loy Fa Bungalow
K.N.T Property & Low Limited Partnership
Mountain Viewpoint
Thong Reng Be
Chai Country/Chills Resort
Nantakarn/Lipstick Cabana
Than Sader Waterfall
Thong Nang Waterfall
Cape Nai Po
Moon Beach/Banana Beach
Srithanu Bay
Pha-Ngan Twilight/Hin Kong Resort
Hinkong Bay
Agama Yoga
Wat Samai Kongka
Wang Mai Daeng Waterfall
Kung Bungalows
Ananda Yoga Resort
Me'n'u
Ko Pha-Ngan Hospital
Wat Madeua Whan (Marble Buddha Image)
Than Prapar Waterfall
Dam Bungalows
Baan Bang Rak Resort & Spa
JJ Resort
385m
Nam Tok Beach
Moo 6 Villa
Bonzai Bar
Sukho Resort
Phaeng Waterfall 400m
Wok Tum Bay
Woktum Bay Resort
Wat Phu Khao Noi
525m
O.K. Bungalows
Wat Amphawan
Yang Beach
Darin/Golden Hill Resort
The Amsterdam Bar and Stone
Baan Tai Elephant Trekking
Cape Nokrang
Asia/Sabai Beach Resort
Hill Resort
Twin Coconut Tree
Haad Yaw Cabana
Sea Scene Resort/Bounty
Pornsawan/Cookies
Yao (East) Beach
Plaaylaem Bay
Beach 99
Montevista Retreat and Yoga Center
Mountain Viewpoint
Ploy Beach
Grand Sea Resort/Tranquil Bungalow
Municipal Office
Hat Yao Bay
Siripun/Suntown
Hope of Pha-Ngan Church
Pha-Ngan Bungalow/Rooung Thip
Wat Pra Yai
Half Moon Festival
Asia/Buakao Inn/Pha-Ngan Chai
Ban Tai Resort/Pimolsuph House
Mountain Viewpoint
Sramanora River Stone
Night Express Boat Pier
525m
Ko Tae Nai
Thong Sala Pier
Pha-Ngan Centrepoint
Wat Pho
Mountain Viewpoint
Wat Nok
Sramanora Waterfall
Ko Tae Nok
Wat Khao Tham
Wainam Huts
Wainam Beach
Health Center
Khao Khai 415m
Haad Thian Resort
Cape Wainam
World Nature/The Sand
Thongsala Guesthouse/Sundance
Phrueksa Resort/White West
Pha-Ngan Villa/Oceanus
Seagate/Weangtha
Pha-Ngan Tropicana Resort
Coco Garden/Holiday Beach
First Villa/Powe Resort
Rungarun/Pha-Ngan Beach Resort
Field Paradise/Tu Shore
Milky Bay/Dew Shore
Ban Tai Resort/Your Family
Island Discovery
Jungle House Resort
Horizon Huts
Bamboo Hut
Jungle Gym
Big Blue/Pariya Haad Yuan
Ta Nouy Garden
Hill Side Resort
Barcelona Resort
Haad Yuan Bungalow
Hat Yuan Bay
Yuan Beach
S Resort/Jub
Pink/Triangle Lodge
My Pha-Ngan/Morning Star
Bay Hut/Pha-Ngan Lodge
Lee Garden/Munchies
Mac's Bay Resort
Liberty
Pha-Ngan Rainbow/Blue Lotus Resort
Papillon/copa
Green Peace/Golden Beach Resort
Jamaica Inn/Sun Sea Resort
Thong Yang Bungalow
Harmony Beach Resort
Cape Ta To
Hat Khontee
Viewpoint
Khontee Resort
Khontee Beach
Health Center
Serenity Hill/Mountain Sea
Venus Resort/Seaview
Silverly Moon/Pha-Ngan Island Resort
Bang Son Villa/Tom Yum Kung
Bangson Bay Boom's Cafe
Seekantang Beach
Tiara Place/Blue Hill Resort
Bird/Starlight Bungalow
Sun Beach/Sandy Bungalow
Seaside/Rainbow Bungalow
Laid Back/Drop In
Blue Marine/Drop In
Palita Lodge/Tommy Resort
Pha-Ngan Bayshore/Sunrise Resort
Haad Rin Resort/Anant
Beach Blue/Paradise
Hua Laem Beach Resort
Hat Rin Bay (Sunrise Beach)
Rin Pier
Coco Hut/Friendly
Sunset Beach/Palm Beach
Laid Back/Coral Bungalow
Family House/Friendly
Sun Cliff/Sea Breeze
Leela Bay
Viewpoint
Cape Hat Rin
Kong Rine

HAT RIN 68

to Ko Tao (45km)
to Ko Samui (34km)
Surat Thani (100km)
to Mae Nam (16km)
to Bo Phut (68km)
to Bo Phut (19.3 km)
to Thongsala Pier (50km)
to Chaweng Mon (13 km)
to Ban Plai (12km)
to Hat Mae Nam (35km)

Hat Rin

View Point
Blue Hill Resort
Blue Bungalow
Star Bungalow
Vimarn Samut
Viewpoint
Bird Bungalow
Starlight Bungalow
Sandy Bungalow
Sunset Beach
Pooltrup Village
5 Starts Padi Facilities
Health Center
Venus Resort
Khonthee Resort
Nees
Serenity Hill
Mountain Sea
Seaview Hat Rin Resort
Fairland Resort
Seaside Bungalow
Rainbow Bungalow
Coral Bungalow
Sorng-taa-ou to Thong Sala
Bakery
Full Moon Party
Palita Lodge
Khontee Beach
Hat Rin Bay (Sunrise Beach)
Sunset Beach
Tommy Resort
Paradise Bungalows
Phangan Bayshore
Hat Rin Nai Bay (Sunset Beach)
Jungle Gym
Phangan Divers
Sunrise Resort
Phangan Buri Resort
Hat Rin Resort
Hat Rin Pier
Anant
Beach Blue
Sea Breeze
Coco Hut
Seekantang Beach
Sarikantang
Friendly
Leela Bss Bungalow
Family House
Rin Beach
Sun Cliff
Hua Laem Beach Resort
Viewpoint
Lighthouse
Cape Hat Rin
Kong Rine

Restaurants:
1. Backyard Club
2. Cactus Bar
3. Chicken Corner
4. Club Paradise
5. Coral Bungalows Bar
6. Da Club
7. Drop-In Bar
8. Lazy House
9. Lucky Crab
10. Mellow Mountain
11. Mr. K
12. Orchid Club
13. Rock
14. Tommy
15. Vinyl
16. Warm Up Bar
17. Zoom

Hotels:
1. Al Colosseo Palace
2. Baan Talay Guesthouse
3. Black and White
4. Blue Marine Resort
5. Bongo
6. Charung
7. Coral Bungalows
8. Delight Resort
9. Drop In Club Resort
10. Garden Hill
11. Had Rin Village
12. Hat Rin Hill
13. Jonathan
14. Laid Back
15. Malai
16. Mr Chaa
17. Nee's
18. Neptune's Villa
19. Oasis Bungalows
20. Palm Beach
21. Phangan Buri Resort
22. Pooltrup Village
23. Ringo
24. Royal Garden
25. Sea Garden Resort
26. Sooksom
27. Sunset Bay
28. Thai House
29. Top Gold

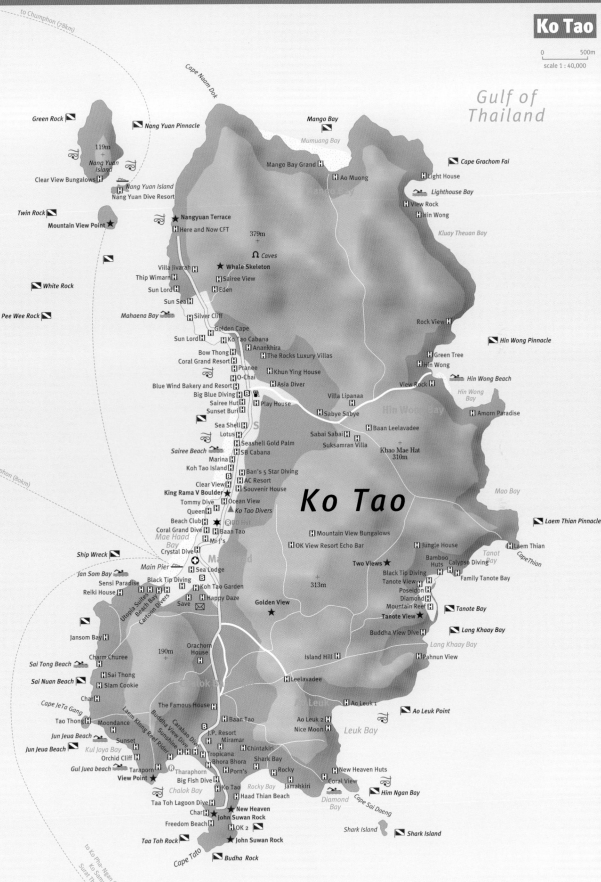

to Chumphon (78km)

0   500m
scale 1 : 40,000

Gulf of Thailand

Green Rock

Nang Yuan Pinnacle

Mango Bay

Cape Naam Dok

Mumuang Bay

Mango Bay Grand

Cape Grachom Fai

119m
Nang Yuan island

Clear View Bungalows

Nang Yuan Island
Nang Yuan Dive Resort

Ao Muong

Light House

Lighthouse Bay

View Rock

Hin Wong

Twin Rock

Mountain View Point

Nangyuan Terrace

Here and Now CFT

379m

Kluay Theuan Bay

White Rock

Caves

Villa Jivarah
Thip Wimarn
Sun Lord
Sun Sea

Whale Skeleton

Sairee View

Eden

Rock View

Pee Wee Rock

Silver Cliff

Mahaena Bay

Golden Cape
Sun Lord
Ko Tao Cabana
Bow Thong
Coral Grand Resort
Pranee
O-Chai
Blue Wind Bakery and Resort
Big Blue Diving
Sairee Hut
Sunset Buri

Anankhira
The Rocks Luxury Villas
Khun Ying House
Asia Diver
Play House

Hin Wong Pinnacle

Green Tree
Hin Wong

Hin Wong Beach

Villa Lipanaa

View Rock

Hin Wong Bay

Amorn Paradise

Sabye Sabye

Sea Shell
Lotus
Sairee Beach
Seashell Gold Palm
SB Cabana
Marina
Koh Tao Island
Ban's 5 Star Diving
Clear View
AC Resort
King Rama V Boulder
Souvenir House
Tommy Dive
Ocean View
Queen
Beach Club
Pub Hut
Coral Grand Dive
Baan Tao
Mr J's
Crystal Dive

Sabai Sabai
Suksamran Villa

Baan Leelavadee

Khao Mae Hat
310m

Mao Bay

Ko Tao Divers

Ko Tao

Laem Thian Pinnacle

Mountain View Bungalows

OK View Resort Echo Bar

Jungle House

Laem Thian

Cape Thian

Tanot Bay

Bamboo
Huts
Calypso Diving
Family Tanote Bay

Ship Wreck

Main Pier

Mae Haad
Bay

Sea Lodge

Two Views
Black Tip Diving
Tanote View
Poseidon
Diamond
Mountain Reef
Tanote View

Tanote Bay

Jan Som Bay
Sensi Paradise
Reiki House
Black Tip Diving
Koh Tao Garden
Cartoon Divers
Happy Daze
Save

Utopia Suites
Beach Bay

190m

Buddha View Dive

Lang Khaay Bay

Lang Khaay Bay

Jansom Bay

Golden View

Island Hill

Pahnun View

Sai Tong Beach
Sai Nuan Beach
Charm Churee
Sai Thong
Siam Cookie
Char

Orachorn
House

Leelavadee

Cape JeTa Gang
Tao Thong
Moondance

The Famous House

Ao Leuk 1

Ao Leuk Point

Jun Jeua Beach
Jun Jeua Beach
Sunset

Kul Jaya Bay

Orchid Cliff
Gul Juea beach
Taraporn

Laem Klong Reef Riders
Buddha View Dive
Sunshine

Carabao Dive
J.P. Resort
Miramar
Chintakiri
Shark Bay

Ao Leuk 2
Nice Moon

Leuk Bay

Tropicana
Bhora Bhora
Porn's

Rocky

New Heaven Huts

View Point

Tharaphorn
Big Fish Dive

Ko Tao

Coral View
Jamahkiri

Chalok Bay

Haad Thian Beach

Rocky Bay

Him Ngan Bay

Taa Toh Lagoon Dive

Char
Freedom Beach

New Heaven
John Suwan Rock
OK 2

Diamond
Bay

Cape Sai Daeng

Taa Toh Rock

John Suwan Rock

Shark Island

Shark Island

Cape Tato

Budha Rock

to Chumphon (80km)

to Ko Pha-Ngan (58km),
Ko Samui (85km),
Surat Thani (120km)

Similan National Park

0   2km
scale 1 : 125,000

North Point
Ko Bangu
Breakfast Bend
Christmas Point
Donald Duck Bay
Cinnamon Bay
The Boulders
Hin Rup Ruea Bai
Turtle Rock
Similan National Park Office
Ko Similan
Fantasy Reef
View Point
Beacon Beach
Beacon Reef
Elephant Head
Beacon Point
Ko Pu Sa
(Elephant Head)
to Tab La Mung Pier 70km

Deep Six
Ko Payu
The Morning Edge
Stonehenge
Princess Bay
Ko Payu
Ko Ha
Ko Miang
Hideaway
Pu Kai
Honeymoon Bay

Ko Payan
Hin Phae
Shark Fin Reef
Boulder City
Ko Payang
Coral Garden
Ko Huyong
Rocky Point
Rocky Bay

Khao Lak

0   2km
scale 1 : 100,000

to Ranong,
Suratthani,
Takuapa

Bang Sak Beach
Royal Bangsak Beach Resort
Hadson Resort
Rajaprajanugroh
School
ATM Krung
Pak Weep Beach
Thai Bank
Le Meridien Khao Lak
Beach & Spa Resort
Sai Rung Waterfall
Similana Resort
Oawthong Beach
The Sarojin
Takolaburi Cultural Resort
Pakarang Bungalow
Cher Fah Resort & Spa
South Sea Grand Resort & Spa
7-eleven
Orathai Seafood
Apsaras Beach Resort & Spa
Blue Village
Pakarang House
Khu Khak Beach
Khuk Khak
School
Health Center
JW Marriott Khao Lak Resort & Spa
Khao Lak Seaview Resort
Khao Lak Orchid Beach Resort
The Andamania Resort Khao Lak
Hotel Garten
Bang Niang Beach
Bangsak Village
Boxing
Stadium
Hotels Chwimmbad Bei Nacht
Khao Lak Orchid
Beach Resort
Garden Salon
Khao Lak Mohin Tara Hotel
Hotel Mukdara Beach
Villa & Spa Resort
Motive Cottage Resort
S. T. C. Khao Lak
Sudala Beach Resort
Khao Lak Summer
House Resort
Fanari Resort Khao Lak
Khao Lak Countryside Resort
Chong Fah Resort Khaolak
Ramada Resort Khao Lak
Khao Lak Laguna Resort
Khao Lak Riverside Resort & Spa Co. Ltd.
ATM Bank of
Ayudhya
Sea Dragon Dive Center
La Flora Resort & Spa
Khaolak Oriental Resort
The Andaburi Resort
Khao Lak Green Beach Resort
T. T. Plaza
Chong Fah Resort Khao Lak
Nang Thong Beach
Khao Lak Grand City
Khao Lak Laguna Resort
Phu Khao Lak Restaurant
Khao Lak Palm Hill Resort
Khao Lak Wanaburee Resort Phang Nga
Khao Lak Beach
Similan Diving Safaris
Khao Lak Paradise Resort
Sunset Beach
Khao Lak Sunset
Ocean Breeze Resort Khao Lak
Baan Krating Khao Lak Resort
Chao Por Khao
Lak Shrine
Khao Lak-Lam Ru National Park Office
Khao Lak National Park
Tsunami Volunteer Center
Ton Pling Waterfall
The Briza Beach Khao Lak
Khao Lak Diamond Beach Resort & Spa
Khao Lak Bhandari Company Limited
Ban Khao Lak
Khao Lak Merlin Resort
Bungalow
Khao Lak Emerald Resort
Wat Lak Kaen
Poseidon
Bungalow
Lam Kaen
School
Kromluang Chumporn
Khet Udamsak Shrine
Office Koh Similan
Thap Lamu Andaman Resort
to Phuket Town,
Phang Nga,
Krabi Town

Ban Pate
to T
Kha
Tha So
N.P.
Thai Muang
Am
Tha
Mu
Thai
Muang
Beach
Thung Wa
Tha
Wang Tha
Unsusampl
Mosque
Ban Khu
Bang
Wat Niche
Samos
Han Bua
Chai Thale
Khao Pilai
Khol
Han Ha
Pi
Bang
Bang Khu
Tha Nun
Th
Beach
Tha Chat Ch
Wat Aronya
Suan Map
Mai Khao Beach
Phuket Int'
Sirinat
Nationa
Nai Yang Beach
Cape Sal Khru
Khao Sai Khr
385m
Nai Thon
Beach
Cape Son
Bang Tao Beach
Bang Tao
Pacific Island
Pansea
Beach
Bang Th
Surin Beach
Phuket Fanta S
Kamala Bay
Kamal
Cape Thai Phao
Kalim Beach
Patong Beach
Pa
Trai Trang
Cape Mai Ngang
Kar
Cape Khok
Karon Noi Beach
Karon Beach
Kata
Kata Yai Beach
Kata Noi Beach
Cape Mum
Cape Mum
Nai Harn
Beach
Phuket
Suns
Ko
to Similan Island

Phuket Province

Phang-Nga

Amphoe Takua Thung

Amphoe Ao Luk

Phang Nga Bay

Phang-Nga Bay National Marine Park

Muang Mai

Pa Yang

Thong Lang

Phuket Sea

Muang Thalang

Phuket Town

Amphoe Kathu

Phuket

Chalong Bay

Andaman Sea

PHUKET ISLAND 72

Yao Noi

Yao Yai

Ko Yao Sea

Krabi Town

AO NANG BEACH 76

KRABI TOWN 77

RAILAY 76

Ao Nang

Railay Beach

Phra Nang Beach

Ko Poda Noi (Dam Hok)

Ko Poda Nok (Dam Khwan)

Ko Yamasan

Ko See

Ko Hah

HAT NOPPHARAT THARA MU KO PHI PHI NATIONAL PARK

Ko Pu

King Cruiser

Ko Dok Mai

Anemone Reef

Shark Point

Ko Yung

Ko Mai Phai

Laem Trong Beach

Phi Phi Natural Resort

Sea Gypsy Village

Erawan Palm Dive Resort

Phi Phi Island Village Resort

Ban Ko

Bay View Resort

Princess & Charlie Beach Resort

Tonsai Village Resort

Ban Laem Trong

Andaman Beach Resort

Araya Buri

Bay View Resort

Ko Phi Phi Don

KO PHI PHI DON 76

Wang Long

Viking Cave

Palong Bay

Maya Bay

Lo Samah Bay

Garang Herg

Phi Le

Ko Bida Nai

Ko Bida Nok

Shark Point

Ko Hay (Coral)

Ko Mai Thon

Ko Lone

Ko Racha Yai

Karon & Kata Beaches

to Patong Beach
Talay-Tai Seafood
South Sea
Woraburi Phuket Resort & Spa
Baan Karonburi Resort
Karon Princess
Krua Mittrapab
Karon Bay View
Coconut Grove Apartment
Nai Phru
Aroona Karon Center
The Old Phuket
Access Resort & Villa
BJ Beach
Sand Resort
Warika Place
4028
Karon Seaview
Pam's
Pizza 2000
Patak Soi 16
My Friend House
Karon Village Resort
Karon Beach
The Hilton Phuket Arcadia Resort & Spa
Phuket Green Valley
Teikano Sea Food
Karon Southern
The Long Beach Terrace

Karon Bay

4233
Bang La
Thavorn Palm Beach
Karon Hospital
Old Siam
Phuket Orchid
The Best House
Patak Soi 14
Karon Palace
Viking GH
Karon Mart
Karon Plaza
Th. Luang Pho Chuan
Holiday Village
Thai Farmers Bank
Karon
Siam Commercial Bank
J&J Inn
Karon Hut
Phuket Island View
Relax Garden Bungalow
Andaman Seaview
Casa Brazil
Karon Silver Resort
Karon GH
Baan Karon Resort
Thoet Phra Kiat Nawamin Stadium
Khok Chang
Patak Soi 12
Prayoon
Karon Tropicana
Patak Soi 9
Ruam Thep Inn
Karon Soi 2
Happy Hut
Boomerang Villages
Karon Beach
Karona Resort
CC Blooms
On the Rock
Euro Daily
Ray's Bluefin Tavern
SAO
Buffalo Steak House
Khok Chang Village
HC Andersen
Marina Phuket Resort
Diamond Cottage
Kata Garden
On Sea
Inter Bungalow
Laem Sai Bungalow
The Bank of Asia
Dino Park Mini Golf
Kata
Watchari
Charlie's Guest House
The Aspasia Phuket
Dino Park
Fantasy Hill
Charlie Chaplin's
Patak Soi 10
White House Inn
SP Inn
Rose Inn
Lucky Guest House
Peach Hill
Smile Inn
Kata Centre Point
Suan Esan Beer Garden
4028
Thai Farmers Bank
Kata Lagoon
Bougainvillea Terrace
Fast Food
Bank of Ayutthaya
Parpa Thai Boxing
Dome Bungalow
Jinta Andaman
Little Mermaid Guest House
Centara Kata Resort
Green Guest House
Sawadee Village
Kata Orient House
Seafood Restaurant
Copenhagen Grill House
Jiva
Fried Rice
Ratri Jasstaurant
Baan Thai Kata
Th. Ket Kwan
Wat Kittisangkaram
Patak Soi 8
Club Mediteranee
Kata Country House
Sumitra Thai House
Kata Sea Breeze Resort
Kata
Kata Yai Beach
Palm Garden Sea Food
Kata Palm Resort
to Phuket Town & Raya Pacific Resort

Kata Yai Bay

The Lagoon
Maleena Bungalow
Kata Plaza Shopping Centre
Shady and Bungalow
Bell Bungalow
Municipality Office
Pomprateep
Kata View Point Resort
Kry Guest House
Khok Tanot
Kata View Guest House
Kata Beach
Siam Commercial Bank
Serena Resort
Nit Guest House
Poolside Mam
Flamingo
Friendship Bungalows
Flamingo
Kata Hill Residence
Bungalow
Boat House
Cool Breeze
The Boat House Y & Grill
Kata Rock Inn Seaview
Kata Delight
Andaman Cannacia
Kata Sun Beach
Tropical Garden Resort
Orchidacea Resort
Katadaman Resort
Baan Kata Villa
Pop Cottage
Katamanda Resort
The Heights Phuket
Luxury Villas
Momtri Boathouse
Seaview Residence
4233

Kata Noi Bay

Western Inn
After Beach
Kata Noi Resort
Kata Noi Beach
Kata Noi GH
Kata Noi
Centara Karon Resort Phuket
Kata Bhuri
Sea Fun Diver Phuket
Soi Thongnak 2
Katathani Phuket Beach Resort
Kok Chong Kata Safari
Kata Noi Club
to Nai Harn Beach

Thanon Patak
Thanon Kata Noi
Th. Pak Bang
Th. Tanot Rd
Kata-Sai Yuan
Soi 5
Soi 6
Soi 3

scale 1 : 20,000
0   500m

---

to Phetchaburi, Bangkok
Khong Tha Nan
402
Dan Yit
Wat Aranya Wiwek
Suan Maphrao
Ko Raet
Yacht Haven Phuket M
Ban Dan
Laem Pi
Ban Yit
Ban Danyit
Kho Ein
Mai Khao Beach
Tu Khun
3016
Khao Kho En 202m
Bo Som
3033
Khao Ban Bang Dok 267m
Mai Khao
Som Po
Bo Sai Klang
402
Bang Rak Mai
Phuket International Airport
Bo Sai
Thep Kra
Sirinat Marine National Park
Din Sai
Yun Ban
Nai Yang Beach
4026
Din Nieo
Hua Hong
Wat Mongkhon Wararam
4026
4031
Tha
Phama Long
Nai Yang
Wat Muang Mai
Muan
Cape Sai Khru
4031
Khao Ta Kliang 225m
Sakhu
Khao Sai Khru 335m
Khao Ta Kliang
3017
402
Nai Thon
Na Sok
Muang Thon Noi Bay
Khao Muang 295m
Mut Dok Khao
Nai Thon Beach
Phru Champa
In Kruai Bay
Phru Somphan
6014
Cape Son
Ban Layan
Wat Phra Nang Sang
Nok Le
Amphoe
Cape Ko Katha
4018
La Yan
Don
Nan Tak To
BANG TAO BEACH 74
Wat
Wat Thepkrasatri
402
Bang Tao Bay
4030
Pa Sak
Bang Kok
Bang Tao Beach
4015
Liphon Bo Rae
08°00'
Choeng Thale
Ton Muang
Pacific Island Club
Phon Hua Han
Pansea Beach
Bang Thao
4025
Surin
Wat Anamai Kasem
Surin Beach
4025
Phuket
Kamala Bay
Phuket Fantasea
Cape Son
Sak Ngam
Khao Bang Nieo Dam 363m
Kamala
Bang Wan
Khao
KAMALA BEACH 74
Ban Klang
Kathu Waterfall
Khao Pak Bang 303m
Khuan Na Kha Le 277m
Nam Tok
Tho Sung
Loch Palm Golf Club
Cape Thai Phao
4233
Wa Kha La By
Khuan Wa 520m
Amph
Cape Yom Ding
Na Kha Le Beach
Jungle Bungy Jump
Kathu
to Similan 100km
Kalim Beach
Patong Bay
4029
Cape Kho Sai Rot
Patong
Chai Le
Phuket Country Club
Wat An Kitsad
Trai
Patong Beach
Na Nai
2036
Cape Mai Ngang
PATONG BEACH 75
Karon Noi
Suan Yang Lo Yong
Cape Khok
Ao Ron Nui
4021
Karon Noi Beach
Na Kok
Na
4233
Karon
Nua Bang
Karon Beach
Tok Wat
Wat Chalong
Ban Karon
Nai Phru
Wat Mai
Phuket z
Bang La
Ban Klang
Khok Tan
Khok Chang
Big Buddha
Bang Rae
Hua Hon
Cape Sai
Kata
3025
Phu
Khao Phlu Ruan 318m
4028
Touris
Harbo
Kata Yai Bay
4024
Kata Yai Beach
Ban Saiyu
KARON & KATA BEACHES 72
4009
Kata Noi Bay
Rawai Rest A
Kata Noi Beach
4233
Cape Mum Nai
Rawai
Nai Harn
Ka Point
Cape Mum Nok
4161
Rawai Beach
Man
Mum Nok Bay
4233
RAWAI 73
Nai Harn Beach
Ko Hay (6 km)
Phuket Famous Sunset View
Ferry to
Ko Hay (5 km
Ka Kaeo (5)
Ko Bon

07°50'
08°00'
08°10'

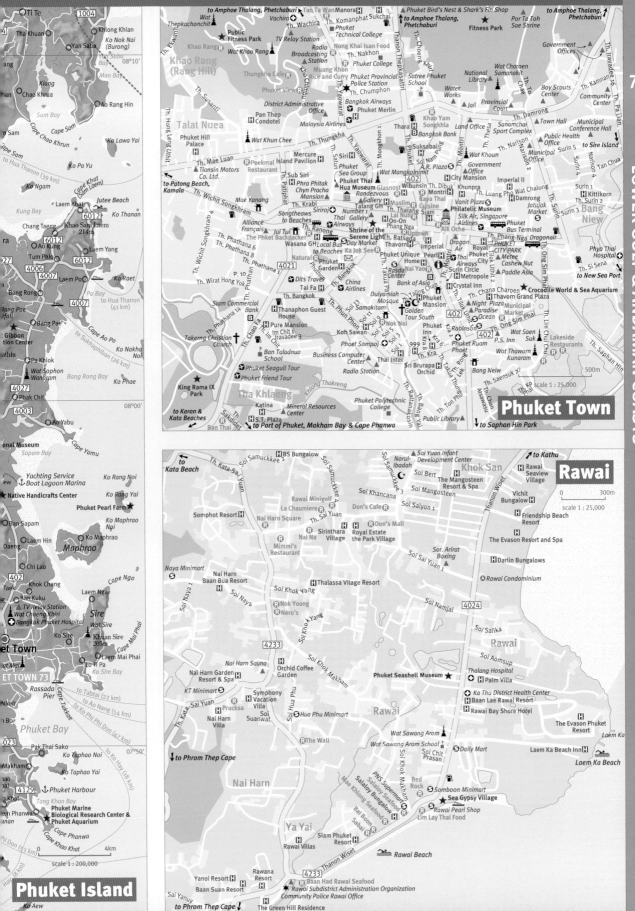

Phuket Town

Rawai

Phuket Island

Bang Tao Beach

0   400m
scale 1 : 20,000

Kamala Beach

0   400m
scale 1 : 20,000

Bang Tao

Rural Roads PK. 4018

Amanpuri
Pansea

Pansea Beach

Banyan Tree
Spa & Gallery

Laguna Fairway

The Chedi Phuket

Bang Tao Beach
Resort

Bang Tao

Banyan Tree
Golf Club

Ruan Thai Re

Surin
Surin Beach
Twin Palm
Benyad
Surin
Oriental

Laguna Phuket
Holiday Residence

Laguna Phuket

Banyan Tree

Allamanda Beach Club

Di A Lamada
Mosque

Laguna Phuket
Golf Club

Laguna Residences
Show House

Laguna Phuket
Golf Club

Angsana
Spa & Gallery

Allamanda
Laguna Phuket

Surin Beach

Albatross
Café

Bang Tao Bay

Sheraton Grande
Laguna Phuket

Laguna Holiday Club
Phuket Resort

Tanamera Resort

Wedding Chapel

Laguna Holiday
Club Office

Laguna Phuket

Cape Laem Singh

Laem Singh Beach

Dusit Thani Laguna Phuket

Canal Shopping
Village

Laguna
Cove

Laguna Beach Resort

Laguna
Grove

Laguna
Waters

Laguna Thai Class

Lanna
Restaurant

Chok Dee Deli

Laguna
Vista

Quest Laguna
Phuket Adventure

Phatthana 2

Quest Adventure &
Camp Laguna

Kamala Bay

Thai Bali Spa

Villa Getaways Phuket

B A N G   T A O   B E A C H

Bang Tao

Choeng Thale Phallana

Pracha
Uthit

Rydges Amora
Beach Resort

Choeng Thale 16

to Phuket Downtown

The Himmaphan

Khaokang Thammachat
Rice and Curry

Sunwing
Resort & Spa

Ki Sai

The Residence Phuket

Dalar Resort
Bangtao Beach

Nuture Place
Bungalow

The Tantawan

Best Western Premier
Bang Tao Beach Resort & Spa

Bang Tao Lagoon
Bungalow

Bang Tao 4/2

Bang Tao 2

Hok Farm
Bungalow

Bang Tao 4/1

The Le Croon
Tasco Lotus

Ochean
Palms

Benjamin Reso
Orchid H

Andaman Bang Tao Bay

Bang Tao
Beach
Chalet

Bang Tao 3

Bangtao Village
Resort

Two Villas
Bang Tao

Senses

Kamala
Beach Inn

Bar

Ka

Bang Tao Beach
Cottage

Bangthao
Piazza

Andaman Seaview Resort
Bangtao Beach 3

Tonsai Retreat
Spa & Villa

Bang Tao 4

Choeng Thalay
Subdistrict
Administration
Organization

Kamala Beach Estate

Naka

Baan Nana Food
& Drink

Baan Chai
Nam Resort

Blue Garden
Hotel & Resort

Ban Coconut

Bang Tao 4

Bang Tao 4/2

4025

Ban Tak Daet

Alila Phuket Villa

Hat Surin 8

Hua Tiam

Orange House
Restaurant

Bang Tao 4

Bang Tao 4

Bang Tao 3

Kamala Mountain View
Gourmet Pizza

Phuket Vacation
Apartments

Club Lursuang

Baan Bang Tao
Health Center

Darul Eahsan
Mosque

Bang Tao 5

The Plantation

Kamala Bay Terrace

Bangtao Tropical
Residence

Zorisunnah
Mosque

Phitakthong
Boxing Gym

Bang Tao 8

Th. Srisoonthorn

Islamic Saving
Cooperative Ltd.

Hat Surin 4

Hat Surin 2

Hua Tiam

Bang Tao 4

Bang Tao Thai 15

4025

Saltwater Dreaming
Surf Shop

Zorisunnah
Mosque

Bukarom
Bang Tao
Mosque

Bang Tao 9

402

Peri Villa

to Patong Beach

Wat Anamai Kasem

to Patong Beach

Kamal

Patong Beach

0   400m
scale 1 : 20,000

Buildings:
1 All 4 Diving
2 Neptune Diving

Hotels/ Resorts:
3 Baan Sukhothai
4 Baanthai Beach Resort
5 Burasari Resort
6 Duang Jitt Resort
7 Jintana Patong Hotel
8 Leelawadee Boutique
9 Nilly's Marina inn
10 Phairin Beach
11 R-mar Resort and SPA
12 Sea Sun Sand Resort
13 Seadream
14 Seaview Patong
15 Tatum Mansion
16 Tony Resort

Shops:
17 Ocean Shopping
18 Siam Commercial

Restaurants:
19 Gonzo Bar
20 Monroe Karaoke

Best Western Premier
Bang Tao Beach Resort & Spa
Andaman Bang Tao Bay
Bang Tao Beach Cottage
Nana Food & Drink
ai Nam Resort
Hat Surin 8

Bang Tao Lagoon Bungalow
Bang Tao Plazza
Bang Tao Beach Chalet
Blue Garden Resort

Villa Santi
Baan Chailay Resort
Ruan Thalay Patong Restaurants
Kalim Cafe
Panyah Restaurants
to Bang Tao & Kamala

Club Lursuang
Tiam

to Phuket Downtown
Hua Tiam
Bang Tao 4
Hat Surin 4
Hat Surin 2

Nakatani Village
Nerntong Resort

Malibu Island Club
The Orchid & Spa
Sunset Beach Resort

Kalim Beach
The Residence Kalim Bay
Phuket Land Ltd

Lim's
Ban Kalim
Argentina Steak Home
Patong Lodge
Kalim Seaview Resort
Blue Marine Resort & Spa
Diamond Cliff

Pen Villa
Surin Estate
TNN Furniture
ow Inn
Sunset
iltops

Wat Anamai Kasem

Da Maurizio
Otowa
Joe's Downstairs
Baan Rim Pa Thai Restaurants
Le Tong Beach
Patong Paragon
Franco Roma Italian Restaurants
Gloria Jean's Coffee
Laemphet Restaurants
On Uma Mansion
Nurul Hudah Mosque
Lim's

Novotel Phuket Resort
Kalim
Seven Seas
Kalim Guesthouse
Villa Archara
Panorama Beach Club
Andaman Divers
Little Chery G.H.
Dog & Duck Inn
Palm Garden
The Mermaid Resort
First Resort
P.S.2 Bungalow
Patong Bayshore

Baan Thai Surin Hill

Arasia Resort
Thai ngthalay
Ayara Surin Villas

AMPHOE THALANG
AMPHOE KATHU

A.A. Villa
Sunset
Phuket Graceland Resort & Spa
Penthouse
Eden
Nordic
Swiss Palm
Shamrock Park Inn
Than Thip Villa
Patong Palace
Beau Rivage
Andatel
Andaman Beach Suites
International Law Office
Public Library
It's alive Seafood
Patong Grand Condotel
Th. Hat Patong
Sawasdee Mansion
Dubai Restaurants
S.V. Phuket Andaman
Patong Comdo
Club Andaman Beach Resort
Sphinx
Patong Premier
Joy Cafe
The Kris

Khok Makham
Green Mountain
Ban Ton Khao
Th. Phra Barami
Kabkloay
Suwankhiriwong School
Marble Inscription of King Rama IX
Khlong Bang Wat
to Kathu

Casuarina
Patong Pearl Resortel
White Sand Resortel
The Chart House
Beach Restaurants
Patong Tour
Patong Beach
Salathai Resort
Thara Patong Beach Resort & Spa
Impiana Phuket Cabana Resort
Tantawan
Poppa
Azzuro Village
Patong Bayshore
Salsa Cocktail Bar
The Beach Resortel
The Union Bank
Molly Malone's
Safari Beach Resort
Savoey
Alice Bar

Moen
Mani Thong
The Green House
Baifern Mansion
Patong City Hall
Ms Guesthouse
Patong Fire Station
Baan Anurak
Baan Boa 1
Jinny Mansion
Chai Le
Butterfly House
The Hill Top

Siam Commercial Bank
Queen Airh Booking Ctr.
Patong City House
FITNESS PARK
7/11
Patong
Royal Paradise
Santana Divers
Tiger Inn

Inter Place Mansion
Sainamyen
Nipa Resort
Wolfies GH
Chaba Villa
Rengaya
Chawit Homes
Andaman Queen Cabaret
Rendez Vous
Soi Sea Dragon
Rock Hard
Neptuna
Expat
Baan Benjamas
BB Cottage
Green Kitchen
Royal Crown
Green View

Centara
Sawaddi Patong
Baan Boa 2
Tana Patong
Royal Kitchen
Baan Nita
Baan Suan Villa 2
Krua Chom View Restaurant
Tavern on the Hill Restaurant
Baan Nam Yen
Phuvaree Resort

Tropical Bungalows
Tropica Restaurants & Cafe
Pizzedelic
Banana Disco
Royal Silk
Aloha Surf Shop
Karlsson's
Family Restaurants
Bel Aire Mansion
Starbucks Cafe
Patong Shopping Center
Royal Palm Resort
Horizon Beach Resort
Paradise
Ocean Plaza
Phuket Grand Tropicana
Bus to Town
Absolute Sea Pearl
Seagull China
QVC Resort
Baan Boa Resort
Crystal Bay
Avantika Boutique Hotel
Swiss
Coconut Village
The Boutique
Maeng Kup Karaoke
Damario Restaurants
Pattana Art Gallery
Si-Fa Restaurants
Snake Farm
Amari Coral Beach Resort
Phuket Palace

Patong
Bang La
Patong Inn
Sand Inn
Pizza
Ocean Plaza
Casa Breeze
Patong Tower
The Dive Inn
Via Rent A Car
Baithong Lifestyle Suites
T & T Service Center Patong
Montana Grand Phuket
Patong Beach Lodge
Nineteen Mansion
Borsalino
Baluchi
Andaman Orchid
O-Top Market
Golden Land Plaza
African Winery
Baumanburi Resort & Spa
Hyton Leelavadee
Ramaburin Resort
Thamdee Inn
C&N
Khun Chai Cafe & Karaoke
Baan
Le Jardin
Drop Inn
The Hill Pub & Restaurant
Sun Set Bar & Restaurant
Suphattra Village

Levele
Grand Orchid
Inn
Holiday Inn
Soho

Nanai Grand Villas
Nanai Resort Patong
Jungceylon
Banzaan Fresh Market

Season Mansion
Na Nai Happy House
F.B.I. Guesthouse
J.R.P. Hotel
Nanai Residence
Sky Restaurants
Rabbit Mansion
Mae Ubol Market
Andaman Villa Resort
Nanai Villa
Patong Cottage
Andaman Hill Hotel
Patong Boxing Gym
Baan Suan Villa
Phairin Hill
Supatra Apartments & G.H.

Phuket Fantasea Office
Phuket Fantasea
Guess Resort
Ban Chaba
Al-Bushra Mosque
Maphrao Resort
Kamala Coco Hut
Kamala
Provincial Police Station of Kamala
Planet Phuket Bungalow
Kamala Resort & Spa
Kamala Best House
amphrakiat Park
Kamala Health Center
Kamala Subdistrict Administration Organization
Kamala Gym Fitness Centre
The Club Residence
Bay Minimart
Phra Niwej Church
Argentina Grill & Steak House
Minimart
Jasmin Kamala
Naka Infant evelopment Center
rul Eahsan
Kamala Mosque
Kamala Subdistrict Administration Organization

Kamala 14
Kamala 12
Kamala Bay Garden Resort
Kamala 10
Kamala Nathong
Kamala Coco Hut
Kamala 8
Thai Vegas Bar & Diner
Ton Kamala
Rim Tha
Tang Thai

Patong Merlin
Baan
Ton Sai
Sun Hill
Club Bamboo

Phuket Simon Cabaret
Tienseng Villa
Bamboubeach
PS Hill
The Artist Studio Gallery
Patong Grand Ville
Patong Hill Estate
The Jungle House
Phuvana Village

Th. Sirirat
Th. Phangmueang
Th. Prachanukhon
Th. Na Nai
Th. Na Nai
Soi Thamdee
Th. Rual
Th. Phisit Karani

Rai Room Yen Restaurants
Baan Khaluang Beer Garden & Restaurants

to Freedom & Paradise Beaches
to Karon & Kata

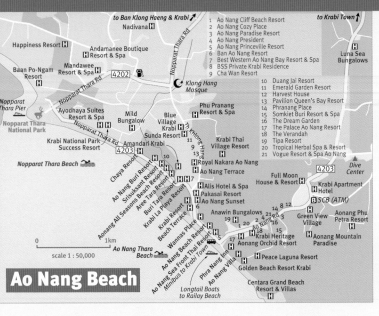
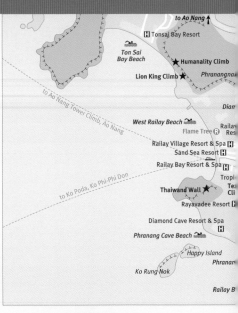
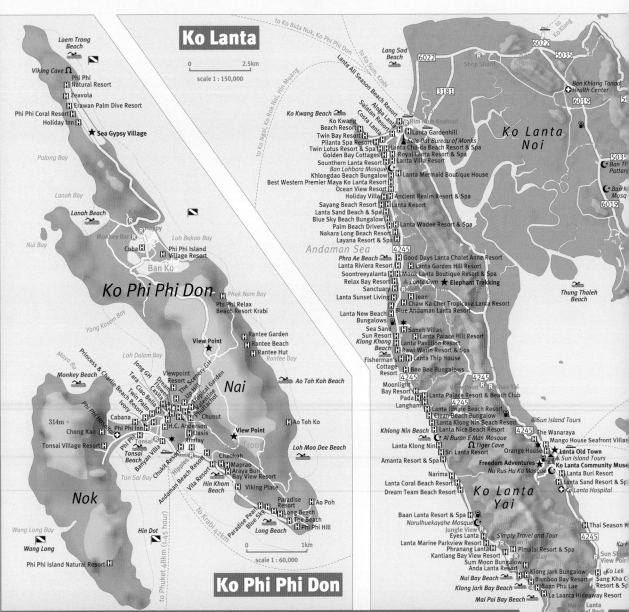

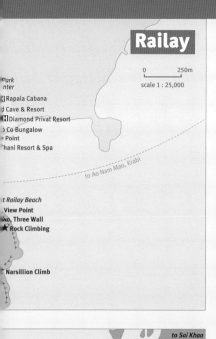

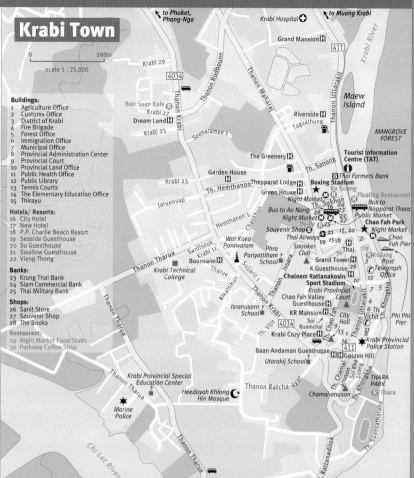

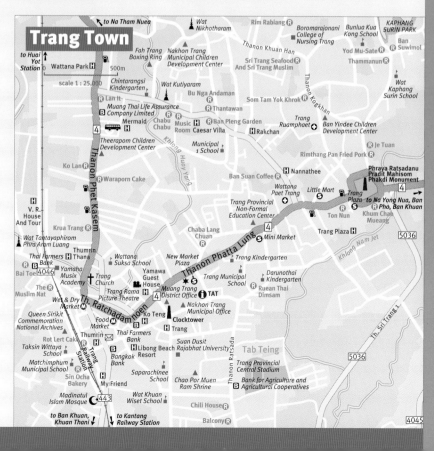

Ko Cham 999 Khun Raya Khlong Phon Bang Di Khao Khao Pun Pa Phayom Mai
Khlong Yang Khlong Raet Tha Pradu Huai Yot 877m Lo Thom Nua Pan Tae Sao Ranot Raw
Tha Thuk Khwai 4 Sai Khao Khlong Yuan Thale Noi Thong Thale Noi 4007 Khlong Yuan Rong Choeng Sae 408
Tha Maphrao 4042 Phru Toei Khuan Kun Na To Mun Nam Phrai 4123 Khao Lak Falls 41 4164 Thung Khung Nang 4048 Lam Pam Thale
Lanta Lanta Noi 4046 Kalase Wang Maprang Lamphu La Khao Pu Khao Ya Taphaen 4163 Khok 4138 Bang Pin Nok Nam Khai Luang
Hua Hin Bo Muang Hua Hin 4158 Na Tham Tai National Park Nam Phut Si Banphot 4048 Phrae Ha 4047 Nok Nam Khai 4196
Mo Mamuang Beach 4245 Thung 4046 4159 Nong Trut Na Ta Luang Na Yong 429m Phatthalung Khao Chai Son Khok Sak Krasae
Sala Dan Phra Ae Khao Mai Kaeo Khok Yang Trang Si Nakharin Na Thom 4122 PHATTHALUNG TOWN 81 4049 Kho Nang Kham Ko Yai
Khlong Ninh Sikao La Mo Si Nakharin Plua Lon Tha Khae Laem Khwai Rap Mae Khli Pak Phayun Hat Yai
Lanta Yai Mai Fat Khuan Pring Na Khao Sia Kachong Falls 1322m Na Som Wang Ko Wut Wildlife Sanctuary Lam Chong Thanon 4081 Khao Chai Son Sathing P
Mu Ko Lanta National Park Bang Sak 403 Thung Khai Sai Khong Kongra 4122 Khlong Chaloem Khao Bang Kaeo Khun Non Bo
Ko Po Pa Tiao 4162 Lam Thu 4124 Lam Plok Falls 1089m Tamot Pak Phayun
Pak Meng Beach Bo Nam Khlong Chi Lom Khok Sai Thung Ko Yuan Charat Lo Chan Kra Tha Yai 4237 Pa Bon Pa Bak
Chang Lang Beach Kantang 404 Phra Sawan Falls Chong Banphot Falls Ton Te Falls 1163m Ban Tamot Pa Bon Khok Sai Huai
Hat Chao Mai National Park Nam Rap Kan Tang Tai Yan Ta Khao Wang Charoen Palian Ton Tok Falls 959m Pa Bak 4111
Ko Ngai Na Klua Na Laem Som Chao Phra Falls Thung Nari 4122 Phru Pho 406
Ko Muk Yong Ling Beach Chao Mai Phra Muang Bawi 4235 Su So Thung Yai 307m Rattaphum Khuan Niang
Ko Kradan Tha Sano Hat Samran Laem Po Khlong Rap 679m Tha Chamuang 43 Bar
Yao Beach Maphrao 311m Laem Po Samran Beach Na Thalot 404 416 Liphang 378m Kamphaeng Phet Khao Khao Rang Kiat 420
Talibong Laem Thuat Ta Se Yong Sata Na Thon 689m Na Luk Nikhom Khao Mai Kaeo Chalung
Ko Rok Nok Palian Thung Wa 689m Phatthana 821m HAT YAI TOWN
Ko Rok Nai Ko Liang Nuea Laem Yong Sata Taban 416 Pam Phatthana 472m 742m Boriphat Falls Ton Nga Chang Ha Rae
Ko Bulao Bot Siam Mai Ko Sukon Wang Charoen Rat Nam Phut King Amphoe Manang Bon Khuan Khao Krai Wildlife Sanctuary Ton Nga Chang Falls Khlong La Kho
Ko Phetra Thung Bu Lang 416 Pa Samet 343m 639m 919m Wang Pha 406
Ko Talui Yai Ko Phetra National Marine Park Khon Khlan Wang Tong Khao Khao Khao Krai Soi Sip Khuan Thung Khlong Hoi
Ko Ta Bai Laem Som Khuan Sanai Phatthana Ka Long Nui Khong
Ko Tongku Son Klang Bo Hin 659m Thung Tam Sao
La-Ngu Pa Fang 4078 416 Satun 4137 Khuan Don Khuan Sato Th
TARUTAO ISLANDS 79 Pak Bara Port Pru Hual Tuai Tha Phae Khuan Pu 4148 Wang Prachan 566m Bang Kwai
Ko Bu Lon Le Mu Ko Phetra National Park Tha Chanuang Sakhon Thung Rin Chin Wat Khao Rup Chang Bang Khoi
Ko Ayam Ko Rang Nok Ko Rifi Rai Ketari Padang Be
Mara Cape Ko Lela 4051 406 Kaki Buki 4054 Sada
Tarutao Islands Jak Bay Ko Tabyong Uma Che Bilang SATUN TOWN 80 Masjid Samna Khar
Ko Ya Ra Tot Noi Che Bilang Pier Satun Ko Nok Kubang Tiga Medang Gajah
TARUTAO ISLANDS NATIONAL MARINE PARK 703m Ko Ya Ra Tot Yai Tanyong Po 4183 Kubang Khlong Phru
Ko Rawi Ko Bitsi Khai Taloh Wow Gauar Padang Asam Padang
Ko Bu Tang Yang Ko Adang Ko Tanga Ko Tarutao Ko Yai Tammalang Jentik 506m Kangar
Ko Lipe Makham Bay Tammalang Border Crossing Point Bt. Ka
THAILAND Tammalang Pier Pauh 194 Ch
Taloh Udang MALAYSIA P. Langgun Kuala Perlis Arau
Langkawi Island Ayer Hangat Kg Surau Kodiang

Ko Lipe

Ko Lipe

0   500m
scale 1 : 30,000

Mountain R Karma
Billa Andaman
Flower Power Fisheries Department Lipe Beach Asia Sunrise Beach Ko Kra
Sunset Beach Porn Jack's Jungle Baan Koh Adang School
Power Station Bonus Tarutao Cabana
Ko Lipe Rain Forest Varin 2
Paradise Pink Sita Kasirin Gipsy
Dayang Peace & Love Lipe Greenview Family Moonlight Varin Forra Dive
Pattaya 2 Ocean Pro Diving Coco
Sanom Beach Barrakud Castaway
Yong Hua Wreck Ao Pattaya Time to Chill Handicraft Sanom Sunrise
Pattaya Beach Blue Tribes Bundhaya Osin Idyllic Resort
Army Ko Usen
Viewpoint Resort

Kuala Sangiang Jitra
Binjai Kg Ala
Ayer Hitam 79 Kepala Batas
Kg Kelompang K363 Zahir Mosque 178
Alor Setar
Kuala Kedah 177
Kuala Kedah Fort
Kuala Kungkong
Simpang Tiga Sungai Dau
P. Bunting Sungai Limau Dalam
Kg Sala
P. Telor Archaeological Museum
P. Bidan Singkir Darat
Bujang Valley Archaeological Site
Sunga Gunung Je

Far South

scale 1 : 1,000,000
0   20km

Tarutao Islands

scale 1 : 500,000
0   10km

to Ko Lantra;
Ko Lantra; to Ko Muk;
Ko Nagai

Private
Accommodation
Ko Bulon Le H

to Ko Lantra

Pak Bara Pier

Ko Bulon
Mai Phai

Ko Un Ying

Ko Phulao Bulon

Mara Cape

Ko Le Lah
(Ta Keang)

Papiyong Cliff ★
Park Headquarters
National Park
Accommodation

Toh-Bo Cliff
Ko Laen
Rusi Bay
Crocodile Cave
Visitors Center

Taloh Wao
Bay

Pante Malacca Bay

Jak Bay

Ao Molae

Ao Taloh Wao
Tarun Cave

Lu Du Waterfall

Ko Putao Na

703m

Ko Klang
Ko Kolo

TARUTAO ISLANDS NATIONAL MARINE PARK

Son Bay

La Po Waterfall

Ko Tarutao

Malaetae Cape

Babi Cape

Nam Tok
Waterfall
Ko Rawi

Pirate's
Waterfall

Ko Bitsi

Ko Klang

Ko Tanga

Fishing Area ★

Tam Nak Tot Waterfall

Makham Bay

Ko Panan

Historical
Sites

Ko Singha
Tam Nok
Nang Cave

Ko Bu Tang

Mu Ko Dong ★
Ko Sagai
Ko Lugoi
Ko Bulu
Ko Ling Kao
Ko Hin Sorn

Ko Yang
Scuba Diving

Ko Adang
Ko Burat
Ko Hin Ngam

Waterfalls

Ko Lipe

Ko Talang

KO LIPE 78

to Langkawi

Taloh U-dong Bay

Ko Beliyung
Besa

ng Ngam Beach

Samira Beach
Wat Matchimawat

Songkhla
SONGKHLA TOWN 81

Chum Pho

Pak Bang Na Thap Beach

ha Chin

Thung Yai

Pak Bang

Hua Thanon

Na Thap

Sakom

7°

43

Khlong Pia

Pa Ching

Sakom

Taling Chan

Sakom
Beach

101°

Cape Pho (Cape Ta Chi)

Laem Pho

Talo Kapo Beach

Talo Kapo Beach

Panare Beach

102°

Chana

Ban Na

Na Wa

Krung I Tam

Laem Ta Chi

Pattani

Yaring

Panare

Chalalai Beach

Chana

Khae

Ban Maeng Lak

Saba

Thepha

PATTANI TOWN 80

Klang

Ngae Ngae

Khae Khae Beach

Thepha

408

Tha Muang

Thepha Sathani

Nong Chik
Bo Thong

Kamiyo

Sadawa

Saban

To Lang

Nam Bo

Bang Kao

iu Tok

Khun Tat Wai

43

Tha Kam Cham

42

Sano

Talal

Krawa

Tha Nam

Na Mo Sri
Ki Kita

Chang

Phru Tu

42

Tha Rua

Na Ket

Pulakong

4075

4157

Thanon

Sakam

Wasu-Kri Beach

Na Thawi

Lam Phai

4085

Khok Pho

Yarang

Mayo

444m

Paen

Paseyawo

Paka Timo Beach

Tha Pradu

Wang Yai

Lamphlai

23

Chang Hai Tak

Pabom

Parai

Muang Tia

Trang

Pado

Sai Buri

Talupan

Kolae Boatmaking Village

Tha Chang

501m

Saba Yoi

Pian

Na Pradu

Thung Pala

Sai Khao

Pak Lo

Yupo

312m

Thung Yang

Daeng

Mai Kaen

Bu-to Su Ngai Padi, Forest & Waterfall

Pa Mai

Pa Mai Beach

1015m

409

Tam Mai

Amphoe
Muang Yala

Talo Nibong

Pu La Mong

4071

Tha Thong

Brae Nua

4168

Bare Tai

Kayomati

4155

Ban Thop

Nara-that Beach

748m

Khao Daeng

Nam Chee

Chahaen

4085

Katong

4065

Na Than

Lidon

Yala

Talo Halo

Noen Ngam

4092

Chakwua

Bacho

42

Lubosawo

Khok Khian

7940m

Prakop

Ba Hoi

Yaha

Posemo

4063

Kototura

Banrangsareng

Suwan

Samakkhi

4060

702m

Bae Ro

Lubobusa

Narathiwat

Phra Tamnak Thaksin Ratchaniwet

Kg Padang Sanai

Ta Pae

486m

La-ae
Purong

4066

Raman

Yata

Sawo

Tapoyo

42

14

San Lamphu

Kg Padang Terab

K11

548m

Kabang

4070

Patae

Bala

4176

Kota Baru

Bumang
Kalo

Riang

Rueso

4067

Chobo

Marubo

4058

Yingo

4055

4055

4048

Gubu-Barn Klong
Ton Beach

385m

Kg Pisang

Kabang

4077

Krong Pinang

1096m

Batong

4060

Lalo

4107

Thaksin Ming Mongkhon
Image Buddha

Phraiwan
Sala Mai

Kuala Nerang

Huai Krathing

4106

Khok Sato

816m

Rangae

Bangosato

Bang Po

Chu Wo

Tak Bai

Kg Tanjung Luar

Tham Thalu

Bannang
Sata

Tan Yong Na Ko

Kalong

Si Sakhon

Tamayung

Ka Nua

Marue Bo-ok

4056

Phron

Kg Telaga Lanos

Kg Bukit

Naka

429m

Kg. Che Song

582m

4106

Yala

Bacho

916m

Si Banphot

Dusongyo

4055

Cho Airong

La Pae

A-18

Na Nak

4057

Meranti

K502

K8

Kg. Gula

K13

Kg.Berhala

Than To

Kiriknet

Khuan Banglang

1054m

4060

Ka To

4217

Todeng

Nami

K157

Nami

Gulau

821m

Rae

Sakai

Ban Phakdi

4115

Chanae

Rom Sai

Paturu

Sungai

Sungai
Kolok

Pasir Mas

Sungai
Tiang

Kg Sungai Batang

928m

Maewat

Ban To

1056m

Than To

1136m

Chang Phuak

672m

Aisure

Sako

Kia

Ku Lu Bi

Sungai Padi

Kg Bakat Hulu

864m

K153

La-ong Rung Waterfall

1034m

1318m

4060

650m

Kg Batu Karang

Jeneri

Kg Jeneri

K8

K10

1003m

Kg. Tanjong Pari

Malong

410

Aiyoeweng

1152m

Hala Bala Forest

THAILAND

1490m

Sukirin

604m

Waeng

Maedong

Kg Alur Pasir

Kg Belgia

773m

Sik

706m

Kg. Surau

Bo Nam Ron

Na Le

MALAYSIA

Ali Timing

Mamong

968m

4057

Kg Bukit Gading

Jenlang

Pekan Batu 5

Bongor

4062

Chantharat

Phukhao
Thong

Lochut

4062

Kg Buyong

Merbau Batang

Tanah
Meran

K17

Bukit Selambau

K15

K10

1145m

Hot
Spring

Betong

Aiyoe Boechang

4062

Bt. Ulu Laho
1203m

To Mo
Gold Mine

Sirithon Falls

4062

787m

D26

Kg China

to Butterworth

4244

Pengkalan
Hulu

Parit Panjang

719m

Kg Kepayang

Batu Melintang

1117m

Jeli

Kg Kerilia

Baling

to Sungai Petani

101°

to Taiping

102°

M A L A Y S I A

MALAYSIA

Satun Town

Hat Yai Town

Pattani Town

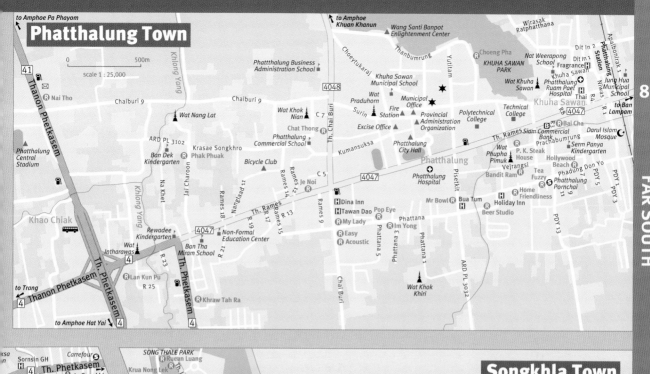

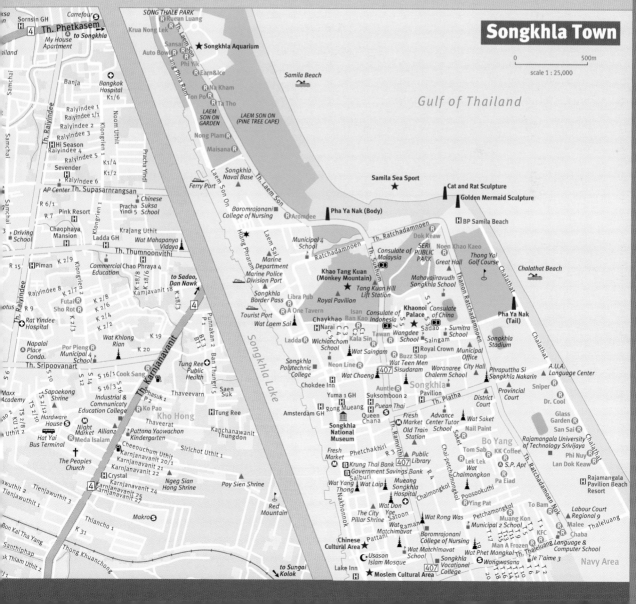

How to use this index
There are two sections. The first lists villages, towns and cities. The second lists significant points of interest, including national parks and reserves. All items give page number and map title. If an entry appears on a large area map and also a more detailed map, only the page with the more detailed map is listed.

Villages, Towns and Cities

Ainshebyin 60 Upper Gulf Coasts
Aisure 79 Far South
Aiyoe Boechang 79 Far South
Aiyoeweng 79 Far South
Akat Amnuai 49 Northeastern Thailand
Ale-man Kyun 60 Upper Gulf Coasts
Ali Timing 79 Far South
Alor Setar 78 Far South
Amnat Charoen 49 Northeastern Thailand
Amphawa 18 Around Bangkok
Amphoe Ao Luk 71 Phuket Province
Amphoe Kathu 72 Phuket Island
Amphoe Takua Thung 71 Phuket Province
Amphoe Thai Muang 70 Phuket Province
Amphoe Thalang 72 Phuket Island
Amphone Muang Yala 79 Far South
An Pao 71 Phuket Province
Ang Hin 18 Around Bangkok
Ang Khao 22 Around Ayutthaya
Ang Maha 17 Central Thailand
Ang Sila 19 Around Bangkok
Ang Thong 18 Around Bangkok
Anoru 80 Pattani Town
Anusawari 5 Greater Bangkok
Ao Bo Thale 71 Phuket Province
Ao Chong Klon 71 Phuket Province
Ao Kung 73 Phuket Island
Ao Leuk 69 Ko Tao
Ao Luek 64 Isthmus of Kra
Ao Luek Noi 64 Isthmus of Kra
Ao Makham 71 Phuket Province
Ao Nam 71 Phuket Province
Ao Nam Bo 73 Phuket Island
Ao Nam Mao 71 Phuket Province
Ao Nang 64 Isthmus of Kra
Ao Ngoen 5 Greater Bangkok
Ao Rang Hin 73 Phuket Island
Ao Ron Nui 72 Phuket Island
Ao Yabu 73 Phuket Island
Ao Yai 28 Southeastern Thailand
Arau 78 Far South
Arun Ammarin 8 Downtown Bangkok
Asa 19 Around Bangkok
Asok Villa 11 Lumphini
At Samat 48 Northeastern Thailand
Aw 60 Upper Gulf Coasts
Awebindat 60 Upper Gulf Coasts
Ayer Hangat 78 Far South
Ayer Hitam 78 Far South
Ba Hoi 79 Far South
Ba Kan 71 Phuket Province
Bacho 79 Far South
Bae Ro 79 Far South
Bak Charang 48 Northeastern Thailand
Bak Dai 50 Around Phanom Rung
Bak Khong 49 Northeastern Thailand
Bala 79 Far South
Baling 79 Far South
Bamnet Narong 17 Central Thailand
Ban Aeng 33 Chiang Mai,
    Mae Hong Son & Lamphun Provinces
Ban Akat 49 Northeastern Thailand
Ban Alang 49 Northeastern Thailand
Ban Ang Thong 66 Ko Samui
Ban bang Bao 28 Southeastern Thailand
Ban Bang Kao 66 Ko Samui
Ban Bang Makham 66 Ko Samui
Ban Bang Rak 66 Ko Samui
Ban Bat 9 Downtown Bangkok
Ban Bo Hin 68 Ko Pha-Ngan
Ban Bo Phut 67 Mae Nam
Ban Boek 22 Around Ayutthaya
Ban Bok 49 Northeastern Thailand
Ban Bok 49 Northeastern Thailand
Ban Bom 33 Chiang Mai,
    Mae Hong Son & Lamphun Provinces
Ban Bong 48 Northeastern Thailand
Ban Bua 51 Buriram Town
Ban Buamthon 48 Northeastern Thailand
Ban Bueng 19 Around Bangkok
Ban Chabok 48 Northeastern Thailand
Ban Chaeng 17 Central Thailand
Ban Chak 49 Northeastern Thailand
Ban Chalok Lum 68 Ko Pha-Ngan
Ban Chan 49 Greater Udon Thani
Ban Chang 22 Around Ayutthaya
Ban Chang Lo 8 Downtown Bangkok
Ban Changom 49 Northeastern Thailand
Ban Charat 49 Northeastern Thailand
Ban Chathu 72 Phuket Island

Ban Chaweng Noi 66 Ko Samui
Ban Chian 24 Around Nakhon Sawan
Ban Chon Khram 66 Ko Samui
Ban Chorakhe Mak
    48 Northeastern Thailand
Ban Chung 22 Around Ayutthaya
Ban Daen 16 Central Thailand
Ban Dan 72 Phuket Island
Ban Dan Na Khom 43 Lampang, Nan,
    Phrae, Uttaradit Provinces
Ban Danyit 72 Phuket Island
Ban Dilang 17 Central Thailand
Ban Dohmen 48 Northeastern Thailand
Ban Don 18 Around Bangkok
Ban Dong 41 Chiang Rai Province
Ban Donhiang 48 Northeastern Thailand
Ban Donkhiao 49 Northeastern Thailand
Ban Dung 48 Northeastern Thailand
Ban Durian 66 Ko Samui
Ban Fa 41 Chiang Rai Province
Ban Faen 41 Chiang Rai Province
Ban Fai Mai 68 Ko Pha-Ngan
Ban Fong 71 Phuket Province
Ban Had Rin 65 Around Samui
Ban Hae 41 Chiang Rai Province
Ban Haeng 41 Chiang Rai Province
Ban Haet 48 Northeastern Thailand
Ban Harn 66 Ko Samui
Ban Hat Rin 68 Hat Rin
Ban Hatkiang 48 Northeastern Thailand
Ban Hiang 49 Northeastern Thailand
Ban Hin 64 Isthmus of Kra
Ban Hin Kong 68 Ko Pha-Ngan
Ban Hinkhan 49 Northeastern Thailand
Ban Hoi 48 Northeastern Thailand
Ban Hong 33 Chiang Mai,
    Mae Hong Son & Lamphun Provinces
Ban Hua Laem 76 Ko Lanta
Ban Hua Lamai 25K 66 Ko Samui
Ban Huat 41 Chiang Rai Province
Ban Hut Taphu 48 Northeastern Thailand
Ban Je Li 76 Ko Lanta
Ban Kaeng 33 Chiang Mai,
    Mae Hong Son & Lamphun Provinces
Ban Kalantha 48 Northeastern Thailand
Ban Kang 16 Central Thailand
Ban Kanong 48 Northeastern Thailand
Ban Kao 24 Around Nakhon Sawan
Ban Kariang 60 Upper Gulf Coasts
Ban Katam 33 Chiang Mai,
    Mae Hong Son & Lamphun Provinces
Ban Keun 48 Northeastern Thailand
Ban Kha 60 Upper Gulf Coasts
Ban Khaen 49 Northeastern Thailand
Ban Khai 68 Ko Pha-Ngan
Ban Khamen 28 Southeastern Thailand
Ban Khiam 49 Northeastern Thailand
Ban Khlang 22 Around Ayutthaya
Ban Khlong Hin 76 Ko Lanta
Ban Khlong Khong 76 Ko Lanta
Ban Khlong Mak 76 Ko Lanta
Ban Khlong Nin 76 Ko Lanta
Ban Khlong Suan 19 Around Bangkok
Ban Khlong Tanod 76 Ko Lanta
Ban Kho 40 Chiang Rai Province
Ban Khok 43 Lampang, Nan, Phrae,
    Uttaradit Provinces
Ban Khok Kruat 66 Ko Samui
Ban Khok Luat
    71 Phuket Province
Ban Khok Pu 17 Central Thailand
Ban Khong 18 Around Bangkok
Ban Khot 30 Chonburi Town
Ban Khuan 72 Phuket Island
Ban Khwan 48 Northeastern Thailand
Ban Khwang 22 Around Ayutthaya
Ban Khwao 48 Northeastern Thailand
Ban Klang 72 Phuket Island
Ban Klap 22 Around Ayutthaya
Ban Kluai 44 New Sukhothai
Ban Klueng 22 Around Ayutthaya
Ban Ko 76 Ko Phi Phi Don
Ban Kok 43 Lampang, Nan, Phrae,
    Uttaradit Provinces
Ban Krang 60 Upper Gulf Coasts
Ban Krathum 22 Around Ayutthaya
Ban Krot 22 Around Ayutthaya
Ban Kruat 50 Around Phanom Rung
Ban Kuku 73 Phuket Island
Ban Kum 22 Around Ayutthaya
Ban Kung 49 Northeastern Thailand
Ban Kusuman 49 Northeastern Thailand
Ban Kwan Chang
    28 Southeastern Thailand

Ban La 71 Phuket Province
Ban Laem 60 Upper Gulf Coasts
Ban Laem 66 Ko Samui
Ban Laem Trang 76 Ko Phi Phi Don
Ban Laeng 42 Lampang, Nan, Phrae,
    Uttaradit Provinces
Ban Lahanam 49 Northeastern Thailand
Ban Lamduan 48 Northeastern Thailand
Ban Lang Sod 76 Ko Lanta
Ban Lang Sot 76 Ko Lanta
Ban Lanta 76 Ko Lanta
Ban Lat 60 Upper Gulf Coasts
Ban Lat-Han 49 Northeastern Thailand
Ban Layan 72 Phuket Island
Ban Len 18 Around Bangkok
Ban Lipa Noi 66 Ko Samui
Ban Lipa Yai 66 Ko Samui
Ban Loh Yai 76 Ko Lanta
Ban Lu Pu 16 Central Thailand
Ban Lu Yong 76 Ko Lanta
Ban Luam 49 Greater Udon Thani
Ban Luan 18 Around Bangkok
Ban Luang 22 Around Ayutthaya
Ban Lueam 48 Northeastern Thailand
Ban Lum 44 New Sukhothai
Ban Ma 22 Around Ayutthaya
Ban Madeua Whan 68 Ko Pha-Ngan
Ban Mae Haad 68 Ko Pha-Ngan
Ban Maeng Lak 79 Far South
Ban Mahaeng 32 Northern Thailand
Ban Mai 4 Greater Bangkok
Ban Mai Chaiyaphot
    48 Northeastern Thailand
Ban Mai Nong Sai
    28 Southeastern Thailand
Ban Mang 41 Chiang Rai Province
Ban Mi 17 Central Thailand
Ban Mo 61 Phetchaburi (Phetburi) Town
Ban Moung 43 Lampang, Nan, Phrae,
    Uttaradit Provinces
Ban Muang 18 Around Bangkok
Ban Muat 49 Northeastern Thailand
Ban Mung 48 Northeastern Thailand
Ban Na 71 Phuket Province
Ban Na Huk 34 Around Chiang Mai
Ban Na Kok 48 Northeastern Thailand
Ban Na Sai 66 Ko Samui
Ban Nahat 48 Northeastern Thailand
Ban Nai 70 Phuket Province
Ban Nai Suan 68 Ko Pha-Ngan
Ban Nai Wok 68 Ko Pha-Ngan
Ban Nakala 49 Northeastern Thailand
Ban Nakep 48 Northeastern Thailand
Ban Nakham 48 Northeastern Thailand
Ban Nakok 49 Northeastern Thailand
Ban Naleng Tai 48 Northeastern Thailand
Ban Nam Pua 43 Lampang, Nan, Phrae,
    Uttaradit Provinces
Ban Nam Tok 68 Ko Pha-Ngan
Ban Namxong 48 Northeastern Thailand
Ban Nangeun 48 Northeastern Thailand
Ban Nathang 49 Northeastern Thailand
Ban Nathon 49 Northeastern Thailand
Ban Natong 48 Northeastern Thailand
Ban Naxong 48 Northeastern Thailand
Ban Ngio 19 Around Bangkok
Ban Ngiu 49 Northeastern Thailand
Ban Nikham 48 Northeastern Thailand
Ban Nok 68 Ko Pha-Ngan
Ban Nok Sai 66 Ko Samui
Ban Non 48 Northeastern Thailand
Ban Nong 48 Northeastern Thailand
Ban Nong Hoi 60 Upper Gulf Coasts
Ban Nong Sang 24 Around Nakhon Sawan
Ban Nongboualao
    49 Northeastern Thailand
Ban Nonghoy 49 Northeastern Thailand
Ban Nongkeun 48 Northeastern Thailand
Ban Nua 68 Ko Pha-Ngan
Ban Nung 43 Lampang, Nan, Phrae,
    Uttaradit Provinces
Ban On 41 Chiang Rai Province
Ban Pa Lai Luang 33 Chiang Mai,
    Mae Hong Son & Lamphun Provinces
Ban Pae 33 Chiang Mai,
    Mae Hong Son & Lamphun Provinces
Ban Paeng 22 Around Ayutthaya
Ban Pah 67 Chaweng
Ban Pakha 49 Northeastern Thailand
Ban Pakman 48 Northeastern Thailand
Ban Paksa 49 Northeastern Thailand
Ban Paksong 49 Northeastern Thailand
Ban Palatha 16 Central Thailand
Ban Pang 17 Central Thailand

Ban Pang Bon 68 Ko Pha-Ngan
Ban Pang Kae 17 Central Thailand
Ban Pao 33 Chiang Mai,
    Mae Hong Son & Lamphun Provinces
Ban Pate 70 Phuket Province
Ban Pathum 19 Around Bangkok
Ban Phaen 22 Around Ayutthaya
Ban Phaeng 48 Northeastern Thailand
Ban Phaeo 18 Around Bangkok
Ban Phai 48 Northeastern Thailand
Ban Phakdi 79 Far South
Ban Pham 49 Northeastern Thailand
Ban Phamuang 49 Northeastern Thailand
Ban Phang Ka 66 Ko Samui
Ban Phao 48 Northeastern Thailand
Ban Phe 28 Ban Phe
Ban Phet 17 Central Thailand
Ban Pho 19 Around Bangkok
Ban Phra Ae 76 Ko Lanta
Ban Phraek 48 Northeastern Thailand
Ban Phran 22 Around Ayutthaya
Ban Phrao 19 Around Bangkok
Ban Phrik 19 Around Bangkok
Ban Phu 48 Northeastern Thailand
Ban Phu Klom 76 Ko Lanta
Ban Plai Laem 67 Ko Samui
Ban Pluang 51 Around Phanom Rung
Ban Pom 23 Ayutthaya Town
Ban Pong 18 Around Bangkok
Ban Prakham 28 Southeastern Thailand
Ban Pramat 18 Around Bangkok
Ban Puang 33 Chiang Mai,
    Mae Hong Son & Lamphun Provinces
Ban Puek 19 Around Bangkok
Ban Puk 17 Central Thailand
Ban Rae 71 Phuket Province
Ban Rai 18 Around Bangkok
Ban Rakat 19 Around Bangkok
Ban Rong 41 Chiang Rai Province
Ban Run 19 Around Bangkok
Ban Sa 33 Chiang Mai,
    Mae Hong Son & Lamphun Provinces
Ban Sa-a 48 Northeastern Thailand
Ban Saiyuan 72 Phuket Island
Ban Sakat 48 Northeastern Thailand
Ban Saket 66 Ko Samui
Ban Sali 48 Northeastern Thailand
Ban Samer 48 Northeastern Thailand
Ban Samphan 48 Northeastern Thailand
Ban Samran 17 Central Thailand
Ban Samrong 49 Northeastern Thailand
Ban San 33 Chiang Mai,
    Mae Hong Son & Lamphun Provinces
Ban San Ga U 76 Ko Lanta
Ban Sang 19 Around Bangkok
Ban Sapam 73 Phuket Island
Ban Saphan Nak 17 Central Thailand
Ban Saphu 49 Northeastern Thailand
Ban Satung 48 Northeastern Thailand
Ban Sawai 48 Northeastern Thailand
Ban Sema 17 Central Thailand
Ban Siam 49 Northeastern Thailand
Ban Sida 48 Northeastern Thailand
Ban Sing 18 Around Bangkok
Ban Siphom 41 Chiang Rai Province
Ban Songkaria (Mon & Karen)
    26 Sangkhlaburi
Ban Srithanu 68 Ko Pha-Ngan
Ban Suan 30 Chonburi Town
Ban Sumthum 17 Central Thailand
Ban Sup 48 Northeastern Thailand
Ban Tai 65 Around Samui
Ban Takao 48 Northeastern Thailand
Ban Talèo Gnai 49 Northeastern Thailand
Ban Tamot 78 Far South
Ban Tan 33 Chiang Mai,
    Mae Hong Son & Lamphun Provinces
Ban Tha Kraden 26 Kanchanaburi Province
Ban Tha Po 66 Ko Samui
Ban Thabok 48 Northeastern Thailand
Ban Thaen 48 Northeastern Thailand
Ban Thaeo 18 Around Bangkok
Ban Thakham 49 Northeastern Thailand
Ban Thalat 48 Northeastern Thailand
Ban Thale 66 Ko Samui
Ban Tham 71 Phuket Province
Ban That 49 Northeastern Thailand
Ban Tho 72 Phuket Island
Ban Thong 48 Northeastern Thailand
Ban Thong Nai Pan 68 Ko Pha-Ngan
Ban Thong Nang 68 Ko Pha-Ngan
Ban Thong Phun 66 Ko Samui
Ban Thong Sai 66 Ko Samui
Ban Thongkha 49 Northeastern Thailand

an Thop 79 Far South
an Thum 48 Northeastern Thailand
an Thung 71 Phuket Province
an Thung Yi Pheng 76 Ko Lanta
an To 71 Phuket Province
an Tong 48 Northeastern Thailand
an Trap 33 Chiang Mai,
    Mae Hong Son & Lamphun Provinces
an Truat 48 Northeastern Thailand
an Tuek 33 Chiang Mai,
    Mae Hong Son & Lamphun Provinces
an Tung 48 Northeastern Thailand
an Udom Thanya
    24 Around Nakhon Sawan
an Vangmon 49 Northeastern Thailand
an Wa 19 Around Bangkok
an Wae 78 Far South
an Waeng 49 Northeastern Thailand
an Wang Ta Kien 68 Ko Pha-Ngan
an Wia Kadi (Karen) 26 Sangkhlaburi
an Woe 48 Northeastern Thailand
an Wok Tum 68 Ko Pha-Ngan
an Xam Nadi 48 Northeastern Thailand
an Yai 71 Phuket Province
an Yang 18 Around Bangkok
an Yit 72 Phuket Island
ang Bai Mai 65 Surat Thani Town
ang Ban 22 Around Ayutthaya
ang Bo 19 Around Bangkok
ang Bon 18 Around Bangkok
ang Bua Thong 4 Greater Bangkok
ang But 28 Southeastern Thailand
ang Chak 64 Isthmus of Kra
ang Chalong 19 Around Bangkok
ang Cham 71 Phuket Province
ang Chan 73 Phuket Island
ang Chang 18 Around Bangkok
ang Chin 71 Phuket Province
ang Di 78 Far South
ang Duan 4 Greater Bangkok
ang Hak 19 Around Bangkok
ang Hoi 64 Isthmus of Kra
ang Kachao 18 Around Bangkok
ang Kadi 19 Around Bangkok
ang Kaeo 22 Around Ayutthaya
ang Kaeo Fa 18 Around Bangkok
ang Kahai 19 Around Bangkok
ang Kao 66 Ko Samui
ang Kapi 7 Central Bangkok
ang Ket 60 Upper Gulf Coasts
ang Khae 4 Greater Bangkok
ang Khae Nuea 4 Greater Bangkok
ang Kham 19 Around Bangkok
ang Khan 64 Isthmus of Kra
ang Khan Taek 18 Around Bangkok
ang Khanak 19 Around Bangkok
ang Khanun 72 Phuket Island
ang Khayaeng 4 Greater Bangkok
ang Khen 4 Greater Bangkok
ang Khian 24 Around Nakhon Sawan
ang Khla 19 Around Bangkok
ang Khli 70 Phuket Province
ang Kho Laem 6 Central Bangkok
ang Khon Thi 60 Upper Gulf Coasts
ang Khram 64 Isthmus of Kra
ang Khrok 71 Phuket Province
ang Khu 73 Phuket Island
ang Khu Rat 4 Greater Bangkok
ang Khu Wat 4 Greater Bangkok
ang Khuan 70 Phuket Province
ang Khum Phrom
    9 Downtown Bangkok
ang Khun Thian 4 Greater Bangkok
ang Khut 24 Around Nakhon Sawan
ang Khwan 70 Phuket Province
ang Klam 78 Far South
ang Klang 19 Around Bangkok
ang Kluea 19 Around Bangkok
ang Kra So 4 Greater Bangkok
ang Krabao 18 Around Bangkok
ang Krabue 24 Around Nakhon Sawan
ang Krachet 19 Around Bangkok
ang Krang 4 Greater Bangkok
ang Krasan 19 Around Bangkok
ang Krasop 4 Greater Bangkok
ang Krathuek 18 Around Bangkok
ang Kruai 6 Central Bangkok
ang Krut 19 Around Bangkok
ang Kung 65 Surat Thani Town
ang Kwai 78 Far South
ang La 72 Karon & Kata Beaches
ang La On 70 Khao Lak
ang Lam 71 Phuket Province
ang Lamphu Lang 12 Silom
ang Lamung 28 Southeastern Thailand
ang Len 18 Around Bangkok
ang Li 22 Around Ayutthaya
ang Luang 18 Around Bangkok
ang Luang Dot 22 Around Ayutthaya

Bang Luk Suea 19 Around Bangkok
Bang Mae Nang 4 Greater Bangkok
Bang Man 22 Singburi Town
Bang Mot 4 Greater Bangkok
Bang Muang 4 Greater Bangkok
Bang Mueang Mai 19 Around Bangkok
Bang Mun Nak 17 Central Thailand
Bang Na 7 Central Bangkok
Bang Nam Chio 22 Around Ayutthaya
Bang Nam Chuet 18 Around Bangkok
Bang Nam Kho 22 Around Ayutthaya
Bang Nam Priao 19 Around Bangkok
Bang Nang 19 Around Bangkok
Bang Nang Ra 22 Around Ayutthaya
Bang Nga 22 Around Ayutthaya
Bang Niang 70 Khao Lak
Bang Niew 73 Phuket Town
Bang Nu 71 Phuket Province
Bang O 19 Around Bangkok
Bang Pa Khai 34 Around Chiang Mai
Bang Pae 73 Phuket Island
Bang Pahan 22 Around Ayutthaya
Bang Pakong 19 Around Bangkok
Bang Pap 18 Around Bangkok
Bang Phae 18 Around Bangkok
Bang Phai 4 Greater Bangkok
Bang Phasi 18 Around Bangkok
Bang Phlap 4 Greater Bangkok
Bang Phlat 6 Central Bangkok
Bang Phli 19 Around Bangkok
Bang Phli Noi 28 Southeastern Thailand
Bang Phli Yai 5 Greater Bangkok
Bang Phnang 28 Southeastern Thailand
Bang Phra 31 Trat Town
Bang Phra Nuea 60 Upper Gulf Coasts
Bang Phrom 4 Greater Bangkok
Bang Phueng 19 Around Bangkok
Bang Phut 4 Greater Bangkok
Bang Phutsa Singburi Town
Bang Pin 78 Far South
Bang Pin Nam 16 Central Thailand
Bang Pla 19 Around Bangkok
Bang Pla Kot 19 Around Bangkok
Bang Pla Ma 17 Central Thailand
Bang Pla Soi 30 Chonburi Town
Bang Po 66 Ko Samui
Bang Pra Luang 24 Around Nakhon Sawan
Bang Pra Mong 24 Around Nakhon Sawan
Bang Prok 19 Around Bangkok
Bang Prong 19 Around Bangkok
Bang Pu 19 Around Bangkok
Bang Pu Mai 19 Around Bangkok
Bang Pung 4 Greater Bangkok
Bang Rachan 24 Around Nakhon Sawan
Bang Rae 72 Phuket Island
Bang Rak 12 Silom
Bang Rak Mai 72 Phuket Island
Bang Rak Noi 4 Greater Bangkok
Bang Rak Phattana 4 Greater Bangkok
Bang Rak Yai 4 Greater Bangkok
Bang Rakam 18 Around Bangkok
Bang Ramat 4 Greater Bangkok
Bang Riang 64 Isthmus of Kra
Bang Rin 60 Upper Gulf Coasts
Bang Rong 73 Phuket Island
Bang Sadet 22 Around Ayutthaya
Bang Sai 30 Chonburi Town
Bang Sai Pa 18 Around Bangkok
Bang Sai Yoi 60 Upper Gulf Coasts
Bang Sak 78 Far South
Bang Sakae 18 Around Bangkok
Bang Samak 19 Around Bangkok
Bang Sao Thong 19 Around Bangkok
Bang Saphan 60 Upper Gulf Coasts
Bang Sare 28 Southeastern Thailand
Bang Si Mueang 4 Greater Bangkok
Bang Sombun 19 Around Bangkok
Bang Son 19 Around Bangkok
Bang Sue 6 Central Bangkok
Bang Ta Khian 18 Around Bangkok
Bang Ta Then 18 Around Bangkok
Bang Taen 19 Around Bangkok
Bang Talat 4 Greater Bangkok
Bang Tanai 4 Greater Bangkok
Bang Tanot 18 Around Bangkok
Bang Tao 74 Bang Tao Beach
Bang Tho Rat 18 Around Bangkok
Bang Thong 71 Phuket Province
Bang Toei 19 Around Bangkok
Bang Wa 4 Greater Bangkok
Bang Wan 72 Phuket Island
Bang Wua 19 Around Bangkok
Bang Ya Phraek 18 Around Bangkok
Bang Yai 4 Greater Bangkok
Bang Yang 18 Around Bangkok
Bang Yi Khan 8 Downtown Bangkok
Bang Yi Tho 19 Around Bangkok
Bangalar 60 Upper Gulf Coasts
Bangbo 60 Upper Gulf Coasts

Bangkok 19 Around Bangkok
Bangkok Noi 8 Downtown Bangkok
Bangosato 79 Far South
Bangpakong 60 Upper Gulf Coasts
Bangphli Yai 19 Around Bangkok
Bangyok 60 Upper Gulf Coasts
Bann Yai 4 Greater Bangkok
Bannang Sata 79 Far South
Bannangsareng 79 Far South
Banphot Phisai 16 Central Thailand
Banpyi 60 Upper Gulf Coasts
BanTo 79 Far South
Bare Tai 79 Far South
Batong 79 Far South
Batu Melintang 79 Far South
Bawi 78 Far South
Be Kluea 32 Northern Thailand
Be-makyauk 60 Upper Gulf Coasts
Benchalak 49 Northeastern Thailand
Beseri 78 Far South
Betong 79 Far South
Binjai 78 Far South
Bo 35 Around Chiang Mai
Bo Daeng 78 Far South
Bo Dan 78 Far South
Bo Hin 35 Around Chiang Mai
Bo In 17 Central Thailand
Bo Kaeo 33 Chiang Mai,
    Mae Hong Son & Lamphun Provinces
Bo Kru 24 Around Nakhon Sawan
Bo Lek Long 42 Lampang,
    Nan, Phrae, Uttaradit Provinces
Bo Lo 64 Isthmus of Kra
Bo Luang 33 Chiang Mai,
    Mae Hong Son & Lamphun Provinces
Bo Muang 78 Far South
Bo Nam 78 Far South
Bo Nam Ron 79 Far South
Bo Ngoen 18 Around Bangkok
Bo Nok 60 Upper Gulf Coasts
Bo Phlap 21 Nakhon Pathom Town
Bo Phloi 26 Kanchanaburi Province
Bo Phong 22 Around Ayutthaya
Bo Phut 66 Ko Samui
Bo Pradu 78 Far South
Bo Pu 35 Around Chiang Mai
Bo Rae 22 Around Ayutthaya
Bo Rai 28 Southeastern Thailand
Bo Sai 72 Phuket Island
Bo Sai Klang 72 Phuket Island
Bo So 79 Far South
Bo Som 72 Phuket Island
Bo Suphan 18 Around Bangkok
Bo Ta Lo 19 Around Bangkok
Bo Tham 16 Central Thailand
Bo Tho 64 Isthmus of Kra
Bo Thong 79 Far South
Bo Win 28 Southeastern Thailand
Bo Yang 81 Songkhla Town
Bobia 48 Northeastern Thailand
Boe 35 Around Chiang Mai
Bok 49 Northeastern Thailand
Bok Yeng 35 Around Chiang Mai
Bokpyin 60 Upper Gulf Coasts
Bon Dan 17 Central Thailand
Bon Khuan 78 Far South
Bong Tan 33 Chiang Mai,
    Mae Hong Son & Lamphun Provinces
Bong Ti 26 Kanchanaburi Province
Bongor 79 Far South
Borabue 48 Northeastern Thailand
Brae Nua 79 Far South
Bu Bak Kung 17 Central Thailand
Bu Hom 48 Northeastern Thailand
Bu Phram 17 Central Thailand
Bua Chet 49 Northeastern Thailand
Bua Khao 34 Around Chiang Mai
Bua Lai 48 Northeastern Thailand
Bua Ngam 18 Around Bangkok
Bua Pak Tha 18 Around Bangkok
Bua Yai 43 Lampang, Nan, Phrae,
    Uttaradit Provinces
Buak 34 Around Chiang Mai
Buak Khang 35 Around Chiang Mai
Buak Khrok Nua 35 Around Chiang Mai
Buak Khrok Tai 35 Around Chiang Mai
Buak Pet 35 Around Chiang Mai
Buak Pha 35 Around Chiang Mai
Bueng 28 Southeastern Thailand
Bueng Ba 19 Around Bangkok
Bueng Bon 19 Around Bangkok
Bueng Bun 49 Northeastern Thailand
Bueng Cham O 19 Around Bangkok
Bueng Ka Sam 19 Around Bangkok
Bueng Kham Phroi 5 Greater Bangkok
Bueng Kho Hai 19 Around Bangkok
Bueng Khong Long
    49 Northeastern Thailand
Bueng Kum 7 Central Bangkok

Bueng Nam Rak 19 Around Bangkok
Bueng Samphan 48 Northeastern Thailand
Bueng San 19 Around Bangkok
Bueng Thong Lang 19 Around Bangkok
Bueng Yitho 19 Around Bangkok
Buengkan 48 Northeastern Thailand
Bukit Jenuh 79 Far South
Bukit Selambau 79 Far South
Bumang 79 Far South
Bung Charoen 50 Around Phanom Rung
Bung Kaeo 22 Ang Thong Town
Bung Khla 32 Northern Thailand
Bung Malu 49 Northeastern Thailand
Bung Na Rang 17 Central Thailand
Bung Sanan 19 Around Bangkok
Buntharik 49 Northeastern Thailand
Buriram 48 Northeastern Thailand
Cha-am 17 Central Thailand
Chabang Tiko 80 Pattani Town
Chachoengsao 19 Around Bangkok
Chae Hom 33 Chiang Mai,
    Mae Hong Son & Lamphun Provinces
Chaem Luang 33 Chiang Mai,
    Mae Hong Son & Lamphun Provinces
Chahaen 79 Far South
Chai Badan 17 Central Thailand
Chai Buri 64 Isthmus of Kra
Chai Le 75 Patong Beach
Chai Na 18 Around Bangkok
Chai Narong 11 Lumphini
Chai Nat 25 Chai Nat Town
Chai Prakan 33 Chiang Mai,
    Mae Hong Son & Lamphun Provinces
Chai Sa Than 35 Around Chiang Mai
Chai Sai 64 Isthmus of Kra
Chai Wan 48 Northeastern Thailand
Chaiya 60 Upper Gulf Coasts
Chaiyaphum 22 Around Ayutthaya
Chaiyarit 22 Around Ayutthaya
Chaiyo 22 Around Ayutthaya
Chak Ngae 60 Upper Gulf Coasts
Chak Si 22 Around Ayutthaya
Chakkarat 48 Northeastern Thailand
Chakkrawat 12 Silom
Chakwua 79 Far South
Chalae 26 Kanchanaburi Province
Chaliang 44 Satchanalai-
    Chaliang National Park
Chaloem Phra Kiat
    50 Around Phanom Rung
Chaloem Phrakiat 64 Isthmus of Kra
Chalok Baan Kao 69 Ko Tao
Chalom Nae 24 Around Nakhon Sawan
Chalong 72 Phuket Island
Chalung 78 Far South
Chamaep 19 Around Bangkok
Chamni 48 Northeastern Thailand
Champa Lo 22 Around Ayutthaya
Chamrak 28 Southeastern Thailand
Chan Bua 49 Northeastern Thailand
Chan Dum 48 Northeastern Thailand
Chan Thop Phet 50 Around Phanom Rung
Chan Yai 49 Northeastern Thailand
Chana Songkhram 8 Downtown Bangkok
Chanae 79 Far South
Chang 79 Far South
Chang Hai Tok 79 Far South
Chang Han 48 Northeastern Thailand
Chang Khoeng 33 Chiang Mai,
    Mae Hong Son & Lamphun Provinces
Chang Klang 64 Isthmus of Kra
Chang Klua 28 Southeastern Thailand
Chang Lek 19 Around Bangkok
Chang Noi 19 Around Bangkok
Chang Nuea 42 Lampang, Nan,
    Phrae, Uttaradit Provinces
Chang Phian 35 Around Chiang Mai
Chang Phuak 35 Around Chiang Mai
Chang Raek 60 Upper Gulf Coasts
Chang Taeng 73 Phuket Island
Chang Talut 48 Northeastern Thailand
Chang Yai 19 Around Bangkok
Changkrang 49 Northeastern Thailand
Changlun 78 Far South
Chanthaburi
    31 Chanthaburi (Chanburi) Town
Chanthanimit
    31 Chanthaburi (Chanburi) Town
Chantharat 79 Far South
Chanumar 49 Northeastern Thailand
Chao Chet 18 Around Bangkok
Chao Khrua 73 Phuket Island
Chao Leh 78 Ko Lipe
Chao Mai 78 Far South
Chao Pluk 22 Around Ayutthaya
Chao Thalang 71 Phuket Province
Char 49 Northeastern Thailand
Charim 43 Lampang, Nan,
    Phrae, Uttaradit Provinces

Charoen Mueang 33 Chiang Mai, Mae Hong Son & Lamphun Provinces
Charoen Sin 48 Northeastern Thailand
Charoen Suk 50 Around Phanom Rung
Chat Trakan 48 Northeastern Thailand
Chatuchak 5 Greater Bangkok
Chaturaphak Phiman 48 Northeastern Thailand
Chaturat 17 Central Thailand
Cha-uat 64 Isthmus of Kra
Chaunghmunwa 60 Upper Gulf Coasts
Chaung-nauk-pyan 60 Upper Gulf Coasts
Chaungwabyin 60 Upper Gulf Coasts
Chawai 22 Around Ayutthaya
Chawang 64 Isthmus of Kra
Chaweng 65 Around Samui
Che Bilang 78 Far South
Chedi Hak 20 Ratchaburi (Ratburi) Town
Chedi Liam 35 Around Chiang Mai
Chedi Luang 33 Chiang Mai, Mae Hong Son & Lamphun Provinces
Chedi Mae Khrua 35 Around Chiang Mai
Cheli 78 Far South
Chet Rio 18 Around Bangkok
Chet Samian 18 Around Bangkok
Chi Lao 73 Phuket Island
Chi Noi 71 Phuket Province
Chian Yai 64 Isthmus of Kra
Chiang Dao 40 Chiang Rai Province
Chiang Khan 48 Northeastern Thailand
Chiang Khian 41 Chiang Rai Province
Chiang Khong 41 Chiang Rai Province
Chiang Khwan 48 Northeastern Thailand
Chiang Klang 41 Chiang Rai Province
Chiang Kong 41 Chiang Kong
Chiang Muan 43 Lampang, Nan, Phrae, Uttaradit Provinces
Chiang Phin 49 Greater Udon Thani
Chiang Raeng 41 Chiang Rai Province
Chiang Rai 40 Chiang Rai Town
Chiang Rak Noi 19 Around Bangkok
Chiang Rak Yai 19 Around Bangkok
Chiang Saen 40 Chiang Saen
Chiang Yuen 48 Northeastern Thailand
Chieng Ngoen 46 Tak Town
Chik Daek 50 Around Phanom Rung
Chik Yao Tai 32 Northern Thailand
Chim Phli 4 Greater Bangkok
Ching Kho 79 Far South
Chitta Townhouse 15 Sukhumvit
Cho Airong 79 Far South
Chobo 79 Far South
Choeng Doi 35 Around Chiang Mai
Choeng Doi Pha Lat 34 Around Chiang Mai
Choeng Klat 24 Around Nakhon Sawan
Choeng Mon 67 Ko Samui
Choeng Noen 28 Southeastern Thailand
Choeng Sae 78 Far South
Choeng Thale 72 Phuket Island
Choho 17 Central Thailand
Chok Chai 17 Central Thailand
Chok Na Sam 50 Around Phanom Rung
Chok Sa-at 50 Around Phanom Rung
Chom Bueng 60 Upper Gulf Coasts
Chom Phra 48 Northeastern Thailand
Chom Phu 41 Chiang Rai Province
Chom Pluak 18 Around Bangkok
Chom Prathat 18 Around Bangkok
Chom Thong 6 Central Bangkok
Chon Daen 17 Central Thailand
Chon Prathan 35 Around Chiang Mai
Chonburi 30 Chonburi Town
Chong Dan 26 Kanchanaburi Province
Chong Khae 24 Around Nakhon Sawan
Chong Kham 38 Around Mae Hong Son
Chong Lat 71 Phuket Province
Chong Mek 49 Northeastern Thailand
Chong Nonsi 14 Sukhumvit
Chong Phli 71 Phuket Province
Chong Sadao 26 Kanchanaburi Province
Chong Samran 17 Central Thailand
Chonlakhram 64 Around Samui
Chonnabot 48 Northeastern Thailand
Chorakhe Bua 5 Greater Bangkok
Chorakhe Mak 50 Around Phanom Rung
Chorakhe Sam Phan 18 Around Bangkok
Chu Wo 79 Far South
Chua Phloeng 48 Northeastern Thailand
Chuen Chom 48 Northeastern Thailand
Chulaphon 64 Isthmus of Kra
Chum Phae 48 Northeastern Thailand
Chum Pho 79 Far South
Chum Phuang 48 Northeastern Thailand
Chum Saeng 24 Around Nakhon Sawan
Chum Ta Bong 32 Northern Thailand
Chumphon 63 Chumphon Town
Chumphon Buri 48 Northeastern Thailand
Chumpu 33 Chiang Mai, Mae Hong Son & Lamphun Provinces

Chumsaeng 24 Around Nakhon Sawan
Chun 41 Chiang Rai Province
Dab Khun Thot 17 Central Thailand
Daen Sawan 49 Northeastern Thailand
Damnoen Saduak 18 Around Bangkok
Dan Chang 16 Central Thailand
Dan Kam 24 Around Nakhon Sawan
Dan Khun Thot 48 Northeastern Thailand
Dan Kwian 17 Central Thailand
Dan Mae Chalap 26 Kanchanaburi Province
Dan Mae Kham Man 42 Lampang, Nan, Phrae, Uttaradit Provinces
Dan Makham Tia 60 Upper Gulf Coasts
Dan Sai 32 Northern Thailand
Dan Yit 72 Phuket Island
Den 35 Around Chiang Mai
Den Chai 43 Lampang, Nan, Phrae, Uttaradit Provinces
Den Lek 43 Lampang, Nan, Phrae, Uttaradit Provinces
Den Yai 24 Around Nakhon Sawan
Det Udom 49 Northeastern Thailand
Deun Phrabat 48 Northeastern Thailand
Di Luang 78 Far South
Din Daeng 11 Lumphini
Din Nieo 72 Phuket Island
Din Sai 72 Phuket Island
Doem Bang Nang Buat 24 Around Nakhon Sawan
Doi Hang 41 Chiang Rai Province
Doi Kaeo 33 Chiang Mai, Mae Hong Son & Lamphun Provinces
Doi Kamphra 35 Around Chiang Mai
Doi Lan 41 Chiang Rai Province
Doi Saket 35 Around Chiang Mai
Doi Tao 33 Chiang Mai, Mae Hong Son & Lamphun Provinces
Doi Yao 35 Around Chiang Mai
Dok Kham Tai 41 Chiang Rai Province
Dok Mai 7 Central Bangkok
Don 35 Around Chiang Mai
Don Ao 49 Northeastern Thailand
Don Bak 49 Northeastern Thailand
Don Cha Em 18 Around Bangkok
Don Chai 35 Around Chiang Mai
Don Chan 48 Northeastern Thailand
Don Ched 16 Central Thailand
Don Chedi 18 Around Bangkok
Don Chimphli 19 Around Bangkok
Don Chin 48 Northeastern Thailand
Don Daeng 48 Northeastern Thailand
Don Faek 18 Around Bangkok
Don Fai 35 Around Chiang Mai
Don Hua Lo 19 Around Bangkok
Don Kaeo 35 Around Chiang Mai
Don Kha 18 Around Bangkok
Don Khlang 18 Around Bangkok
Don Klang 60 Upper Gulf Coasts
Don Kloy 24 Around Nakhon Sawan
Don Ko Ka 19 Around Bangkok
Don Krabuang 18 Around Bangkok
Don Li 49 Northeastern Thailand
Don Makluea 18 Around Bangkok
Don Manao 18 Around Bangkok
Don Manora 18 Around Bangkok
Don Mong 48 Northeastern Thailand
Don Mot Daeng 49 Northeastern Thailand
Don Muang 5 Greater Bangkok
Don Phai 18 Around Bangkok
Don Phut 22 Around Ayutthaya
Don Phutsa 18 Around Bangkok
Don Rae 18 Around Bangkok
Don Rin 35 Around Chiang Mai
Don Ruak 18 Around Bangkok
Don Sai 18 Around Bangkok
Don Sak 64 Around Samui
Don Salap 18 Around Bangkok
Don Ta Phet 18 Around Bangkok
Don Tako 18 Around Bangkok
Don Tan 35 Around Chiang Mai
Don Thong 18 Around Bangkok
Don Tum 18 Around Bangkok
Don Wai 17 Central Thailand
Don Yai Horn 18 Around Bangkok
Don Yang 48 Northeastern Thailand
Don Yo 19 Around Bangkok
Dong 35 Around Chiang Mai
Dong Bang 48 Northeastern Thailand
Dong Chang 17 Central Thailand
Dong Chang Kaeo 34 Around Chiang Mai
Dong Charoen 32 Northern Thailand
Dong Dam 33 Chiang Mai, Mae Hong Son & Lamphun Provinces
Dong Duan 49 Northeastern Thailand
Dong Khit Lek 35 Around Chiang Mai
Dong Khon 24 Around Nakhon Sawan
Dong Khwang 24 Around Nakhon Sawan
Dong La Khon 34 Around Chiang Mai

Dong Lakhon 19 Around Bangkok
Dong Luang 49 Northeastern Thailand
Dong Mafai 48 Northeastern Thailand
Dong Man 49 Northeastern Thailand
Dong Noi 16 Central Thailand
Dong Nok 34 Around Chiang Mai
Dong Prathun 24 Around Nakhon Sawan
Dong Ta-ngao 22 Around Ayutthaya
Dong Yang 24 Around Nakhon Sawan
Dot Tong Ton 17 Central Thailand
Dusit 6 Central Bangkok
Dusongyo 79 Far South
E-San 51 Buriram Town
E-san Khet 50 Around Phanom Rung
Erawan 48 Northeastern Thailand
Fa Mui 35 Around Chiang Mai
Faek 48 Northeastern Thailand
Fai Kaeo 43 Nan
Fai Kwang 41 Chiang Rai Province
Fai Tha 64 Isthmus of Kra
Fak Tha 43 Lampang, Nan, Phrae, Uttaradit Provinces
Fang 33 Chiang Mai, Mae Hong Son & Lamphun Provinces
Fao Rai 48 Northeastern Thailand
Fao Rai Hang Talat 17 Central Thailand
Fhu Toei 17 Central Thailand
Fon 34 Around Chiang Mai
Gauar Jentik 78 Far South
Gong Mong Tha (Karen) 26 Sangkhlaburi
Guar Chempedak 78 Far South
Gulau 79 Far South
Had Sai Ri 64 Around Samui
Hae 80 Hat Yai Town
Hai 34 Around Chiang Mai
Halaukhani 26 Sangkhlaburi
Han Bua 70 Phuket Province
Han Hak 70 Phuket Province
Han Sai 28 Southeastern Thailand
Han Taphao 19 Around Bangkok
Han Thao 78 Far South
Han Tra 23 Ayutthaya Town
Hang Chat 33 Chiang Mai, Mae Hong Son & Lamphun Provinces
Hang Dong 34 Around Chiang Mai
Hang Khwae 35 Around Chiang Mai
Hang Nam Sekhon 24 Around Nakhon Sawan
Hangapru 60 Upper Gulf Coasts
Hankadin 60 Upper Gulf Coasts
Hankha 24 Around Nakhon Sawan
Hantra 22 Around Ayutthaya
Hat Chao Samran 60 Upper Gulf Coasts
Hat Chik 60 Upper Gulf Coasts
Hat Jomtien 29 Pattaya
Hat Khamphi 48 Northeastern Thailand
Hat La 43 Lampang, Nan, Phrae, Uttaradit Provinces
Hat Lieo 33 Chiang Mai, Mae Hong Son & Lamphun Provinces
Hat Makok 17 Central Thailand
Hat Ngio 43 Lampang, Nan, Phrae, Uttaradit Provinces
Hat Noi 28 Southeastern Thailand
Hat Samran 78 Far South
Hat Sung 24 Around Nakhon Sawan
Hat Tha Sao 24 Around Nakhon Sawan
Hat Yai 80 Hat Yai Town
Hat Yao Nua 71 Phuket Province
Hat Yao Tai 71 Phuket Province
Hin Bun 49 Northeastern Thailand
Hin D'at 48 Northeastern Thailand
Hin Dat 26 Kanchanaburi Province
Hin Khan 49 Northeastern Thailand
Hin Kong 18 Around Bangkok
Hin Lat 50 Around Phanom Rung
Hin Mun 18 Around Bangkok
Hin Rao 71 Phuket Province
Hin Tang 48 Northeastern Thailand
Hin Wong Bay 69 Ko Tao
Ho Rattanachai 23 Ayutthaya Town
Hokki 33 Chiang Mai, Mae Hong Son & Lamphun Provinces
Hom Sin 19 Around Bangkok
Home in Park 34 Around Chiang Mai
Homok 19 Around Bangkok
Hong Charoen 60 Upper Gulf Coasts
Hong Hae 35 Around Chiang Mai
Hong Khuan 71 Phuket Province
Hong Kok 35 Around Chiang Mai
Hong Nok 34 Around Chiang Mai
Horathep 22 Around Ayutthaya
Hot 33 Chiang Mai, Mae Hong Son & Lamphun Provinces
Hpaktu Möng 33 Chiang Mai, Mae Hong Son & Lamphun Provinces
Hu Rae 78 Far South
Hu Thamnop 50 Around Phanom Rung

Hua Chang 49 Northeastern Thailand
Hua Diat 47 Tak Town
Hua Dong 34 Around Chiang Mai
Hua Fai 35 Around Chiang Mai
Hua Fai Ko Ngua 35 Around Chiang Mai
Hua Hin 78 Far South
Hua Hong 72 Phuket Island
Hua Khao 17 Central Thailand
Hua Khok 48 Northeastern Thailand
Hua Khua 48 Northeastern Thailand
Hua Laem 71 Phuket Province
Hua Lamai 25K 67 Lamai
Hua Lim 35 Around Chiang Mai
Hua Lin 35 Around Chiang Mai
Hua Mueang 33 Chiang Mai, Mae Hong Son & Lamphun Provinces
Hua Na 24 Around Nakhon Sawan
Hua Nam Mae Sakud 39 Around Mae Hong Son
Hua Non 72 Phuket Island
Hua Pa 22 Around Ayutthaya
Hua Phai 22 Around Ayutthaya
Hua Phluang 32 Northern Thailand
Hua Pho 18 Around Bangkok
Hua Po 18 Around Bangkok
Hua Rai 35 Around Chiang Mai
Hua Rin 35 Around Chiang Mai
Hua Rua 35 Around Chiang Mai
Hua Sai 70 Phuket Province
Hua Suea 33 Chiang Mai, Mae Hong Son & Lamphun Provinces
Hua Taphan 49 Northeastern Thailand
Hua Thale 49 Greater Nakhon Ratchasim
Hua Thanon 67 Lamai
Hua Thung 34 Around Chiang Mai
Hua Wai 24 Around Nakhon Sawan
Hua Wiang 42 Lampang Town
Huai Chan 24 Around Nakhon Sawan
Huai Cholakhe 20 Nakhon Pathom Town
Huai Deau 38 Around Mae Hong Son
Huai Duan 18 Around Bangkok
Huai Fai 43 Lampang, Nan, Phrae, Uttaradit Provinces
Huai Hom 33 Chiang Mai, Mae Hong Son & Lamphun Provinces
Huai Kayeng 26 Kanchanaburi Province
Huai Kho 48 Northeastern Thailand
Huai Khot 32 Northern Thailand
Huai Khwang 11 Lumphini
Huai Krachao 18 Around Bangkok
Huai Krathing 79 Far South
Huai Krot Pattanan 24 Around Nakhon Sawan
Huai Lat 48 Northeastern Thailand
Huai Luek 78 Far South
Huai Mai 42 Lampang, Nan, Phrae, Uttaradit Provinces
Huai Mek 48 Northeastern Thailand
Huai Mon Thong 18 Around Bangkok
Huai Muang 18 Around Bangkok
Huai Mut 64 Isthmus of Kra
Huai Na 17 Central Thailand
Huai Nam Daeng 71 Phuket Province
Huai Nang 64 Isthmus of Kra
Huai Ngu 24 Around Nakhon Sawan
Huai Niam 48 Northeastern Thailand
Huai Noi 48 Northeastern Thailand
Huai O 33 Chiang Mai, Mae Hong Son & Lamphun Provinces
Huai Phai 18 Around Bangkok
Huai Phra 18 Around Bangkok
Huai Pling 64 Isthmus of Kra
Huai Pong 33 Chiang Mai, Mae Hong Son & Lamphun Provinces
Huai Prik 64 Isthmus of Kra
Huai Pu Ling 33 Chiang Mai, Mae Hong Son & Lamphun Provinces
Huai Rai 17 Central Thailand
Huai Rat 48 Northeastern Thailand
Huai Rong 18 Around Bangkok
Huai Sai 78 Far South
Huai Sak 41 Chiang Rai Province
Huai Som 48 Northeastern Thailand
Huai Tha Chang 60 Upper Gulf Coasts
Huai Thalaeng 48 Northeastern Thailand
Huai Thap Than 49 Northeastern Thailan
Huai Thua Tai 24 Around Nakhon Sawan
Huai To 71 Phuket Province
Huai Yai 24 Around Nakhon Sawan
Huai Yang 60 Upper Gulf Coasts
Huai Yang Kham 41 Chiang Rai Province
Huai Yang Ton 18 Around Bangkok
Huai Yot 78 Far South
Huay Bon 35 Around Chiang Mai
Huay Bong 35 Around Chiang Mai
Huay Chaek Tai 34 Around Chiang Mai
Huay Hiam 48 Northeastern Thailand
Huay Kaeo 35 Around Chiang Mai
Huay Kho 34 Around Chiang Mai

luay Khok 34 Around Chiang Mai
luay Khok Khwar 35 Around Chiang Mai
luay Khrai 41 Chiang Rai Province
luay Kom 35 Around Chiang Mai
luay Muang 35 Around Chiang Mai
luay Nam Kat 33 Chiang Mai,
    Mae Hong Son & Lamphun Provinces
luay Nam Yen 16 Central Thailand
luay Not 32 Northern Thailand
luay Pha 33 Chiang Mai,
    Mae Hong Son & Lamphun Provinces
luay Pu 34 Around Chiang Mai
luay Rai 35 Around Chiang Mai
luay Sai 35 Around Chiang Mai
luay Sai Nua 35 Around Chiang Mai
luay Sai Tai 35 Around Chiang Mai
luay Siaw 34 Around Chiang Mai
luay Som 35 Around Chiang Mai
luay Tao Hai 35 Around Chiang Mai
luay Thong 34 Around Chiang Mai
luay Wai 34 Around Chiang Mai
luay Xai 41 Chiang Rai Province
luay Yuak 34 Around Chiang Mai
n Buri 24 Around Nakhon Sawan
ntha Pramun 22 Around Ayutthaya
eli 79 Far South
eniang 79 Far South
tra 78 Far South
a Lai 71 Phuket Province
a Nua 79 Far South
a To 79 Far South
abang 79 Far South
abin Buri 17 Central Thailand
abingyaung 60 Upper Gulf Coasts
aboktia 24 Around Nakhon Sawan
achong 78 Far South
adin 60 Upper Gulf Coasts
adwe 60 Upper Gulf Coasts
ae Dam 48 Northeastern Thailand
ae Makrut 26 Kanchanaburi Province
aen Nua 41 Chiang Rai Province
aen Sai 48 Northeastern Thailand
aen Thao 48 Northeastern Thailand
aeng Hip 17 Central Thailand
aeng Khoi 17 Central Thailand
aeng Khro 17 Central Thailand
aeng Krachan 60 Upper Gulf Coasts
aeng Ruang 49 Northeastern Thailand
aeng Sanam Nang 17 Central Thailand
aeng Sian 26 Kanchanaburi Province
aeo Fa 18 Around Bangkok
aki Bukit 78 Far South
alase 78 Far South
alasin Town 48 Northeastern Thailand
alim 75 Patong Beach
alo 79 Far South
along 18 Around Bangkok
amala 75 Kamala Beach
amalasai 48 Northeastern Thailand
amiyo 79 Far South
amnoet Phet 48 Northeastern Thailand
amphaen Saen 18 Around Bangkok
amphaeng Phet 78 Far South
amphaeng Phet Historical Park
    47 Kamphaeng Phet Town
ampong- Mah Puteh
    60 Upper Gulf Coasts
ampong Ulu 64 Isthmus of Kra
ampung Temiang
    20 Nakhon Pathom Town
an Chu 17 Central Thailand
an Tang Tai 78 Far South
anchanaburi 27 Kanchanaburi Town
anchanadit 60 Upper Gulf Coasts
anetthiri 60 Upper Gulf Coasts
angar 78 Far South
angyi 60 Upper Gulf Coasts
anmaw 60 Upper Gulf Coasts
antang 78 Far South
antharalak 49 Northeastern Thailand
anthararom 49 Northeastern Thailand
antharawichai 48 Northeastern Thailand
anti 60 Upper Gulf Coasts
ao 35 Around Chiang Mai
ao Cha Ngum 18 Around Bangkok
ao Chai Thong 24 Around Nakhon Sawan
ao Din Nua 50 Around Phanom Rung
ao Dua 34 Around Chiang Mai
ao Liao 24 Around Nakhon Sawan
ap Choeng 48 Northeastern Thailand
apa 60 Upper Gulf Coasts
apang 64 Isthmus of Kra
apoe 60 Upper Gulf Coasts
apong 64 Isthmus of Kra
araket 64 Isthmus of Kra
araturi 60 Upper Gulf Coasts
ariang Piya Cho 32 Northern Thailand
aron 72 Karon & Kata Beaches
aron Noi 72 Phuket Island

Kaset Phatthana 18 Around Bangkok
Kaset Sin 35 Around Chiang Mai
Kaset Sombun 48 Northeastern Thailand
Kaset Wisai 48 Northeastern Thailand
Kat Mai 35 Around Chiang Mai
Kata 72 Karon & Kata Beaches
Kata Noi 72 Karon & Kata Beaches
Kathu 72 Phuket Island
Kathun 64 Isthmus of Kra
Katong 79 Far South
Kawmapyin 60 Upper Gulf Coasts
Kawsaing 60 Upper Gulf Coasts
Kawthaung 60 Upper Gulf Coasts
Kayomati 79 Far South
Ketari 78 Far South
Khae 79 Far South
Khae Don 49 Northeastern Thailand
Khae Ok 19 Around Bangkok
Khae Rai 4 Greater Bangkok
Khae Tok 19 Around Bangkok
Khaen Dong 48 Northeastern Thailand
Kham 48 Northeastern Thailand
Kham Hai 48 Northeastern Thailand
Kham Khuan Kaeo
    49 Northeastern Thailand
Kham Klang 49 Northeastern Thailand
Kham Muang 48 Northeastern Thailand
Kham Phak 49 Northeastern Thailand
Kham Phon 48 Northeastern Thailand
Kham Sakae Saeng 17 Central Thailand
Kham Ta Kla 48 Northeastern Thailand
Kham Tai 24 Around Nakhon Sawan
Kham Thale So 48 Northeastern Thailand
Kham Yat 22 Around Ayutthaya
Khan Ham 19 Around Bangkok
Khan Na Yao 7 Central Bangkok
Khan Thuli 60 Upper Gulf Coasts
Khang Nam 35 Around Chiang Mai
Khanna Yao 5 Greater Bangkok
Khanom 65 Around Samui
Khanon Luang 19 Around Bangkok
Khanuworalak Buri 16 Central Thailand
Khao 78 Far South
Khao Baisi 28 Southeastern Thailand
Khao Bin Cave 60 Upper Gulf Coasts
Khao Chai Son 78 Far South
Khao Chakan 17 Central Thailand
Khao Chamao 28 Southeastern Thailand
Khao Chiak 81 Phatthalung Town
Khao Daeng 79 Far South
Khao Din 19 Around Bangkok
Khao Fachi 60 Upper Gulf Coasts
Khao Hin Son 17 Central Thailand
Khao Hua Khwai 64 Isthmus of Kra
Khao Huat 26 Kanchanaburi Province
Khao Kaeo 24 Around Nakhon Sawan
Khao Kala 24 Around Nakhon Sawan
Khao Khansong 28 Southeastern Thailand
Khao Khao 78 Far South
Khao Khlung 18 Around Bangkok
Khao Kho 32 Northern Thailand
Khao Khok 50 Around Phanom Rung
Khao Khom 71 Phuket Province
Khao Klom 71 Phuket Province
Khao Krai 78 Far South
Khao Mai Kaeo 78 Far South
Khao Mai Kaew 71 Phuket Province
Khao Mi Kita 79 Far South
Khao Ngam 71 Phuket Province
Khao Noi 18 Around Bangkok
Khao Pahanom 64 Isthmus of Kra
Khao Phanom Baek 64 Isthmus of Kra
Khao Pho 64 Isthmus of Kra
Khao Phoem 28 Southeastern Thailand
Khao Phra 19 Around Bangkok
Khao Phra Ngam 22 Around Ayutthaya
Khao Phra Thong 64 Isthmus of Kra
Khao Pip 60 Upper Gulf Coasts
Khao Po 71 Phuket Province
Khao Pu 78 Far South
Khao Pun 78 Far South
Khao Raeng 18 Around Bangkok
Khao Rang (Rang Hill) 73 Phuket Town
Khao Rang Kiat 78 Far South
Khao Sam Sip Hap 18 Around Bangkok
Khao Sam Yot 23 Lopburi Town
Khao Saming 28 Southeastern Thailand
Khao Samsip 28 Southeastern Thailand
Khao Sok 28 Southeastern Thailand
Khao Suan Kwang
    48 Northeastern Thailand
Khao Ta Kliang 72 Phuket Island
Khao Tao 60 Upper Gulf Coasts
Khao Thalu 64 Isthmus of Kra
Khao Tham Nam 71 Phuket Province
Khao Thao 71 Phuket Province
Khao Thong 71 Phuket Province
Khao Thong Tai 71 Phuket Province
Khao To 64 Isthmus of Kra

Khao Tok 64 Isthmus of Kra
Khao Wong 49 Northeastern Thailand
Khao Ya 78 Far South
Khao Yoi 60 Upper Gulf Coasts
Khap I Mui 49 Northeastern Thailand
Khayai 22 Around Ayutthaya
Khemmarat 49 Northeastern Thailand
Khian Sa 64 Isthmus of Kra
Khiat 78 Far South
Khiri Ratthanikhom 64 Isthmus of Kra
Khlang 65 Nakhon Si Thammarat Town
Khlong 80 Hat Yai Town
Khlong Ban Pho 19 Around Bangkok
Khlong Bon 71 Phuket Province
Khlong Chaloem 78 Far South
Khlong Chet 19 Around Bangkok
Khlong Chi Lom 78 Far South
Khlong Chiang Mai 71 Phuket Province
Khlong Chik 19 Around Bangkok
Khlong Chinda 18 Around Bangkok
Khlong Chong 60 Upper Gulf Coasts
Khlong Dan 19 Around Bangkok
Khlong Din Niaw 71 Phuket Province
Khlong Ha 19 Around Bangkok
Khlong Hae 78 Far South
Khlong hat 28 Southeastern Thailand
Khlong Hia 71 Phuket Province
Khlong Hin 71 Phuket Province
Khlong Hoi Khong 78 Far South
Khlong Huk 19 Around Bangkok
Khlong Kha Chen 45 Phichit Town
Khlong Kha Yaeng 16 Central Thailand
Khlong Khaek 71 Phuket Province
Khlong Khanak 22 Around Ayutthaya
Khlong Khanan 17 Central Thailand
Khlong Khian 73 Phuket Island
Khlong Khlung 16 Central Thailand
Khlong Khoi 4 Greater Bangkok
Khlong Khon 18 Around Bangkok
Khlong Khuean 19 Around Bangkok
Khlong Khut 28 Southeastern Thailand
Khlong Khwai 19 Around Bangkok
Khlong Khwang 18 Around Bangkok
Khlong Kluea 4 Greater Bangkok
Khlong Kra Saeng
    61 Phetchaburi (Phetburi) Town
Khlong Kua 78 Far South
Khlong Kwang 4 Greater Bangkok
Khlong La 78 Far South
Khlong Luang 19 Around Bangkok
Khlong Luang Phaeng 19 Around Bangkok
Khlong Maha Nak 9 Downtown Bangkok
Khlong Mai 18 Around Bangkok
Khlong Nakhon Nueang Khet
    19 Around Bangkok
Khlong Nin 78 Far South
Khlong Niyom Yatra 19 Around Bangkok
Khlong Noi 64 Isthmus of Kra
Khlong Nok Krathung 18 Around Bangkok
Khlong Nueng 19 Around Bangkok
Khlong Pha 60 Upper Gulf Coasts
Khlong Phlu 28 Southeastern Thailand
Khlong Phon 78 Far South
Khlong Phra Udom 4 Greater Bangkok
Khlong Phraya Banlue 18 Around Bangkok
Khlong Phruan 78 Far South
Khlong Pia 79 Far South
Khlong Pom 78 Far South
Khlong Prado 17 Central Thailand
Khlong Prasong 71 Phuket Province
Khlong Prawet 19 Around Bangkok
Khlong Preng 19 Around Bangkok
Khlong Raet 71 Phuket Province
Khlong Rap 78 Far South
Khlong Sa 64 Isthmus of Kra
Khlong Sai 71 Phuket Province
Khlong Sakae 22 Around Ayutthaya
Khlong Sam 19 Around Bangkok
Khlong Sam Prawet 5 Greater Bangkok
Khlong Sam Wa 5 Greater Bangkok
Khlong San 12 Silom
Khlong Si 19 Around Bangkok
Khlong Sip 5 Greater Bangkok
Khlong Sip Song 19 Around Bangkok
Khlong Son 71 Phuket Province
Khlong Song 19 Around Bangkok
Khlong Song Ton Nun 5 Greater Bangkok
Khlong Suan 19 Around Bangkok
Khlong Suan Phlu 23 Ayutthaya Town
Khlong Takrao 28 Southeastern Thailand
Khlong Tamru 19 Around Bangkok
Khlong Tan 15 Sukhumvit
Khlong Tan Nua 11 Lumphini
Khlong Tapan 64 Isthmus of Kra
Khlong Thanon 5 Greater Bangkok
Khlong Thom 71 Phuket Province
Khlong Toei 14 Sukhumvit
Khlong Toei Niwet 14 Sukhumvit
Khlong Toei Nua 10 Lumphini

Khlong Ton Sai 12 Silom
Khlong Udom Chonlachon
    19 Around Bangkok
Khlong Ya 71 Phuket Province
Khlong Yai 28 Southeastern Thailand
Khlong Yang 78 Far South
Khlong Yong 18 Around Bangkok
Khlong Yuan 78 Far South
Khlung 28 Southeastern Thailand
Kho Ein 72 Phuket Island
Kho Hong 80 Hat Yai Town
Kho Kalok 60 Upper Gulf Coasts
Kho Nang Kham 78 Far South
Kho Sai 22 Around Ayutthaya
Kho Wang 49 Northeastern Thailand
Khoh Tan 35 Around Chiang Mai
Khok Chang 72 Karon & Kata Beaches
Khok Charoen 17 Central Thailand
Khok Don 48 Northeastern Thailand
Khok Faet 19 Around Bangkok
Khok Han 64 Isthmus of Kra
Khok Kachai 48 Northeastern Thailand
Khok Kham Tai 32 Northern Thailand
Khok Khathiam 22 Around Ayutthaya
Khok Khi Non 19 Around Bangkok
Khok Khian 79 Far South
Khok Kho 48 Northeastern Thailand
Khok Khrai 71 Phuket Province
Khok Klang 48 Northeastern Thailand
Khok Kloi 70 Phuket Province
Khok Krabue 18 Around Bangkok
Khok Lamphan 22 Around Ayutthaya
Khok Lan Koi 48 Northeastern Thailand
Khok Lo 16 Central Thailand
Khok Ma 50 Around Phanom Rung
Khok Mai Ngam 48 Northeastern Thailand
Khok Makham 75 Patong Beach
Khok Mamuang 50 Around Phanom Rung
Khok Mo 24 Around Nakhon Sawan
Khok Mon 48 Northeastern Thailand
Khok Muang 78 Far South
Khok Nong Khamoi 17 Central Thailand
Khok Nong Waeng
    48 Northeastern Thailand
Khok Pak Wan 48 Northeastern Thailand
Khok Phek 28 Southeastern Thailand
Khok Phlo 19 Around Bangkok
Khok Pho 79 Far South
Khok Phochai 48 Northeastern Thailand
Khok Phra Chedi 18 Around Bangkok
Khok Phutsa 22 Around Ayutthaya
Khok Saba 78 Far South
Khok Sai 49 Northeastern Thailand
Khok Sak 78 Far South
Khok Samaesan 17 Central Thailand
Khok Samrong 17 Central Thailand
Khok San 73 Rawai
Khok Sato 79 Far South
Khok Sawang 49 Northeastern Thailand
Khok Si Suphan 49 Northeastern Thailand
Khok Sung 17 Central Thailand
Khok Tabong 18 Around Bangkok
Khok Tanot 72 Phuket Island
Khok Ya 78 Far South
Khok Yai 22 Around Ayutthaya
Khok Yang 78 Far South
Khon Buri 17 Central Thailand
Khon Hat 64 Isthmus of Kra
Khon Kaen 48 Northeastern Thailand
Khon Kam 49 Northeastern Thailand
Khon Khlan 78 Far South
Khon San 48 Northeastern Thailand
Khon Sawan 48 Northeastern Thailand
Khong 17 Central Thailand
Khong Chai 48 Northeastern Thailand
Khong Jiam 49 Northeastern Thailand
Khong Khao 34 Around Chiang Mai
Khonh Chiam 49 Northeastern Thailand
Khreng 64 Isthmus of Kra
Khron 60 Upper Gulf Coasts
Khrueng 41 Chiang Rai Province
Khu Bua 18 Around Bangkok
Khu Fang Nuea 5 Greater Bangkok
Khu Ha 79 Far South
Khu Khot 5 Greater Bangkok
Khu Khwang 19 Around Bangkok
Khu Mueang 48 Northeastern Thailand
Khu Salot 18 Around Bangkok
Khu Yai Mi 28 Southeastern Thailand
Khua Deng Ko Sai 35 Around Chiang Mai
Khua Sung 35 Around Chiang Mai
Khuan Banglang 79 Far South
Khuan Din Daeng 73 Phuket Island
Khuan Don 78 Far South
Khuan Ka Long 78 Far South
Khuan Kalong 78 Far South
Khuan Khanun 78 Far South
Khuan Kun 78 Far South
Khuan Niang 78 Far South

Khuan Pring 78 Far South
Khuan Pu 78 Far South
Khuan Sanai 78 Far South
Khuan Sato 78 Far South
Khuan Thong 64 Around Samui
Khueang Nai 49 Northeastern Thailand
Khuha Sawan 81 Phatthalung Town
Khuk Khak 70 Khao Lak
Khukhan 49 Northeastern Thailand
Khum Thong 19 Around Bangkok
Khun Han 49 Northeastern Thailand
Khun Kaeo 18 Around Bangkok
Khun Khuan 41 Chiang Rai Province
Khun Krathing 64 Isthmus of Kra
Khun Lam 19 Around Bangkok
Khun Mae La Noi 33 Chiang Mai, Mae
   Hong Son & Lamphun Provinces
Khun Non 78 Far South
Khun Raya 64 Isthmus of Kra
Khun Si 18 Around Bangkok
Khun Song 28 Southeastern Thailand
Khun Tat Wai 79 Far South
Khun Yuam 33 Chiang Mai,
   Mae Hong Son & Lamphun Provinces
Khung Nam Won 18 Around Bangkok
Khung Phayom 18 Around Bangkok
Khung Tanot 60 Upper Gulf Coasts
Khung Taphao 42 Lampang, Nan, Phrae,
   Uttaradit Provinces
Khura 64 Isthmus of Kra
Khura Buri 60 Upper Gulf Coasts
Khwan Mueang 22 Around Ayutthaya
Khwao Sin Rin 48 Northeastern Thailand
Kia 79 Far South
Kiang Kha Mai 35 Around Chiang Mai
King Amphoe Manang 78 Far South
Kinso 60 Upper Gulf Coasts
Kirikhet 79 Far South
Kiu 35 Around Chiang Mai
Kiu Lae 35 Around Chiang Mai
Klaeng 28 Southeastern Thailand
Klai 64 Isthmus of Kra
Klang 35 Around Chiang Mai
Klang Dong 33 Chiang Mai,
   Mae Hong Son & Lamphun Provinces
Klang No 49 Northeastern Thailand
Klang Wiang 43 Lampang,
   Nan, Phrae, Uttaradit Provinces
Klong Sok 71 Phuket Province
Klong Son 28 Southeastern Thailand
Kluai Phae 33 Chiang Mai,
   Mae Hong Son & Lamphun Provinces
Ko 35 Around Chiang Mai
Ko Boi 71 Phuket Province
Ko Chan 28 Southeastern Thailand
Ko Chang 30 Ko Chang
Ko Chang Tai 31 Ko Chang
Ko Kaew 73 Phuket Island
Ko Khiam Klang 71 Phuket Province
Ko Klang 76 Ko Lanta
Ko Koet 19 Around Bangkok
Ko Kret 4 Greater Bangkok
Ko Kwang 71 Phuket Province
Ko Loi 19 Around Bangkok
Ko Lon 72 Phuket Island
Ko Mai Phai 71 Phuket Province
Ko Maphrao 73 Phuket Island
Ko Muang 35 Around Chiang Mai
Ko Nakha Yai 71 Phuket Province
Ko Nok 78 Far South
Ko Phlappa 18 Around Bangkok
Ko Pho 19 Around Bangkok
Ko Raet 72 Phuket Island
Ko Rai 19 Around Bangkok
Ko Rian 19 Around Bangkok
Ko Roi 71 Phuket Province
Ko Saliam 35 Around Chiang Mai
Ko Samet 28 Ko Samet
Ko San Phra 18 Around Bangkok
Ko Satoeng (Karen) 26 Sangkhlaburi
Ko Sire 73 Phuket Island
Ko Wut 78 Far South
Ko Yai 78 Far South
Kodiang 78 Far South
Kok Kaeo Burapha 19 Around Bangkok
Kok Ko 22 Around Ayutthaya
Kok Kok 49 Northeastern Thailand
Kok Makham 50 Around Phanom Rung
Kok Mamuang 48 Northeastern Thailand
Kok Pho 48 Northeastern Thailand
Kok Sai 48 Northeastern Thailand
Kok Wan 50 Around Phanom Rung
Kon Kaeo 19 Around Bangkok
Kong Hae 34 Around Chiang Mai
Kong Khaek 33 Chiang Mai,
   Mae Hong Son & Lamphun Provinces
Kong Khak Luang 34 Around Chiang Mai
Kong Khak Noi 34 Around Chiang Mai
Kong Khak Nua 34 Around Chiang Mai

Kong Khan 34 Around Chiang Mai
Kong Khing 34 Around Chiang Mai
Kong Koi 33 Chiang Mai,
   Mae Hong Son & Lamphun Provinces
Kong Sai 35 Around Chiang Mai
Kong Sua 35 Around Chiang Mai
Kong Thanu 22 Around Ayutthaya
Kongra 78 Far South
Kosum Phisai 48 Northeastern Thailand
Kota Baru 79 Far South
Kototura 79 Far South
Kra Buri 60 Upper Gulf Coasts
Krabi 64 Isthmus of Kra
Krabi Noi 64 Isthmus of Kra
Krabi Town 71 Phuket Province
Krachaeng 19 Around Bangkok
Krachio 22 Around Ayutthaya
Kradon Yai 17 Central Thailand
Kramang 23 Ayutthaya Town
Krang Satu 60 Upper Gulf Coasts
Kranuan 48 Northeastern Thailand
Krasae Bon 28 Southeastern Thailand
Krasae Sin 78 Far South
Krasang 51 Buriram Town
Krathum 16 Central Thailand
Krathum Baen 18 Around Bangkok
Krathum Lom 4 Greater Bangkok
Krathum Rai 19 Around Bangkok
Kratip 18 Around Bangkok
Krawa 79 Far South
Kritsana 18 Around Bangkok
Krok Kaeo 50 Around Phanom Rung
Krok Phra 24 Around Nakhon Sawan
Krong Pinang 79 Far South
Krung I Tam 79 Far South
Krut 64 Isthmus of Kra
Ku Daeng 35 Around Chiang Mai
Ku Ka Sing 48 Northeastern Thailand
Ku Kaeo 48 Northeastern Thailand
Ku Lu Bi 79 Far South
Kuala Kedah 78 Far South
Kuala Kungkong 78 Far South
Kuala Nerang 79 Far South
Kuala Perlis 78 Far South
Kuala Sanglang 78 Far South
Kubang Tiga 78 Far South
Kubor Panjang 79 Far South
Kuchinari 49 Northeastern Thailand
Kudi 22 Around Ayutthaya
Kui Buri (Kui Nua) 60 Upper Gulf Coasts
Kum Hak 19 Around Bangkok
Kumphawapi 48 Northeastern Thailand
Kungyaunggale 60 Upper Gulf Coasts
Kut Bak 48 Northeastern Thailand
Kut Chap 48 Northeastern Thailand
Kut Chim Khum Kao
   49 Northeastern Thailand
Kut Chum 49 Northeastern Thailand
Kut Du 48 Northeastern Thailand
Kut Hae 49 Northeastern Thailand
Kut Khaopun 49 Northeastern Thailand
Kut Nao 17 Central Thailand
Kut Rang 48 Northeastern Thailand
Kut Sra 49 Greater Udon Thani
Kyaukmigyaung 60 Upper Gulf Coasts
Kyaukmithwe 60 Upper Gulf Coasts
Kyaukpa 60 Upper Gulf Coasts
Kyauk-pyu 60 Upper Gulf Coasts
Kyaukse 60 Upper Gulf Coasts
Kyi-upha 33 Chiang Mai,
   Mae Hong Son & Lamphun Provinces
La Khone P'heng49 Northeastern Thailand
La Mo 78 Far South
La Pae 79 Far South
La Yan 72 Phuket Island
La-ae 79 Far South
Laem Bua 18 Around Bangkok
Laem Din 60 Upper Gulf Coasts
Laem Hat 78 Far South
Laem Hin 72 Phuket Island
Laem Hua Lan 71 Phuket Province
Laem Khao Khat 73 Phuket Island
Laem Khat 73 Phuket Island
Laem Kho 71 Phuket Province
Laem Klat 28 Southeastern Thailand
Laem Mai Phai 73 Phuket Island
Laem Nga 73 Phuket Island
Laem Phanwa 73 Phuket Island
Laem Pho 79 Far South
Laem Phrao 72 Phuket Island
Laem Po 73 Phuket Island
Laem Pradu 19 Around Bangkok
Laem Sai 72 Phuket Island
Laem Sak 71 Phuket Province
Laem Sam 73 Phuket Island
Laem Som 78 Far South
Laem Son 78 Far South
Laem Son Lake 68 Ko Pha-Ngan
Laem Sop 71 Phuket Province

Laem Thanot 64 Isthmus of Kra
Laem Trong 71 Phuket Province
Laem Yai 71 Phuket Province
Laem Yang 73 Phuket Island
Lahan 28 Southeastern Thailand
Lahan Sai 50 Around Phanom Rung
Lak 35 Around Chiang Mai
Lak Chai 18 Around Bangkok
Lak Chan 78 Far South
Lak Fa 22 Around Ayutthaya
Lak Hok 5 Greater Bangkok
Lak Kaeo 22 Around Ayutthaya
Lak Pan 35 Around Chiang Mai
Lak Si 4 Greater Bangkok
Lak Song 4 Greater Bangkok
Lakhon Phen 49 Northeastern Thailand
Lalo 79 Far South
Lam Chong Thanon 78 Far South
Lam Chuat 28 Southeastern Thailand
Lam Hoei 18 Around Bangkok
Lam Kachuan 17 Central Thailand
Lam Liang 64 Isthmus of Kra
Lam Luk Bua 18 Around Bangkok
Lam Luk Ka 5 Greater Bangkok
Lam Mai 79 Far South
Lam Narai 17 Central Thailand
Lam Pam 78 Far South
Lam Phai 79 Far South
Lam Phak Kut 19 Around Bangkok
Lam Phakchi 19 Around Bangkok
Lam Phara 18 Around Bangkok
Lam Phaya 20 Nakhon Pathom Town
Lam Pho 4 Greater Bangkok
Lam Plai Mat 48 Northeastern Thailand
Lam Plathew 5 Greater Bangkok
Lam Poeng 35 Around Chiang Mai
Lam Ru 64 Isthmus of Kra
Lam Sai 19 Around Bangkok
Lam Sonthi 32 Northern Thailand
Lam Ta Sao 19 Around Bangkok
Lam Takhian 22 Around Ayutthaya
Lam Tha Men Chai
   48 Northeastern Thailand
Lam Thap 64 Isthmus of Kra
Lam Thu 78 Far South
Lam Toi Ting 19 Around Bangkok
Lamae 60 Upper Gulf Coasts
Lampang 33 Chiang Mai, Mae Hong Son &
   Lamphun Provinces
Lamphaya 79 Far South
Lamphlai 79 Far South
Lamphu La 78 Far South
Lamphun 39 Lamphun Town
Lan Sak 32 Northern Thailand
Lan Saka 64 Isthmus of Kra
Lan Tak 18 Around Bangkok
Lang Hin Dtat 50 Around Phanom Rung
Lang Khao 78 Far South
Lang Suan 60 Upper Gulf Coasts
Langgar 78 Far South
Langka 35 Around Chiang Mai
Langu 64 Isthmus of Kra
La-Ngu 78 Far South
Lanta 78 Far South
Lao 35 Around Chiang Mai
Lao Khwan 16 Central Thailand
Lao Suea Kok 49 Northeastern Thailand
Lat Bua Khao 18 Around Bangkok
Lat Bua Luang 18 Around Bangkok
Lat Chit 22 Around Ayutthaya
Lat Khwang 19 Around Bangkok
Lat Krabang 5 Greater Bangkok
Lat Phrao 5 Greater Bangkok
Lat Sali 22 Around Ayutthaya
Lat Sawai 5 Greater Bangkok
Lat Ya 26 Kanchanaburi Province
Lat Yai 18 Around Bangkok
Lat Yao 4 Greater Bangkok
Lato 33 Chiang Mai, Mae Hong Son &
   Lamphun Provinces
Latphrao 7 Central Bangkok
La-un 64 Isthmus of Kra
Lawia 50 Around Phanom Rung
Li Phuan Bang Kok 72 Phuket Island
Lidon 79 Far South
Lin Fa 49 Northeastern Thailand
Lin Fo 48 Northeastern Thailand
Ling Ha 35 Around Chiang Mai
Liphang 78 Far South
Liphon Bo Rae 72 Phuket Island
Liphon Hua Han 72 Phuket Island
Lo Ba Kao 71 Phuket Province
Lo Chan Kra 78 Far South
Lo Pa La Nam Tok 71 Phuket Province
Lo Pa Lai Ok 71 Phuket Province
Lo Po Noi 71 Phuket Province
Lo Thom Nua 78 Far South
Lo Ti Pa 73 Phuket Island
Lo Yung 64 Isthmus of Kra

Lochut 79 Far South
Loei 48 Northeastern Thailand
Loeng Nok Tha 49 Northeastern Thailand
Lom Kao 48 Northeastern Thailand
Lom Sak 48 Northeastern Thailand
Long Khe 16 Central Thailand
Long Khot 33 Chiang Mai,
   Mae Hong Son & Lamphun Provinces
Lop Buri 48 Northeastern Thailand
Lopburi 23 Lopburi Town
Luang 34 Around Chiang Mai
Luang Nua 35 Around Chiang Mai
Luang Tai 35 Around Chiang Mai
Lubobusa 79 Far South
Lubosawo 79 Far South
Lue Amnat 49 Northeastern Thailand
Lum 35 Around Chiang Mai
Lum Khao 24 Around Nakhon Sawan
Lum Phli 23 Ayutthaya Town
Lum Rang 26 Kanchanaburi Province
Lum Than 71 Phuket Province
Lume 79 Far South
Lumphini 10 Lumphini
Lun Moe 41 Chiang Rai Province
Lutlut 60 Upper Gulf Coasts
Ma Pea 33 Chiang Mai,
   Mae Hong Son & Lamphun Provinces
Ma Wa 33 Chiang Mai,
   Mae Hong Son & Lamphun Provinces
Madeua Whan 65 Around Samui
Mae Aen 34 Around Chiang Mai
Mae Ai 33 Chiang Mai,
   Mae Hong Son & Lamphun Provinces
Mae Aw 33 Chiang Mai,
   Mae Hong Son & Lamphun Provinces
Mae Bong 41 Chiang Rai Province
Mae Chaem 33 Chiang Mai, Mae Hong Son
   & Lamphun Provinces
Mae Chai Tai 41 Chiang Rai Province
Mae Chan 40 Mae Chan
Mae Charim 43 Lampang, Nan, Phrae,
   Uttaradit Provinces
Mae Chayuang 35 Around Chiang Mai
Mae Chedi 33 Chiang Mai, Mae Hong Son
   & Lamphun Provinces
Mae Chedi Mai 33 Chiang Mai,
   Mae Hong Son & Lamphun Provinces
Mae Cheo 33 Chiang Mai, Mae Hong Son
   & Lamphun Provinces
Mae Chong 35 Around Chiang Mai
Mae Chong Noi 35 Around Chiang Mai
Mae Chua 43 Lampang, Nan, Phrae,
   Uttaradit Provinces
Mae Daet 33 Chiang Mai,
   Mae Hong Son & Lamphun Provinces
Mae Dok Daeng 35 Around Chiang Mai
Mae Faek 40 Chiang Rai Province
Mae Ha 34 Around Chiang Mai
Mae Haad 69 Ko Tao
Mae Hat 64 Around Samui
Mae Hat Luang 35 Around Chiang Mai
Mae Hat Noi 35 Around Chiang Mai
Mae Hia 35 Around Chiang Mai
Mae Hia Nai 34 Around Chiang Mai
Mae Ho 33 Chiang Mai,
   Mae Hong Son & Lamphun Provinces
Mae Ho Phra 33 Chiang Mai, Mae Hong
   Son & Lamphun Provinces
Mae Hoi Ngoen Tai 35 Around Chiang Mai
Mae Hong Son Town
   38 Mae Hong Son Town
Mae Huay Ngoen 35 Around Chiang Mai
Mae Jo 35 Around Chiang Mai
Mae Ka 41 Chiang Rai Province
Mae Ka Nua 35 Around Chiang Mai
Mae Ka Tai 35 Around Chiang Mai
Mae Ka Talat Yai 35 Around Chiang Mai
Mae Kha 33 Chiang Mai,
   Mae Hong Son & Lamphun Provinces
Mae Khak 34 Around Chiang Mai
Mae Kham 41 Chiang Rai Province
Mae Kham Mi Tamnak 43 Lampang,
   Nan, Phrae, Uttaradit Provinces
Mae Khanin Nua 34 Around Chiang Mai
Mae Khanin Tai 34 Around Chiang Mai
Mae Khaning 41 Chiang Rai Province
Mae Khao 35 Around Chiang Mai
Mae Khatuan 33 Chiang Mai,
   Mae Hong Son & Lamphun Provinces
Mae Khi 34 Around Chiang Mai
Mae Khli 78 Far South
Mae Kho 35 Around Chiang Mai
Mae Khu 35 Around Chiang Mai
Mae Ki 33 Chiang Mai,
   Mae Hong Son & Lamphun Provinces
Mae Klong Mai 16 Central Thailand
Mae Kra Bung 26 Kanchanaburi Province
Mae Kua 33 Chiang Mai,
   Mae Hong Son & Lamphun Provinces

Mae La 22 Around Ayutthaya
Mae La Luang 33 Chiang Mai,
    Mae Hong Son & Lamphun Provinces
Mae La Noi 33 Chiang Mai, Mae Hong Son
    & Lamphun Provinces
Mae Lai 43 Lampang, Nan, Phrae,
    Uttaradit Provinces
Mae Lan 33 Chiang Mai,
    Mae Hong Son & Lamphun Provinces
Mae Lop 33 Chiang Mai,
    Mae Hong Son & Lamphun Provinces
Mae Mae 34 Around Chiang Mai
Mae Mak 33 Chiang Mai,
    Mae Hong Son & Lamphun Provinces
Mae Mo 42 Lampang, Nan, Phrae,
    Uttaradit Provinces
Mae Mok 33 Chiang Mai,
    Mae Hong Son & Lamphun Provinces
Mae Na Chang 33 Chiang Mai,
Mae Na Cnon 33 Chiang Mai,
Mae Na Sai 34 Around Chiang Mai
Mae Na Toeng 33 Chiang Mai,
Mae Na Wang 33 Chiang Mai,
    Mae Hong Son & Lamphun Provinces
Mae Nai 34 Around Chiang Mai
Mae Nam 65 Around Samui
Mae Nam Khu 28 Southeastern Thailand
Mae Nang Khao 60 Upper Gulf Coasts
Mae Ngam 35 Around Chiang Mai
Mae Ngao 33 Chiang Mai,
    Mae Hong Son & Lamphun Provinces
Mae Pa 46 Mae Sot
Mae pang 33 Chiang Mai, Mae Hong Son
    & Lamphun Provinces
Mae Phrik 33 Chiang Mai,
    Mae Hong Son & Lamphun Provinces
Mae Pong 35 Around Chiang Mai
Mae Pu 33 Chiang Mai,
    Mae Hong Son & Lamphun Provinces
Mae Raen 34 Around Chiang Mai
Mae Rim 35 Around Chiang Mai
Mae Roi Ngoen Nua 35 Around Chiang Mai
Mae Sa Luang 35 Around Chiang Mai
Mae Sa Noi 35 Around Chiang Mai
Mae Sai 25K 40 Mae Sai
Mae Sakhon 43 Lampang, Nan,
    Phrae, Uttaradit Provinces
Mae Salap 35 Around Chiang Mai
Mae Salit 33 Chiang Mai,
    Mae Hong Son & Lamphun Provinces
Mae Sam 33 Chiang Mai,
    Mae Hong Son & Lamphun Provinces
Mae Sam Laep 33 Chiang Mai,
    Mae Hong Son & Lamphun Provinces
Mae Sameng 33 Chiang Mai,
    Mae Hong Son & Lamphun Provinces
Mae Sap 33 Chiang Mai,
    Mae Hong Son & Lamphun Provinces
Mae Sap Mai 34 Around Chiang Mai
Mae Sap Tai 34 Around Chiang Mai
Mae Sariang 38 Mae Sariang
Mae Sin 33 Chiang Mai,
    Mae Hong Son & Lamphun Provinces
Mae Soa 33 Chiang Mai,
    Mae Hong Son & Lamphun Provinces
Mae Soi 33 Chiang Mai,
    Mae Hong Son & Lamphun Provinces
Mae Song 33 Chiang Mai,
    Mae Hong Son & Lamphun Provinces
Mae Sot 25K 46 Mae Sot
Mae Suai 33 Chiang Mai,
    Mae Hong Son & Lamphun Provinces
Mae Suat 33 Chiang Mai,
    Mae Hong Son & Lamphun Provinces
Mae Suek 33 Chiang Mai,
    Mae Hong Son & Lamphun Provinces
Mae Suk 33 Chiang Mai,
    Mae Hong Son & Lamphun Provinces
Mae Sun 33 Chiang Mai,
    Mae Hong Son & Lamphun Provinces
Mae Suya 33 Chiang Mai,
    Mae Hong Son & Lamphun Provinces
Mae Tae 35 Around Chiang Mai
Mae Taeng 33 Chiang Mai,
    Mae Hong Son & Lamphun Provinces
Mae Tan 33 Chiang Mai,
    Mae Hong Son & Lamphun Provinces
Mae Tao 46 Mae Sot
Mae Tao Hai 35 Around Chiang Mai
Mae Tat 35 Around Chiang Mai
Mae Tha 33 Chiang Mai,
    Mae Hong Son & Lamphun Provinces
Mae Thalop 33 Chiang Mai,
    Mae Hong Son & Lamphun Provinces
Mae Tho 33 Chiang Mai,
    Mae Hong Son & Lamphun Provinces

Mae Tip 42 Lampang, Nan, Phrae,
    Uttaradit Provinces
Mae Tom 34 Around Chiang Mai
Mae Tuen 33 Chiang Mai,
    Mae Hong Son & Lamphun Provinces
Mae Tung Ting 34 Around Chiang Mai
Mae Ukho 33 Chiang Mai,
    Mae Hong Son & Lamphun Provinces
Mae Usu 33 Chiang Mai,
    Mae Hong Son & Lamphun Provinces
Mae Wa Luang 33 Chiang Mai,
    Mae Hong Son & Lamphun Provinces
Mae Wang 33 Chiang Mai,
    Mae Hong Son & Lamphun Provinces
Mae Win 33 Chiang Mai,
    Mae Hong Son & Lamphun Provinces
Mae Yoi 35 Around Chiang Mai
Mae Yuak 35 Around Chiang Mai
Mae Yuam Noi 33 Chiang Mai,
    Mae Hong Son & Lamphun Provinces
Mae Yum Luang 33 Chiang Mai,
    Mae Hong Son & Lamphun Provinces
Maedong 79 Far South
Maen Huay Mae Nai34 Around Chiang Mai
Maew 34 Around Chiang Mai
Maew Chang Khian 34 Around Chiang Mai
Maew Doi Pui 34 Around Chiang Mai
Maewat 79 Far South
Maha Chanachai 49 Northeastern Thailand
Maha Pho 24 Around Nakhon Sawan
Maha Phruettharam 13 Silom
Maha Rat 22 Around Ayutthaya
Maha Sarakham 48 Northeastern Thailand
Maha Sawat 18 Around Bangkok
Maharchai 21 Samut Sakhon Town
Mahat Thai 22 Around Ayutthaya
Mai 35 Around Chiang Mai
Mai Dat 24 Around Nakhon Sawan
Mai Fat 78 Far South
Mai Kaen 79 Far South
Mai Khao 72 Phuket Island
Mai Lamphup 35 Around Chiang Mai
Mai Lav 64 Isthmus of Kra
Mai Na Hi 34 Around Chiang Mai
Mai San Khong 35 Around Chiang Mai
Mai Siap 64 Isthmus of Kra
Mai Tra 19 Around Bangkok
Mak 78 Far South
Mak Khaeng 49 Greater Udon Thani
Makham 28 Southeastern Thailand
Makham Klu 28 Southeastern Thailand
Makham Thao 24 Around Nakhon Sawan
Makham Yai 35 Around Chiang Mai
Makham Yong 30 Chonburi Town
Makkasan 11 Lumphini
Makot Tai 78 Far South
Maliwun 60 Upper Gulf Coasts
Malong 79 Far South
Maluan 64 Isthmus of Kra
Mamae 34 Around Chiang Mai
Mamong 79 Far South
Mancha Khiri 48 Northeastern Thailand
Mango Bay 69 Ko Tao
Manorom 24 Around Nakhon Sawan
Manwichai 18 Around Bangkok
Mao Ta Phut 28 Southeastern Thailand
Map Ammarit 64 Isthmus of Kra
Map Kae 24 Around Nakhon Sawan
Map Khla 28 Southeastern Thailand
Map Phai 19 Around Bangkok
Map Pong 19 Around Bangkok
Maphrao 78 Far South
Marang 60 Upper Gulf Coasts
Marubo 79 Far South
Marue Bo-ok 79 Far South
Masjid 78 Far South
Mawton 60 Upper Gulf Coasts
Mayanchaung 60 Upper Gulf Coasts
Mayo 79 Far South
Mayom 48 Northeastern Thailand
Medang Gatal 78 Far South
Medaw 60 Upper Gulf Coasts
Meng 35 Around Chiang Mai
Meranti 79 Far South
Merbau Batang 79 Far South
Mergui 60 Upper Gulf Coasts
Methi Niwet 15 Sukhumvit
Min Buri 5 Greater Bangkok
Min-ngaw 16 Central Thailand
Mittraphap 17 Central Thailand
Mo 35 Around Chiang Mai
Mo Mawi 79 Far South
Mo Thai 64 Isthmus of Kra
Moeiwadi 49 Northeastern Thailand
Moen 75 Patong Beach
Mok Cham Pae 33 Chiang Mai,
    Mae Hong Son & Lamphun Provinces
Mok Lan 64 Isthmus of Kra
Momaka 60 Upper Gulf Coasts

Mon 35 Around Chiang Mai
Mon Nang 19 Around Bangkok
Mon Pin 33 Chiang Mai,
    Mae Hong Son & Lamphun Provinces
Mon Thong 19 Around Bangkok
Mong Mum 48 Northeastern Thailand
Mu Mon 49 Greater Udon Thani
Muaklek 17 Central Thailand
Muang Chet Ton 43 Lampang,
    Nan, Phrae, Uttaradit Provinces
Muang Chum 35 Around Chiang Mai
Muang Ha 35 Around Chiang Mai
Muang Khammouan
    49 Northeastern Thailand
Muang Khiaw 35 Around Chiang Mai
Muang Khon 35 Around Chiang Mai
Muang Klang 60 Upper Gulf Coasts
Muang Krabi 71 Phuket Province
Muang Lang 35 Around Chiang Mai
Muang Liap 48 Northeastern Thailand
Muang Ma 35 Around Chiang Mai
Muang Mai 72 Phuket Island
Muang Mu 22 Around Ayutthaya
Muang Ngam 64 Isthmus of Kra
Muang Nonthaburi 4 Greater Bangkok
Muang Nua 53 Si Saket Town
Muang Pakxan 48 Northeastern Thailand
Muang Phan 33 Chiang Mai,
    Mae Hong Son & Lamphun Provinces
Muang Sam Sip 49 Northeastern Thailand
Muang San Kham Tai
    35 Around Chiang Mai
Muang Sonkhon 49 Northeastern Thailand
Muang Suang 48 Northeastern Thailand
Muang Tai 53 Si Saket Town
Muang Tao 48 Northeastern Thailand
Muang Tia 79 Far South
Muang Ton 35 Around Chiang Mai
Muang Uthai Thani
    24 Around Nakhon Sawan
Muang Wa 35 Around Chiang Mai
Mueang Chan 49 Northeastern Thailand
Mueang Chang 41 Chiang Rai Province
Mueang Chi 33 Chiang Mai,
    Mae Hong Son & Lamphun Provinces
Mueang Khong 33 Chiang Mai,
    Mae Hong Son & Lamphun Provinces
Mueang Lampang 33 Chiang Mai,
    Mae Hong Son & Lamphun Provinces
Mueang Len 35 Around Chiang Mai
Mueang Mai 18 Around Bangkok
Mueang Mo 42 Phrae Town
Mueang Na 33 Chiang Mai,
    Mae Hong Son & Lamphun Provinces
Mueang Nan 41 Chiang Rai Province
Mueang Paeng 33 Chiang Mai,
    Mae Hong Son & Lamphun Provinces
Mueang Yang 48 Northeastern Thailand
Mueang Yao 33 Chiang Mai,
    Mae Hong Son & Lamphun Provinces
Muet Ka 33 Chiang Mai,
    Mae Hong Son & Lamphun Provinces
Mukdahan 49 Northeastern Thailand
Mun Wai 49 Greater Nakhon Ratchasima
Mut Dok Khao 72 Phuket Island
Na 78 Far South
Na Bon 72 Phuket Island
Na Bua 48 Northeastern Thailand
Na Chaluai 49 Northeastern Thailand
Na Chan 73 Phuket Island
Na Chik 17 Central Thailand
Na Chueak 48 Northeastern Thailand
Na Di 49 Greater Udon Thani
Na Doem 64 Isthmus of Kra
Na Duang 48 Northeastern Thailand
Na Dun 48 Northeastern Thailand
Na Fai 17 Central Thailand
Na Fan 34 Around Chiang Mai
Na Haew 48 Northeastern Thailand
Na Hi 34 Around Chiang Mai
Na Ho 35 Around Chiang Mai
Na Hua Non 71 Phuket Province
Na Inh Noi 49 Northeastern Thailand
Na Kae 49 Northeastern Thailand
Na Kaoe 33 Chiang Mai,
    Mae Hong Son & Lamphun Provinces
Na Ken 48 Northeastern Thailand
Na Ket 79 Far South
Na Kha 72 Phuket Island
Na Khae Rang 48 Northeastern Thailand
Na Kham Hai 48 Northeastern Thailand
Na Khao Sia 78 Far South
Na Khlong Sai 17 Central Thailand
Na Kho 48 Northeastern Thailand
Na Khok 18 Around Bangkok
Na Khu 49 Northeastern Thailand
Na Khuan 19 Around Bangkok
Na Khum 43 Lampang, Nan,
    Phrae, Uttaradit Provinces

Na Khun Krai 33 Chiang Mai,
    Mae Hong Son & Lamphun Provinces
Na Kian 33 Chiang Mai,
    Mae Hong Son & Lamphun Provinces
Na Klang 48 Northeastern Thailand
Na Klua 78 Far South
Na Kluea 19 Around Bangkok
Na Kok 72 Phuket Island
Na Lak 49 Northeastern Thailand
Na Lan Khao 48 Northeastern Thailand
Na Lao 48 Northeastern Thailand
Na Le 79 Far South
Na Luk 78 Far South
Na Mafuang 48 Northeastern Thailand
Na Mahieo 48 Northeastern Thailand
Na Mai 18 Around Bangkok
Na Mathum 19 Around Bangkok
Na Meun 43 Lampang, Nan,
    Phrae, Uttaradit Provinces
Na Mo Sri 79 Far South
Na Mon 79 Far South
Na Mueang 20 Ratchaburi (Ratburi) Town
Na Nai 72 Phuket Island
Na Nak 79 Far South
Na Noi 48 Northeastern Thailand
Na Nong Thum 17 Central Thailand
Na Nua 71 Phuket Province
Na Oy Nou 48 Northeastern Thailand
Na Pa 19 Around Bangkok
Na Pho 48 Northeastern Thailand
Na Pho Klang 49 Northeastern Thailand
Na Phrathat 19 Around Bangkok
Na Phru 60 Upper Gulf Coasts
Na Phun 33 Chiang Mai,
    Mae Hong Son & Lamphun Provinces
Na Pradu 19 Around Bangkok
Na Prang 41 Chiang Rai Province
Na Pu 32 Northern Thailand
Na Pu Pom 33 Chiang Mai,
    Mae Hong Son & Lamphun Provinces
Na Riang 48 Northeastern Thailand
Na Roek 19 Around Bangkok
Na Sa 48 Northeastern Thailand
Na Saeng 48 Northeastern Thailand
Na Sak 60 Upper Gulf Coasts
Na San 64 Isthmus of Kra
Na Sat 72 Phuket Island
Na Si Noi 49 Northeastern Thailand
Na Sok 72 Phuket Island
Na Suan 26 Kanchanaburi Province
Na Ta Luang 78 Far South
Na Tha Nung 43 Lampang,
    Nan, Phrae, Uttaradit Provinces
Na Thalot 78 Far South
Na Tham Tai 78 Far South
Na Than 79 Far South
Na Thap 79 Far South
Na Thawi 79 Far South
Na Thom 78 Far South
Na Thon 78 Far South
Na Thong 78 Far South
Na To Mun 78 Far South
Na Wa 79 Far South
Na Wa Yai 49 Northeastern Thailand
Na Wang 48 Northeastern Thailand
Na Wang Hin 19 Around Bangkok
Na Wua 48 Northeastern Thailand
Na Yai Am 28 Southeastern Thailand
Na Yang Klak 17 Central Thailand
Na Yao 48 Northeastern Thailand
Na Yia 49 Northeastern Thailand
Na Yong 78 Far South
Na Yung 48 Northeastern Thailand
Naeng Mut 50 Around Phanom Rung
Nai 35 Around Chiang Mai
Nai Chok 64 Isthmus of Kra
Nai Harn 73 Rawai
Nai Lat 71 Phuket Province
Nai Mo 71 Phuket Province
Nai Muang 45 Phitsanulok Town
Nai Muang V 53 Ubon Ratchathani Town
Nai Muang VI 52 Yasothon Town
Nai Muang XIX 45 Phichit Town
Nai Muang XVI 47 Kamphaeng Phet Town
Nai Na 71 Phuket Province
Nai Phru 72 Karon & Kata Beaches
Nai Sai 71 Phuket Province
Nai Thon 72 Phuket Island
Nai Wiang 42 Phrae Town
Nai Yang 72 Phuket Island
Nai Yong 71 Phuket Province
Nak Reng 64 Isthmus of Kra
Naka 79 Far South
Nakhon 18 Around Bangkok
Nakhon Chum 47 Kamphaeng Phet Town
Nakhon Luang 22 Around Ayutthaya
Nakhon Nayok 19 Around Bangkok
Nakhon Pathom 20 Nakhon Pathom Town
Nakhon Phanom 49 Northeastern Thailand

INDEX

Nakhon Ratchasima
  51 Nakhon Ratchasima City
Nakhon Ratchasima (Khorat)
  48 Northeastern Thailand
Nakhon Sawan 25 Nakhon Sawan Town
Nakhon Si Thammarat 64 Isthmus of Kra
Nakhon Thai 48 Northeastern Thailand
Naklua 29 Pattaya
Nam Bo Luang 33 Chiang Mai,
  Mae Hong Son & Lamphun Provinces
Nam Cha 28 Southeastern Thailand
Nam Cham 35 Around Chiang Mai
Nam Chan 17 Central Thailand
Nam Chan Nua 71 Phuket Province
Nam Chee 79 Far South
Nam Daeng 19 Around Bangkok
Nam Khrai 43 Lampang,
  Nan, Phrae, Uttaradit Provinces
Nam Khun 49 Northeastern Thailand
Nam Kliang 49 Northeastern Thailand
Nam Len 48 Northeastern Thailand
Nam Lom 35 Around Chiang Mai
Nam Long 35 Around Chiang Mai
Nam Magroeg (Mam) 26 Sangkhlaburi
Nam Muap 43 Lampang, Nan, Phrae,
  Uttaradit Provinces
Nam Nao 48 Northeastern Thailand
Nam Om 48 Northeastern Thailand
Nam Pat 43 Lampang, Nan, Phrae,
  Uttaradit Provinces
Nam Phai 43 Lampang, Nan, Phrae,
  Uttaradit Provinces
Nam Phi 43 Lampang, Nan, Phrae,
  Uttaradit Provinces
Nam Phong 48 Northeastern Thailand
Nam Phra 71 Phuket Province
Nam Phrae 35 Around Chiang Mai
Nam Phrai 78 Far South
Nam Phu 18 Around Bangkok
Nam Phut 78 Far South
Nam Rap 78 Far South
Nam Rin 35 Around Chiang Mai
Nam Rit 42 Lampang, Nan, Phrae,
  Uttaradit Provinces
Nam Ron 17 Central Thailand
Nam Ruem 47 Tak Town
Nam Som 48 Northeastern Thailand
Nam Song 24 Around Nakhon Sawan
Nam Sum 48 Northeastern Thailand
Nam Tao 22 Around Ayutthaya
Nam Thong 35 Around Chiang Mai
Nam Tok 72 Phuket Island
Nam Tok Krating
  28 Southeastern Thailand
Nam Ton 35 Around Chiang Mai
Nam Waen 41 Chiang Rai Province
Nam Wing 17 Central Thailand
Nam Yen 48 Northeastern Thailand
Nam Yuen 49 Northeastern Thailand
Nami 79 Far South
Nan 43 Nan
Nan Ka Phrao 60 Upper Gulf Coasts
Nan Kok 17 Central Thailand
Nanai 75 Patong Beach
Nang Kaeo 18 Around Bangkok
Nang Klang 24 Around Nakhon Sawan
Nang Lu 24 Around Nakhon Sawan
Nang Rong 50 Around Phanom Rung
Naraphirom 18 Around Bangkok
Narathiwat 79 Far South
Nathom 49 Northeastern Thailand
Nathon 66 Ko Samui
National Park 71 Phuket Province
Navy Area 81 Songkhla Town
New Sukhothai 44 New Sukhothai
Nga Maeng Nua 34 Around Chiang Mai
Nga Maeng Tai 34 Around Chiang Mai
Ngae Ngae 79 Far South
Ngao 64 Isthmus of Kra
Ngio Ngam 43 Lampang, Nan, Phrae,
  Uttaradit Provinces
Ngio Rai 18 Around Bangkok
Ngoi 48 Northeastern Thailand
Ngop 41 Chiang Rai Province
Nikhom Ban Nong
  48 Northeastern Thailand
Nikhom Kao Bo Kaeo
  24 Around Nakhon Sawan
Nikhom Kham Soi
  49 Northeastern Thailand
Nikhom Makkasan 11 Lumphini
Nikhom Nam Un 48 Northeastern Thailand
Nikhom Sahako 64 Isthmus of Kra
Nikhom Sahakon Nong Hai
  35 Around Chiang Mai
Nin Phet 18 Around Bangkok
Nng Phai 17 Central Thailand
No Ri 28 Southeastern Thailand

Noen Hin 17 Central Thailand
Noen Kham 24 Around Nakhon Sawan
Noen Khi Lek 24 Around Nakhon Sawan
Noen Kwao 24 Around Nakhon Sawan
Noen Ngam 79 Far South
Noen Phra Prang 18 Around Bangkok
Noen Sa Nga 48 Northeastern Thailand
Noi 35 Around Chiang Mai
Nok Le 72 Phuket Island
Nok Mueang 52 Surin Town
Non Bua 24 Around Nakhon Sawan
Non Champa 48 Northeastern Thailand
Non Chan 49 Northeastern Thailand
Non Charoen 50 Around Phanom Rung
Non Daeng 48 Northeastern Thailand
Non Din Daeng 48 Northeastern Thailand
Non Faek 49 Northeastern Thailand
Non Han 48 Northeastern Thailand
Non Hua Na 48 Northeastern Thailand
Non Kham 49 Northeastern Thailand
Non Kheng 48 Northeastern Thailand
Non Khun 49 Northeastern Thailand
Non Kok 48 Northeastern Thailand
Non Krabuang 48 Northeastern Thailand
Non Lek 24 Around Nakhon Sawan
Non Mak Kheng 17 Central Thailand
Non Na Yao 48 Northeastern Thailand
Non Narai 49 Northeastern Thailand
Non Phet 17 Central Thailand
Non Po Daeng 48 Northeastern Thailand
Non Rawiang 17 Central Thailand
Non Sa-at 48 Northeastern Thailand
Non Sang 48 Northeastern Thailand
Non Sila 48 Northeastern Thailand
Non Sung 17 Central Thailand
Non Suwan 50 Around Phanom Rung
Non Thai 17 Central Thailand
Non Thong lang 17 Central Thailand
Nong 32 Northern Thailand
Nong Ap Chang 35 Around Chiang Mai
Nong Bo 18 Around Bangkok
Nong Bom Klui 24 Around Nakhon Sawan
Nong Bon 7 Central Bangkok
Nong Bon Daeng 19 Around Bangkok
Nong Bot 50 Around Phanom Rung
Nong Bua 35 Around Chiang Mai
Nong Bua Daeng
  48 Northeastern Thailand
Nong Bua Khok 17 Central Thailand
Nong Bua Lam Phu
  48 Northeastern Thailand
Nong Bua Nok 35 Around Chiang Mai
Nong Bua Phak Kwian 17 Central Thailand
Nong Bua Rawe 48 Northeastern Thailand
Nong Bunnak 48 Northeastern Thailand
Nong Chaeng 17 Central Thailand
Nong Chak 19 Around Bangkok
Nong Chang 24 Around Nakhon Sawan
Nong Chik 79 Far South
Nong Chim 28 Southeastern Thailand
Nong Chok 19 Around Bangkok
Nong Chon 49 Northeastern Thailand
Nong Chorakhe 19 Around Bangkok
Nong Chot 48 Northeastern Thailand
Nong Chumphon 18 Around Bangkok
Nong Daeng 43 Lampang, Nan, Phrae,
  Uttaradit Provinces
Nong Don 48 Northeastern Thailand
Nong Fa 16 Central Thailand
Nong Faek 35 Around Chiang Mai
Nong Fan 35 Around Chiang Mai
Nong Ha 34 Around Chiang Mai
Nong Hai 35 Around Chiang Mai
Nong Han 48 Northeastern Thailand
Nong Hat Sai 48 Northeastern Thailand
Nong Hi 49 Northeastern Thailand
Nong Hian 49 Northeastern Thailand
Nong Hin 48 Northeastern Thailand
Nong Hoi 35 Around Chiang Mai
Nong Hoi Maew 34 Around Chiang Mai
Nong Hong 19 Around Bangkok
Nong Hua Rat 17 Central Thailand
Nong Irun 19 Around Bangkok
Nong Kae 24 Around Nakhon Sawan
Nong Kakha 19 Around Bangkok
Nong Kha Yang 32 Northern Thailand
Nong Khae 17 Central Thailand
Nong Khaem 4 Greater Bangkok
Nong Khai 48 Northeastern Thailand
Nong Kham 48 Northeastern Thailand
Nong Khan 17 Central Thailand
Nong Khang Khok 19 Around Bangkok
Nong Khang Phlu 4 Greater Bangkok
Nong Khao 18 Around Bangkok
Nong Khayang 24 Around Nakhon Sawan
Nong Khayat 19 Around Bangkok
Nong Khi Khwai 35 Around Chiang Mai
Nong Khiam 17 Central Thailand
Nong Khon 71 Phuket Province

Nong Khon Kwang 49 Greater Udon Thani
Nong Khrai Luang 35 Around Chiang Mai
Nong Khrai Nang Liaw
  35 Around Chiang Mai
Nong Khratum 26 Kanchanaburi Province
Nong Khum 49 Northeastern Thailand
Nong Ki 28 Southeastern Thailand
Nong Klang Na 18 Around Bangkok
Nong Klot 48 Northeastern Thailand
Nong Kok Hoi 17 Central Thailand
Nong Kop 18 Around Bangkok
Nong Krachao 24 Around Nakhon Sawan
Nong Kradon 24 Around Nakhon Sawan
Nong Krathao 48 Northeastern Thailand
Nong Krathing 33 Chiang Mai, Mae Hong
  Son & Lamphun Provinces
Nong Krathum 18 Around Bangkok
Nong Kratum
  49 Greater Nakhon Ratchasima
Nong Krot 24 Around Nakhon Sawan
Nong Kum 26 Kanchanaburi Province
Nong Kung 48 Northeastern Thailand
Nong Kung Noi 48 Northeastern Thailand
Nong Kung Si 48 Northeastern Thailand
Nong Kwang 18 Around Bangkok
Nong Lam 18 Around Bangkok
Nong Lek 35 Around Chiang Mai
Nong Lu 26 Sangkhlaburi
Nong Luang 46 Tak Town
Nong Lum Phuk 17 Central Thailand
Nong Lung 49 Northeastern Thailand
Nong Mae Kai 22 Around Ayutthaya
Nong Mai Kaen 28 Southeastern Thailand
Nong Mai Ngam 50 Around Phanom Rung
Nong Mamong 24 Around Nakhon Sawan
Nong Me 24 Around Nakhon Sawan
Nong Mek 48 Northeastern Thailand
Nong Mu 19 Around Bangkok
Nong Muang 48 Northeastern Thailand
Nong Na Kham 48 Northeastern Thailand
Nong Nam 33 Chiang Mai,
  Mae Hong Son & Lamphun Provinces
Nong Nam Som 19 Around Bangkok
Nong Nam Yai 22 Around Ayutthaya
Nong Ngu Lueam 18 Around Bangkok
Nong Niang 35 Around Chiang Mai
Nong Noi 24 Around Nakhon Sawan
Nong Nok Khu 48 Northeastern Thailand
Nong Nom Wua 24 Around Nakhon Sawan
Nong Pak Long 18 Around Bangkok
Nong Pet 26 Kanchanaburi Province
Nong Phai 48 Northeastern Thailand
Nong Phai Kaeo 28 Southeastern Thailand
Nong Phai Lom
  50 Nakhon Ratchasima City
Nong Pham 35 Around Chiang Mai
Nong Phikun 24 Around Nakhon Sawan
Nong Phlam 35 Around Chiang Mai
Nong Pho 24 Around Nakhon Sawan
Nong Phok 49 Northeastern Thailand
Nong Phrao Ngai 4 Greater Bangkok
Nong Phu 49 Northeastern Thailand
Nong Phut 71 Phuket Province
Nong Pla 34 Around Chiang Mai
Nong Pla Lai 28 Southeastern Thailand
Nong Pla Man 34 Around Chiang Mai
Nong Pla Mo 18 Around Bangkok
Nong Pla Sawai 33 Chiang Mai,
  Mae Hong Son & Lamphun Provinces
Nong Pling 22 Around Ayutthaya
Nong Po 18 Around Bangkok
Nong Pom 35 Around Chiang Mai
Nong Pradu 16 Central Thailand
Nong Pru 16 Central Thailand
Nong Prue 5 Greater Bangkok
Nong Pu 35 Around Chiang Mai
Nong Rang 48 Northeastern Thailand
Nong Ri 19 Around Bangkok
Nong Rong 18 Around Bangkok
Nong Ruea 48 Northeastern Thailand
Nong Sae 35 Around Chiang Mai
Nong Saeng 48 Northeastern Thailand
Nong Sai 50 Around Phanom Rung
Nong Sam Wang 19 Around Bangkok
Nong Samat 28 Southeastern Thailand
Nong Samnak 19 Around Bangkok
Nong San 49 Northeastern Thailand
Nong Sano 17 Central Thailand
Nong Sarai 18 Around Bangkok
Nong Si Chaeng 35 Around Chiang Mai
Nong Si Ma 17 Central Thailand
Nong Soeng 48 Northeastern Thailand
Nong Song Hong
  48 Northeastern Thailand
Nong Song Yae 49 Northeastern Thailand
Nong Sra 24 Around Nakhon Sawan
Nong Suang 19 Around Bangkok
Nong Suea 48 Northeastern Thailand
Nong Sung 49 Northeastern Thailand

Nong Tai 48 Northeastern Thailand
Nong Takhai 17 Central Thailand
Nong Takhian 17 Central Thailand
Nong Takrong 50 Around Phanom Rung
Nong Tamlueng 19 Around Bangkok
Nong Thale 71 Phuket Province
Nong Tho 17 Central Thailand
Nong Thom 48 Northeastern Thailand
Nong Thung Yai 48 Northeastern Thailand
Nong Tian 60 Upper Gulf Coasts
Nong Tin Nok 19 Around Bangkok
Nong To Soem 60 Upper Gulf Coasts
Nong Trut 78 Far South
Nong Um 48 Northeastern Thailand
Nong Ung 35 Around Chiang Mai
Nong Wa 48 Northeastern Thailand
Nong Waeng 48 Northeastern Thailand
Nong Wai 34 Around Chiang Mai
Nong Wua So 48 Northeastern Thailand
Nong Ya Khao 17 Central Thailand
Nong Ya Khao Nak 17 Central Thailand
Nong Ya Phraek 48 Northeastern Thailand
Nong Ya Plong 60 Upper Gulf Coasts
Nong Yai 51 Around Phanom Rung
Nong Yai Da 24 Around Nakhon Sawan
Nong Yang 24 Around Nakhon Sawan
Nong Yao 48 Northeastern Thailand
NongTae 49 Northeastern Thailand
Nonthaburi 60 Upper Gulf Coasts
Noppharat 19 Around Bangkok
Nopphitam 64 Isthmus of Kra
Not 79 Far South
Nua Bang 72 Phuket Island
Nuea 64 Isthmus of Kra
Nuea Khlong 64 Isthmus of Kra
Nuen Maprang 48 Northeastern Thailand
Old Town 47 Kamphaeng Phet Town
Om Ko 48 Northeastern Thailand
Om Noi 4 Greater Bangkok
Om Phanom 17 Central Thailand
Om Yai 18 Around Bangkok
Omkai 33 Chiang Mai,
  Mae Hong Son & Lamphun Provinces
Ong Phra 26 Kanchanaburi Province
Ongkharak 19 Around Bangkok
Op Luang 33 Chiang Mai,
  Mae Hong Son & Lamphun Provinces
Pa Bak 78 Far South
Pa Bon 78 Far South
Pa Bong 35 Around Chiang Mai
Pa Ching 79 Far South
Pa Daeng 32 Northern Thailand
Pa Daet 35 Around Chiang Mai
Pa Dua 35 Around Chiang Mai
Pa Fang 35 Around Chiang Mai
Pa Ha 41 Chiang Rai Province
Pa Hiang 35 Around Chiang Mai
Pa Hung 35 Around Chiang Mai
Pa Kha Nua 35 Around Chiang Mai
Pa Kha Tai 35 Around Chiang Mai
Pa Khai 43 Lampang, Nan,
  Phrae, Uttaradit Provinces
Pa Kham 35 Around Chiang Mai
Pa Khlok 73 Phuket Island
Pa Khoi Tai 35 Around Chiang Mai
Pa Khui 35 Around Chiang Mai
Pa Kluai 35 Around Chiang Mai
Pa Kluai Luang 35 Around Chiang Mai
Pa Laeo Luang 43 Lampang,
  Nan, Phrae, Uttaradit Provinces
Pa Lai 72 Phuket Island
Pa Lan 35 Around Chiang Mai
Pa Maet 42 Phrae Town
Pa Mai 79 Far South
Pa Mai Daeng 35 Around Chiang Mai
Pa Mak 35 Around Chiang Mai
Pa Miang 33 Chiang Mai,
  Mae Hong Son & Lamphun Provinces
Pa Miang Pang Thong Daeng
  34 Around Chiang Mai
Pa Miang Pang Ton Lung
  34 Around Chiang Mai
Pa Mok 22 Around Ayutthaya
Pa Muat 35 Around Chiang Mai
Pa Nai 33 Chiang Mai,
  Mae Hong Son & Lamphun Provinces
Pa Nat 35 Around Chiang Mai
Pa Ngae 35 Around Chiang Mai
Pa Ngio 33 Chiang Mai,
  Mae Hong Son & Lamphun Provinces
Pa Ngiu 35 Around Chiang Mai
Pa Nom Dong Rak
  48 Northeastern Thailand
Pa Pae 33 Chiang Mai,
  Mae Hong Son & Lamphun Provinces
Pa Pang 33 Chiang Mai,
  Mae Hong Son & Lamphun Provinces
Pa Pao 35 Around Chiang Mai
Pa Phai 35 Around Chiang Mai

Phang 49 Northeastern Thailand
Phayom 64 Isthmus of Kra
Phlu 33 Chiang Mai,
  Mae Hong Son & Lamphun Provinces
Po 48 Northeastern Thailand
Pong 33 Chiang Mai,
  Mae Hong Son & Lamphun Provinces
Pong Tai Rong 35 Around Chiang Mai
Sai 71 Phuket Province
Sak 72 Phuket Island
Sak Khwang 35 Around Chiang Mai
Sak Luang 35 Around Chiang Mai
Sak Ngam 35 Around Chiang Mai
Sak Noi 35 Around Chiang Mai
Sakae 24 Around Nakhon Sawan
Samet 78 Far South
Sang 48 Northeastern Thailand
Tan 23 Lopburi Town
Tiao 78 Far South
Tiu 35 Around Chiang Mai
Tueng 40 Mae Chan
Tung 35 Around Chiang Mai
Tung Mai 35 Around Chiang Mai
Tung Noi 35 Around Chiang Mai
Tung Pa Mok 35 Around Chiang Mai
Yang 71 Phuket Province
Yang Thong 35 Around Chiang Mai
Yup Nai 28 Southeastern Thailand
bon 79 Far South
byin 60 Upper Gulf Coasts
dang Asam 78 Far South
dang Besar 78 Far South
dang Donan 78 Far South
dang Lembu 79 Far South
do 79 Far South
en 79 Far South
i 20K 38 Pai
i 20Kling 23 Ayutthaya Town
k Bang 79 Far South
k Bong 33 Chiang Mai,
  Mae Hong Son & Lamphun Provinces
k Chan 60 Upper Gulf Coasts
k Chap 17 Central Thailand
k Chong 18 Around Bangkok
k Kading 49 Northeastern Thailand
k Kang 33 Chiang Mai,
  Mae Hong Son & Lamphun Provinces
k Khat 48 Northeastern Thailand
k Khem 48 Northeastern Thailand
k Khlong 71 Phuket Province
k Lai 48 Northeastern Thailand
k Lat 78 Far South
k Lo 79 Far South
k Mak 60 Upper Gulf Coasts
k Meng 78 Far South
k Muang 35 Around Chiang Mai
k Nam 19 Around Bangkok
k Nam Pran 60 Upper Gulf Coasts
k Nam Tako 60 Upper Gulf Coasts
k Ngam 16 Central Thailand
k Phanang 64 Isthmus of Kra
k Phayun 78 Far South
k Phli 48 Northeastern Thailand
k Phraek 27 Kanchanaburi Town
k Phreak 60 Upper Gulf Coasts
k Raet 18 Around Bangkok
k Thai Sako 73 Phuket Island
k Than 24 Around Nakhon Sawan
k Thang 71 Phuket Province
k Tho 18 Around Bangkok
k Thong Chai 48 Northeastern Thailand
kchom 48 Northeastern Thailand
kham 50 Around Phanom Rung
alauk 60 Upper Gulf Coasts
alaw 60 Upper Gulf Coasts
alian 78 Far South
aluru 79 Far South
am Phatthana 78 Far South
an Tae 78 Far South
anare 79 Far South
anebo 60 Upper Gulf Coasts
ang 35 Around Chiang Mai
ang Haew 34 Around Chiang Mai
ang Hai 34 Around Chiang Mai
ang Hin Fon 33 Chiang Mai,
  Mae Hong Son & Lamphun Provinces
ang Ku 50 Around Phanom Rung
ang Kwao 34 Around Chiang Mai
ang Mapha 20K 39 Pang Mapha
ang Mu 38 Around Mae Hong Son
ang Nga 71 Phuket Province
ang Ta Wai 16 Central Thailand
ang Yang 34 Around Chiang Mai
antin Sakan 33 Chiang Mai,
  Mae Hong Son & Lamphun Provinces
arai 79 Far South
arit Panjong 79 Far South
aseyawo 79 Far South
asir Mas 79 Far South

Patae 79 Far South
Patan 35 Around Chiang Mai
Pathiu 60 Upper Gulf Coasts
Pathom 18 Around Bangkok
Pathum 53 Ubon Ratchathani Town
Pathum Thani 19 Around Bangkok
Pathum Wan 10 Lumphini
Pathumrat 48 Northeastern Thailand
Pathumratwongsa
  49 Northeastern Thailand
Pathumwan 13 Silom
Patong 75 Patong Beach
Pattani 80 Pattani Town
Pattaya 29 Pattaya
Pauh 78 Far South
Pawapya 60 Upper Gulf Coasts
Pawut 60 Upper Gulf Coasts
Payatwet 60 Upper Gulf Coasts
Pe 60 Upper Gulf Coasts
Pedaing 60 Upper Gulf Coasts
Peinchaung 60 Upper Gulf Coasts
Pekan Batu 5 79 Far South
Pendang 79 Far South
Pengkalan Hulu 79 Far South
Pha Bong 39 Around Mae Hong Son
Pha Chino 34 Around Chiang Mai
Pha Chuk 43 Lampang, Nan,
  Phrae, Uttaradit Provinces
Pha Khao 48 Northeastern Thailand
Pha Lak 41 Chiang Rai Province
Pha Luat 48 Northeastern Thailand
Pha Nok Khao 48 Northeastern Thailand
Pha Sing 41 Chiang Rai Province
Pha Taek 35 Around Chiang Mai
Pha Tale 17 Central Thailand
Phae 35 Around Chiang Mai
Phae Huay Bong 35 Around Chiang Mai
Phae Khwang 34 Around Chiang Mai
Phae Nam Kham 34 Around Chiang Mai
Phae Nua 35 Around Chiang Mai
Phae Pa Kha 35 Around Chiang Mai
Phae Pa Tiu 35 Around Chiang Mai
Phae Phrabat 35 Around Chiang Mai
Phai Cha 17 Central Thailand
Phai Cham Sin 22 Around Ayutthaya
Phai Hu Chang 18 Around Bangkok
Phai Khiao 24 Around Nakhon Sawan
Phai Khwang 22 Around Ayutthaya
Phai Kong Din 18 Around Bangkok
Phai Lio 22 Around Ayutthaya
Phai Lom 35 Around Chiang Mai
Phai Phra 19 Around Bangkok
Phai Sali 48 Northeastern Thailand
Phai San 50 Around Phanom Rung
Phai Sing 24 Around Nakhon Sawan
Phai Thong 60 Upper Gulf Coasts
Phaisali (Khok Dua) 17 Central Thailand
Phak Chit 73 Phuket Island
Phak Hai 22 Around Ayutthaya
Phak Khaya Noi 49 Northeastern Thailand
Phak Khuang 43 Lampang,
  Nan, Phrae, Uttaradit Provinces
Phak Kong Thang 17 Central Thailand
Phak Madoe 34 Around Chiang Mai
Phama Long 72 Phuket Island
Phan 33 Chiang Mai,
  Mae Hong Son & Lamphun Provinces
Phan Lan 24 Around Nakhon Sawan
Phan Lang 35 Around Chiang Mai
Phan Soeng 43 Lampang,
  Nan, Phrae, Uttaradit Provinces
Phan Tao 34 Around Chiang Mai
Phan Thong 19 Around Bangkok
Phana 49 Northeastern Thailand
Phanat Nikhom 19 Around Bangkok
Phang Khon 48 Northeastern Thailand
Phang La 78 Far South
Phang Tru 18 Around Bangkok
Phang Yang 78 Far South
Phangnga 64 Isthmus of Kra
Phanna Nikhom 48 Northeastern Thailand
Phanom 64 Isthmus of Kra
Phanom Dong Rak
  50 Around Phanom Rung
Phanom Sarakham 19 Around Bangkok
Phanom Sat 24 Around Nakhon Sawan
Phanom Thuan 18 Around Bangkok
Phanon Phrai 49 Northeastern Thailand
Phanthai Norasing 18 Around Bangkok
Phao Tan 71 Phuket Province
Phara 73 Phuket Island
Phato 60 Upper Gulf Coasts
Phattalung 64 Isthmus of Kra
Phatthalung 81 Phatthalung Town
Phatthana Nikhom 17 Central Thailand
Phaya Chomphu 35 Around Chiang Mai
Phayakkhaphum Phisal
  48 Northeastern Thailand
Phayao 41 Phayao Town

Phayu 49 Northeastern Thailand
Phayuha Khir 24 Around Nakhon Sawan
Phayuha Khiri 24 Around Nakhon Sawan
Phe 28 Ban Phe
Phen 48 Northeastern Thailand
Phetchabun 32 Northern Thailand
Phetchaburi 60 Upper Gulf Coasts
Phibun Mangsahan
  49 Northeastern Thailand
Phibun Rak 48 Northeastern Thailand
Phichai 42 Lampang Town
Phichit 45 Phichit Town
Phikul Thong 22 Around Ayutthaya
Phikun Ok 19 Around Bangkok
Phikun Thong 18 Around Bangkok
Phimai 48 Northeastern Thailand
Phiman 80 Satun Town
Phimon Rat 4 Greater Bangkok
Phimpha 19 Around Bangkok
Phipun 64 Isthmus of Kra
Phitsanulok 45 Pitsanulok,
  Sukhothai & Phichit Provinces
Phitsanulok Town 25K
  45 Phitsanulok Town
Phlao 60 Upper Gulf Coasts
Phlapphla Chai 48 Northeastern Thailand
Phlio 28 Southeastern Thailand
Phlu Ta Luang 28 Southeastern Thailand
Phlu Thuean 64 Isthmus of Kra
Phluang Song Nang
  24 Around Nakhon Sawan
Pho Chai 48 Northeastern Thailand
Pho En 22 Around Ayutthaya
Pho Hak 18 Around Bangkok
Pho Kao Ton 23 Lopburi Town
Pho Klang 49 Greater Nakhon Ratchasima
Pho Mak Khaeng
  49 Northeastern Thailand
Pho Nang Dam Ok
  24 Around Nakhon Sawan
Pho Ngam 24 Around Nakhon Sawan
Pho Prachak 22 Around Ayutthaya
Pho Sai 49 Northeastern Thailand
Pho Sam Ton 22 Around Ayutthaya
Pho Sang 22 Around Ayutthaya
Pho Sao Han 19 Around Bangkok
Pho Si Suwan 49 Northeastern Thailand
Pho So 33 Chiang Mai,
  Mae Hong Son & Lamphun Provinces
Pho Taeng 19 Around Bangkok
Pho Tak 48 Northeastern Thailand
Pho Talat Kaeo 22 Around Ayutthaya
Pho Tale 24 Around Nakhon Sawan
Pho Taru 22 Around Ayutthaya
Pho Thaen 19 Around Bangkok
Pho Thong 22 Around Ayutthaya
Pho Thong Charoen 35 Around Chiang Mai
Phochai 24 Around Nakhon Sawan
Phon 48 Northeastern Thailand
Phon Charoen 48 Northeastern Thailand
Phon Duan 49 Northeastern Thailand
Phon Hong 48 Northeastern Thailand
Phon Hua Han 72 Phuket Island
Phon Na Kaeo 49 Northeastern Thailand
Phon Ngam 48 Northeastern Thailand
Phon Phek 48 Northeastern Thailand
Phon Phisai 48 Northeastern Thailand
Phon Sai 49 Northeastern Thailand
Phon Sawan 49 Northeastern Thailand
Phon Soung 48 Northeastern Thailand
Phon Sung 32 Northern Thailand
Phon Thong 49 Northeastern Thailand
Phon Yang 49 Northeastern Thailand
Phong 43 Lampang, Nan, Phrae,
  Uttaradit Provinces
Phong Tuk 18 Around Bangkok
Phonsavang 48 Northeastern Thailand
Phot 64 Isthmus of Kra
Photharam 60 Upper Gulf Coasts
Phra Achan 19 Around Bangkok
Phra Ae 78 Far South
Phra Chedi Sam Ong 26 Sangkhlaburi
Phra Kha Wan 34 Around Chiang Mai
Phra Khanong 15 Sukhumvit
Phra Khanong Nuea 15 Sukhumvit
Phra Khao 22 Around Ayutthaya
Phra Muang 78 Far South
Phra Nakhon 8 Downtown Bangkok
Phra Ngam 22 Around Ayutthaya
Phra Non 35 Around Chiang Mai
Phra Pathom Chedi 18 Around Bangkok
Phra Phloeng 17 Central Thailand
Phra Phrom 64 Isthmus of Kra
Phra Phuttabat 17 Central Thailand
Phra Pradaeng 7 Central Bangkok
Phra Prathon 18 Around Bangkok
Phra Saeng 64 Isthmus of Kra
Phra Thaen 18 Around Bangkok
Phra That Doi Siu 35 Around Chiang Mai

Phra That Doi Suthep
  35 Around Chiang Mai
Phra Thong Kham
  48 Northeastern Thailand
Phra Yuen 48 Northeastern Thailand
Phrabat 42 Lampang Town
Phrachi 17 Central Thailand
Phrae 42 Phrae Town
Phraek Ha 78 Far South
Phraek Nam Daeng 18 Around Bangkok
Phraek Sa Mai 19 Around Bangkok
Phrai Bueng 49 Northeastern Thailand
Phraiwan 79 Far South
Phrao 33 Chiang Mai,
  Mae Hong Son & Lamphun Provinces
Phrasaeng 64 Isthmus of Kra
Phra That Khing kaeng
  41 Chiang Rai Province
Phraya Banlue 19 Around Bangkok
Phri Nok 24 Around Nakhon Sawan
Phrom Buri 22 Around Ayutthaya
Phrom Khiri 64 Isthmus of Kra
Phromburi 22 Around Ayutthaya
Phrommani 19 Around Bangkok
Phromsuk 23 Ayutthaya Town
Phron 79 Far South
Phrong Akat 19 Around Bangkok
Phrong Maduea 18 Around Bangkok
Phru 78 Far South
Phru Champa 72 Phuket Island
Phru Nai 64 Isthmus of Kra
Phru Pho 78 Far South
Phru Phri 64 Isthmus of Kra
Phru Somphan 72 Phuket Island
Phru Thai 64 Isthmus of Kra
Phru Tiao 64 Isthmus of Kra
Phru Toei 78 Far South
Phru Tu 79 Far South
Phru Yai 71 Phuket Province
Phu Jue 16 Central Thailand
Phu Kao Thong 23 Ayutthaya Town
Phu Khao Din 17 Central Thailand
Phu Khiao 48 Northeastern Thailand
Phu Khie 17 Central Thailand
Phu Kradueng 48 Northeastern Thailand
Phu Luang 48 Northeastern Thailand
Phu Nam Ron 26 Kanchanaburi Province
Phu Not 60 Upper Gulf Coasts
Phu Pha Man 48 Northeastern Thailand
Phu Phan 49 Northeastern Thailand
Phu Rakam 16 Central Thailand
Phu Ruea 48 Northeastern Thailand
Phu Sing 49 Northeastern Thailand
Phu Wiang 48 Northeastern Thailand
Phuet Udom 19 Around Bangkok
Phuket Town 64 Isthmus of Kra
Phukhao Thong 22 Around Ayutthaya
Phunphin 60 Upper Gulf Coasts
Phut Lao 22 Around Ayutthaya
Phutthaisong
  48 Northeastern Thailand
Pi Lai 70 Phuket Province
Pian 79 Far South
Piang Luang 33 Chiang Mai,
  Mae Hong Son & Lamphun Provinces
Pilok 26 Kanchanaburi Province
Pisandaungsaung 60 Upper Gulf Coasts
Pla Kang 35 Around Chiang Mai
Pla Khao 49 Northeastern Thailand
Plaeng Yao 28 Southeastern Thailand
Plai Bang 4 Greater Bangkok
Plai Nam 60 Upper Gulf Coasts
Plai Phongphang 18 Around Bangkok
Plai Phraya 64 Isthmus of Kra
Plua Lon 78 Far South
Pluak Daeng 28 Southeastern Thailand
Po Daeng 17 Central Thailand
Po Faek Nua 33 Chiang Mai,
  Mae Hong Son & Lamphun Provinces
Pok 34 Around Chiang Mai
Pom Phra Chunlachomkiao
  60 Upper Gulf Coasts
Pom Pi Nai 26 Kanchanaburi Province
Pom Prap 9 Downtown Bangkok
Pom Prap Sattru Phai
  9 Downtown Bangkok
Pong 35 Around Chiang Mai
Pong Din 40 Chiang Rai Province
Pong Don 33 Chiang Mai, Mae Hong Son &
  Lamphun Provinces
Pong Kadon 17 Central Thailand
Pong Khlong Nua 17 Central Thailand
Pong Kho Noi 35 Around Chiang Mai
Pong Khrai 34 Around Chiang Mai
Pong Kluo 41 Chiang Rai Province
Pong Ko 60 Upper Gulf Coasts
Pong Luang 33 Chiang Mai,
  Mae Hong Son & Lamphun Provinces
Pong Mu 35 Around Chiang Mai

Pong Nam Rong 33 Chiang Mai,
    Mae Hong Son & Lamphun Provinces
Pong Noi 35 Around Chiang Mai
Pong Nua 34 Around Chiang Mai
Pong Pa Lang 35 Around Chiang Mai
Pong Sa 33 Chiang Mai,
    Mae Hong Son & Lamphun Provinces
Pong Sawai 20 Ratchaburi (Ratburi) Town
Pong Tai 34 Around Chiang Mai
Pong Tao 41 Chiang Rai Province
Pong Thung 33 Chiang Mai,
    Mae Hong Son & Lamphun Provinces
Pong Yaeng Nai 34 Around Chiang Mai
Pong Yaeng Nok 34 Around Chiang Mai
Pong Yang Khok 33 Chiang Mai,
    Mae Hong Son & Lamphun Provinces
Poseng 79 Far South
Pra Tha 64 Isthmus of Kra
Prachak Silapakhom
    48 Northeastern Thailand
Prachan Khirikhet 17 Central Thailand
Prachinburi 17 Central Thailand
Prachuap Khiri Khan 60 Upper Gulf Coasts
Prakham 48 Northeastern Thailand
Prakhon Chai 50 Around Phanom Rung
Prakop 79 Far South
Pran Buri 60 Upper Gulf Coasts
Prang Ku 49 Northeastern Thailand
Prang Phe 26 Kanchanaburi Province
Prasat 48 Northeastern Thailand
Prasatsit 18 Around Bangkok
Pratatbhu 50 Around Phanom Rung
Prathai 48 Northeastern Thailand
Pratuchai 23 Ayutthaya Town
Prawet 7 Central Bangkok
Preng 19 Around Bangkok
Prey Phdau 49 Northeastern Thailand
Prik 78 Far South
Pring 48 Northeastern Thailand
Prommat 23 Lopburi Town
Pru 50 Around Phanom Rung
Pru Yai 17 Central Thailand
Pu Dok 33 Chiang Mai,
    Mae Hong Son & Lamphun Provinces
Pu Kha Hua 35 Around Chiang Mai
Pu Kha Nua 35 Around Chiang Mai
Pu Kha Tai 35 Around Chiang Mai
Pu La Mong 79 Far South
Puang 33 Chiang Mai,
    Mae Hong Son & Lamphun Provinces
Pueai Noi 48 Northeastern Thailand
Puek Tiean 60 Upper Gulf Coasts
Pulakong 79 Far South
Purong 79 Far South
Puyo 79 Far South
Pyinbutha Sakan 60 Upper Gulf Coasts
Pyinbyugyi 60 Upper Gulf Coasts
Pyingyi 60 Upper Gulf Coasts
Pyinletku 60 Upper Gulf Coasts
Ra Mat 78 Far South
Racha 71 Phuket Province
Racha Thewa 5 Greater Bangkok
Rae 79 Far South
Rahaeng 46 Tak Town
Rai 35 Around Chiang Mai
Rai Lak Thong 19 Around Bangkok
Rai Lamang 17 Central Thailand
Rai Nong Ho 35 Around Chiang Mai
Rai Patthana 24 Around Nakhon Sawan
Rai Salai 49 Northeastern Thailand
Rai Sayam 60 Upper Gulf Coasts
Rai Suan Khwan 60 Upper Gulf Coasts
Ram 64 Isthmus of Kra
Raman 79 Far South
Ran Tong 35 Around Chiang Mai
Rang Wai 18 Around Bangkok
Rangae 79 Far South
Rangsan Resort 50 Around Phanom Rung
Rangsit 28 Southeastern Thailand
Ranong 60 Upper Gulf Coasts
Ranot 78 Far South
Rat 35 Around Chiang Mai
Rat Sathit 22 Around Ayutthaya
Ratchaburi 20 Ratchaburi (Ratburi) Town
Ratchakrut 60 Upper Gulf Coasts
Ratchathewi 10 Lumphini
Ratsada 64 Isthmus of Kra
Rattana Buri 48 Northeastern Thailand
Rattana Wapi 48 Northeastern Thailand
Rattaphum 78 Far South
Rawa 78 Far South
Rawai 25K 73 Rawai
Rawang Si Yang 78 Far South
Rayong 30 Rayong Town
Rhong Kham 48 Northeastern Thailand
Riang 72 Phuket Island
Rim Thale 71 Phuket Province
Roi Chan 34 Around Chiang Mai
Roi Et 48 Northeastern Thailand

Rom Sai 79 Far South
Ron Phibun 64 Isthmus of Kra
Ron Thong 60 Upper Gulf Coasts
Rong 35 Around Chiang Mai
Rong Chang 22 Around Ayutthaya
Rong Ha 41 Chiang Rai Province
Rong Khe 18 Around Bangkok
Rong Khi Lek 35 Around Chiang Mai
Rong Kho 33 Chiang Mai,
    Mae Hong Son & Lamphun Provinces
Rong Khun 35 Around Chiang Mai
Rong Kong Khao 35 Around Chiang Mai
Rong Kwang 43 Lampang,
    Nan, Phrae, Uttaradit Provinces
Rong Muang 9 Downtown Bangkok
Rong Wua 35 Around Chiang Mai
Rong Wuai 34 Around Chiang Mai
Royal Palace 8 Downtown Bangkok
Ruam Chit Townhouse 14 Sukhumvit
Ruang 34 Around Chiang Mai
Rueso 79 Far South
Sa Bot 48 Northeastern Thailand
Sa Dai Tha 16 Central Thailand
Sa Kaeo 24 Around Nakhon Sawan
Sa Kaew 17 Central Thailand
Sa Khrai 48 Northeastern Thailand
Sa Krathiam 18 Around Bangkok
Sa Phatthana 18 Around Bangkok
Sa Prathip 28 Southeastern Thailand
Sa Si Liam 19 Around Bangkok
Saba 79 Far South
Saba Yoi 79 Far South
Saban 79 Far South
Sabarang 81 Pattani Town
Sadao 48 Northeastern Thailand
Sadawa 79 Far South
Sadeinchaungby 60 Upper Gulf Coasts
Sae O 28 Southeastern Thailand
Sae Sa 35 Around Chiang Mai
Saen Phu Dat 19 Around Bangkok
Saen Saep 5 Greater Bangkok
Saen Suk 19 Around Bangkok
Saen To 18 Around Bangkok
Saen Tung 28 Southeastern Thailand
Sahakon Nikhom
    26 Kanchanaburi Province
Sahatsakhan 48 Northeastern Thailand
Sai Buri 79 Far South
Sai Daeng 60 Upper Gulf Coasts
Sai Khao 78 Far South
Sai Khlong Haeng 17 Central Thailand
Sai Khong 78 Far South
Sai Kong Din 5 Greater Bangkok
Sai Kong Din Tai 5 Greater Bangkok
Sai Lamphong 24 Around Nakhon Sawan
Sai Ma 4 Greater Bangkok
Sai Mai 5 Greater Bangkok
Sai Mun 35 Around Chiang Mai
Sai Ngam 18 Around Bangkok
Sai Noi 18 Around Bangkok
Sai Riang 71 Phuket Province
Sai Ta Ku 50 Around Phanom Rung
Sai Tai 35 Around Chiang Mai
Sai Thao 71 Phuket Province
Sai Thong 28 Southeastern Thailand
Sai Yoi 42 Lampang, Nan,
    Phrae, Uttaradit Provinces
Sai Yok 27 Sai Yok National Park
Sa-iap 41 Chiang Rai Province
Sairee 69 Ko Tao
Sak Ngam 72 Phuket Island
Sakae Khrua 48 Northeastern Thailand
Sakai 79 Far South
Sakam 79 Far South
Sakanthit 60 Upper Gulf Coasts
Sakhon 78 Far South
Sakhon Nakhon 48 Northeastern Thailand
Sakhu 72 Phuket Island
Sako 79 Far South
Sakom 79 Far South
Sala 35 Around Chiang Mai
Sala Chao Kai To
    24 Around Nakhon Sawan
Sala Daeng 22 Ang Thong Town
Sala Dan 76 Ko Lanta
Sala Khru 19 Around Bangkok
Sala Klang 4 Greater Bangkok
Sala Mai 79 Far South
Sala Thammasop 4 Greater Bangkok
Sala Thung Lung 78 Far South
Salaeng 41 Chiang Rai Province
Salaeng Thon 48 Northeastern Thailand
Salai Chiang Thong 33 Chiang Mai,
    Mae Hong Son & Lamphun Provinces
Salawin 33 Chiang Mai,
    Mae Hong Son & Lamphun Provinces
Salaya 4 Greater Bangkok
Salik 43 Lampang, Nan, Phrae,
    Uttaradit Provinces

Sam Chai 48 Northeastern Thailand
Sam Chong Nue 71 Phuket Province
Sam Chuk 17 Central Thailand
Sam Kha 49 Northeastern Thailand
Sam Khok 19 Around Bangkok
Sam Ko 22 Around Ayutthaya
Sam Kong 73 Phuket Island
Sam Mueang 18 Around Bangkok
Sam Ngam 18 Around Bangkok
Sam Phaniang 22 Around Ayutthaya
Sam Phrao 48 Northeastern Thailand
Sam Roi Yot 60 Upper Gulf Coasts
Sam Ruan 18 Around Bangkok
Sam Sa-at 49 Northeastern Thailand
Sam Sung 48 Northeastern Thailand
Sam Thai 22 Around Ayutthaya
Sam Tum 19 Around Bangkok
Sam Wa Tawan Ok 5 Greater Bangkok
Sam Wa Tawan Tok 5 Greater Bangkok
Samae Dam 18 Around Bangkok
Samae San 60 Upper Gulf Coasts
Samaesan 28 Southeastern Thailand
Samai 33 Chiang Mai,
    Mae Hong Son & Lamphun Provinces
Samakkhi 79 Far South
Samet 19 Around Bangkok
Samet Nuea 19 Around Bangkok
Samet Tai 19 Around Bangkok
Sami Lang 71 Phuket Province
Samnak Bok 19 Around Bangkok
Samnak Kham 78 Far South
Samnak Taeo 79 Far South
Samnak Thong 28 Southeastern Thailand
Samnak Tin Lao 28 Southeastern Thailand
Samoeng 34 Around Chiang Mai
Sampathuan 18 Around Bangkok
Samphan Thawong 12 Silom
Samphao 64 Isthmus of Kra
Samphao Lom 23 Ayutthaya Town
Samran 52 Yasothon Town
Samran Rat 8 Downtown Bangkok
Samrong 5 Greater Bangkok
Samrong Mae 50 Around Phanom Rung
Samrong Nua 5 Greater Bangkok
Samrong Phlan 49 Northeastern Thailand
Samrong Thap 49 Northeastern Thailand
Samut Prakan 19 Around Bangkok
Samut Prakan Town 21
    Samut Prakan Town
Samut Sakhon 21 Samut Sakhon Town
Samut Songkhram 18 Around Bangkok
San Chang Mup 35 Around Chiang Mai
San Chao Rong Thong 22
    Around Ayutthaya
San Chaopho Suea 8 Downtown Bangkok
San Dok Kham Tai 35 Around Chiang Mai
San Dong 33 Chiang Mai,
    Mae Hong Son & Lamphun Provinces
San Khao Khaep Klang
    35 Around Chiang Mai
San Khong Kao 35 Around Chiang Mai
San Khong Mai 35 Around Chiang Mai
San Khu 35 Around Chiang Mai
San Klang Tai 35 Around Chiang Mai
San Kracho 35 Around Chiang Mai
San Lamphu 79 Far South
San Mamuang 33 Chiang Mai, Mae Hong
    Son & Lamphun Provinces
San Mapaep 35 Around Chiang Mai
San Muang 35 Around Chiang Mai
San Na Nong Mai 43 Lampang,
    Nan, Phrae, Uttaradit Provinces
San Pa Kha 35 Around Chiang Mai
San Pa Sak 35 Around Chiang Mai
San Pa Sak Noi 35 Around Chiang Mai
San Pa Yang 33 Chiang Mai, Mae Hong
    Son & Lamphun Provinces
San Phak Wan Noi 35 Around Chiang Mai
San Phi Sua 35 Around Chiang Mai
San Phra Net 35 Around Chiang Mai
San Pu Loei 35 Around Chiang Mai
San Ro Changan
    28 Southeastern Thailand
San Sai 35 Around Chiang Mai
San Sai Kom 35 Around Chiang Mai
San Sai Luang 35 Around Chiang Mai
San Sali 33 Chiang Mai,
    Mae Hong Son & Lamphun Provinces
San Ton Du 35 Around Chiang Mai
San Um 35 Around Chiang Mai
Sanam Chai 28 Southeastern Thailand
Sanam Chai Khet 17 Central Thailand
Sanam Chan 20 Nakhon Pathom Town
Sanap Thuep 28 Southeastern Thailand
Sang Khla Buri 32 Northern Thailand
Sang Kho 49 Northeastern Thailand
Sang Ming 49 Northeastern Thailand
Sangka-U 78 Far South
Sangkha 48 Northeastern Thailand

Sangkhlaburi 32 Northern Thailand
Sangkhom 48 Northeastern Thailand
Sankamphaeng 35 Around Chiang Mai
Sankhaburi 24 Around Nakhon Sawan
Sano 79 Far South
Sano Loi 4 Greater Bangkok
Sanom 48 Northeastern Thailand
Sanphaya 24 Around Nakhon Sawan
Sao Hin 33 Chiang Mai,
    Mae Hong Son & Lamphun Provinces
Sao Thong 22 Around Ayutthaya
Sao Thong Hin 4 Greater Bangkok
Sap Malua 17 Central Thailand
Sap Yai 48 Northeastern Thailand
Saphan Hih 24 Around Nakhon Sawan
Saphan Sung 7 Central Bangkok
Saphan Thai 22 Around Ayutthaya
Saraburi 17 Central Thailand
Saraphi 35 Around Chiang Mai
Sathan 43 Lampang, Nan,
    Phrae, Uttaradit Provinces
Sathing Phra 78 Far South
Sathon 79 Far South
Sathorn 13 Silom
Sato 28 Southeastern Thailand
Sattahip 28 Southeastern Thailand
Satuek 48 Northeastern Thailand
Satun 80 Satun Town
Savannakhét 49 Northeastern Thailand
Sawa So 48 Northeastern Thailand
Sawaeng Ha 22 Around Ayutthaya
Sawang Arom 24 Around Nakhon Sawan
Sawang Daen Din
    48 Northeastern Thailand
Sawang Wirawong
    49 Northeastern Thailand
Sawi 60 Upper Gulf Coasts
Sawiat 60 Upper Gulf Coasts
Sawo 79 Far South
Seka 49 Northeastern Thailand
Selaphum 49 Northeastern Thailand
Semeling 78 Far South
Sena 18 Around Bangkok
Sena Nikhom 5 Greater Bangkok
Senangkhanikhom
    49 Northeastern Thailand
Si Banphot 79 Far South
Si Bua Ban 33 Chiang Mai,
    Mae Hong Son & Lamphun Provinces
Si Bun Ruang 35 Around Chiang Mai
Si Bunruang 35 Around Chiang Mai
Si Chang District 29 Ko Si Chang
Si Chiang Mai 48 Northeastern Thailand
Si Chomphu 48 Northeastern Thailand
Si Chula 19 Around Bangkok
Si Ka-ang 19 Around Bangkok
Si Kan 5 Greater Bangkok
Si Khiu 17 Central Thailand
Si Khlong 22 Around Ayutthaya
Si Khoraphum 48 Northeastern Thailand
Si Lom 13 Silom
Si Maha Pho 18 Around Bangkok
Si Maha Phot 17 Central Thailand
Si Mahosot 17 Central Thailand
Si Mueang Mai 49 Northeastern Thailand
Si Muen 18 Around Bangkok
Si Nakharin 78 Far South
Si Narong 48 Northeastern Thailand
Si Photharam 35 Around Chiang Mai
Si Phran 22 Around Ayutthaya
Si Phraya 13 Silom
Si Prachan 17 Central Thailand
Si Racha 29 Si Racha
Si Rattana 49 Northeastern Thailand
Si Roi 22 Around Ayutthaya
Si Sa ket 43 Lampang, Nan,
    Phrae, Uttaradit Provinces
Si Saket 49 Northeastern Thailand
Si Sakhon 79 Far South
Si Satchanalai 44
    Satchanalai-Chaliang National Park
Si Sawat 26 Kanchanaburi Province
Si Somdet 48 Northeastern Thailand
Si Songkhram 49 Northeastern Thailand
Si Than 49 Northeastern Thailand
Si That 48 Northeastern Thailand
Si Thep 17 Central Thailand
Si Wichai 64 Isthmus of Kra
Si Yaak 48 Northeastern Thailand
Si Yaek 48 Northeastern Thailand
Siam Mai 78 Far South
Sichon 64 Isthmus of Kra
Sik 79 Far South
Sikao 78 Far South
Sila Lat 49 Northeastern Thailand
Silom 15K 13 Silom
Simpang Empat 78 Far South
Simpang Tiga Sungai Daun 78 Far South
Sin Don Chai 41 Chiang Rai Province

indin 60 Upper Gulf Coasts
ing 26 Kanchanaburi Province
ingburi 22 Singburi Town
inghanat 18 Around Bangkok
ingkir Darat 78 Far South
ingto Thong 19 Around Bangkok
intok 79 Far South
ip Et Sok 19 Around Bangkok
irinthon 49 Northeastern Thailand
iriraj 8 Downtown Bangkok
isa Chorakhe Noi 5 Greater Bangkok
isa Chorakhe Yai 5 Greater Bangkok
isa Krabue 19 Around Bangkok
itara 66 Ko Samui
iwilai 48 Northeastern Thailand
o Phisai 48 Northeastern Thailand
ob Soi 38 Around Mae Hong Son
oem Khwa 33 Chiang Mai,
    Mae Hong Son & Lamphun Provinces
oem Klang 33 Chiang Mai,
    Mae Hong Son & Lamphun Provinces
oem Sai 33 Chiang Mai,
    Mae Hong Son & Lamphun Provinces
oeng Sang 48 Northeastern Thailand
oi Hok 35 Around Chiang Mai
oi Lakhon 24 Around Nakhon Sawan
oi Sip 78 Far South
oi Thong 24 Around Nakhon Sawan
om Fo 49 Northeastern Thailand
om Poi 72 Phuket Island
om Wang 78 Far South
omdet 48 Northeastern Thailand
omdet Chao Phraya 12 Silom
omdet Charoen
    26 Kanchanaburi Province
on Klang 78 Far South
ong 43 Lampang,
    Nan, Phrae, Uttaradit Provinces
ong Dao 48 Northeastern Thailand
ong Hong 48 Northeastern Thailand
ong Khlong 19 Around Bangkok
ong Khwae 41 Chiang Rai Province
ong Phi Nong 18 Around Bangkok
ong Phraek 64 Isthmus of Kra
ong Salueng 28 Southeastern Thailand
ongkhla 81 Songkhla Town
op Huay Yao 34 Around Chiang Mai
op Khong 33 Chiang Mai,
    Mae Hong Son & Lamphun Provinces
op Moei 33 Chiang Mai,
    Mae Hong Son & Lamphun Provinces
op Poeng 33 Chiang Mai,
    Mae Hong Son & Lamphun Provinces
op Pong 39 Pang Mapha
op Prap 33 Chiang Mai,
    Mae Hong Son & Lamphun Provinces
op Sa 41 Chiang Rai Province
op Tui 42 Lampang Town
oppong 33 Chiang Mai,
    Mae Hong Son & Lamphun Provinces
ra Chaeng 24 Around Nakhon Sawan
ra Khuan 17 Central Thailand
ra Lung Rua 18 Around Bangkok
ra Phang Lan 18 Around Bangkok
ra Yai Som 18 Around Bangkok
u So 78 Far South
uan Chai Leng 71 Phuket Province
uan Chitlada 9 Downtown Bangkok
uan Chitladda 9 Downtown Bangkok
uan Dok 35 Around Chiang Mai
uan Hom 48 Northeastern Thailand
uan Luang 4 Greater Bangkok
uan Maphrao 72 Phuket Island
uan Phrik Thai 19 Around Bangkok
uan Phueng 60 Upper Gulf Coasts
uan Phung 60 Upper Gulf Coasts
uan Som 18 Around Bangkok
uan Yai 4 Greater Bangkok
uan Yang Lo Yong 72 Phuket Island
uat 41 Chiang Rai Province
ub Samoh Tod 17 Central Thailand
ub Sombun 17 Central Thailand
uea Hueng 64 Isthmus of Kra
uk Samran 60 Upper Gulf Coasts
ukhothai 44 Pitsanulok,
    Sukhothai & Phichit Provinces
ukirin 79 Far South
ung Men 42 Lampang, Nan,
    Phrae, Uttaradit Provinces
ung Noen 48 Northeastern Thailand
ungai Kolok 79 Far South
ungai Limau Dalam 78 Far South
ungai Padi 79 Far South
ungai Petani 78 Far South
ungai Tiang 79 Far South
ungei Bati 60 Upper Gulf Coasts
ungei Makuang 60 Upper Gulf Coasts
up Phraya 50 Around Phanom Rung
uphanburi 17 Central Thailand

Surat Thani 60 Upper Gulf Coasts
Surin 48 Northeastern Thailand
Suthep 36 Central Chiang Mai
Suwan 79 Far South
Suwan Khuha 48 Northeastern Thailand
Suwannaphum 48 Northeastern Thailand
Ta Bao 51 Around Phanom Rung
Ta Chong 50 Around Phanom Rung
Ta Khli 32 Northern Thailand
Ta Khram En 18 Around Bangkok
Ta Khun 60 Upper Gulf Coasts
Ta Lang Nai 28 Southeastern Thailand
Ta Luang 41 Chiang Rai Province
Ta Miang 50 Around Phanom Rung
Ta Ni 50 Around Phanom Rung
Ta Pae 79 Far South
Ta Pek 50 Around Phanom Rung
Ta Pha Mok 42 Lampang, Nan,
    Phrae, Uttaradit Provinces
Ta Pring 71 Phuket Province
Ta Se 78 Far South
Ta Sit 28 Southeastern Thailand
Taa Than 32 Northern Thailand
Tab Teing 77 Trang Town
Tachi 79 Far South
Tachilek 41 Chiang Rai Province
Tagu 60 Upper Gulf Coasts
Tailing Chan 60 Upper Gulf Coasts
Tak 46 Kamphaeng Phet & Tak Provinces
Tak Bai 79 Far South
Tak Fa 17 Central Thailand
Takhian Thong 28 Southeastern Thailand
Takhli 24 Around Nakhon Sawan
Takhro 48 Northeastern Thailand
Tako 48 Northeastern Thailand
Tako Ta Phi 50 Around Phanom Rung
Takua Pa 64 Isthmus of Kra
Takua Thung 64 Isthmus of Kra
Takuk Tai 60 Upper Gulf Coasts
Talan 22 Around Ayutthaya
Talat 65 Surat Thani Town
Talat Bang Bo 28 Southeastern Thailand
Talat Bang Khen 5 Greater Bangkok
Talat Khwan 4 Greater Bangkok
Talat Krathum Baen 18 Around Bangkok
Talat Luang 22 Ang Thong Town
Talat Mai 22 Around Ayutthaya
Talat Noi 12 Silom
Talat Nua 73 Phuket Island
Talat Nua 73 Phuket Town
Talat Yot 8 Downtown Bangkok
Talial 79 Far South
Taling Chan 4 Greater Bangkok
Taling Ngam 66 Ko Samui
Taling Sung 16 Central Thailand
Talo Due Raman 79 Far South
Talo Halo 79 Far South
Talo Nibong 79 Far South
Talok Babai 60 Upper Gulf Coasts
Taluk Do 24 Around Nakhon Sawan
Taluk Hin 17 Central Thailand
Talung 22 Around Ayutthaya
Talupan 79 Far South
Tamayung 79 Far South
Tambon Chang Khlan
    37 Central Chiang Mai
Tambon Chang Moi 37 Central Chiang Mai
Tambon Chet Yot 36 Central Chiang Mai
Tambon Chiang Mai 36 Central Chiang Mai
Tambon Haiya 36 Central Chiang Mai
Tambon Nong Pa Krang
    37 Central Chiang Mai
Tambon Phra Sing 36 Central Chiang Mai
Tambon Si Phum 36 Central Chiang Mai
Tambon Suan Dok 36 Central Chiang Mai
Tambon Tha Sala 37 Central Chiang Mai
Tambon Wat Ket 37 Central Chiang Mai
Tammalang 78 Far South
Tamnak 35 Around Chiang Mai
Tamot 78 Far South
Tan Sum 49 Northeastern Thailand
Tan Yong Na Ko 79 Far South
Tanah Merah 79 Far South
Taninthari 60 Upper Gulf Coasts
Tanyong Po 78 Far South
Tao Bo 48 Northeastern Thailand
Tao Pun 18 Around Bangkok
Tao Than 71 Phuket Island
Taphaen 78 Far South
Taphan Hin 17 Central Thailand
Tapo 60 Upper Gulf Coasts
Tapon 28 Southeastern Thailand
Tapoyo 79 Far South
Tase 79 Far South
Taubye 60 Upper Gulf Coasts
Taungzin 60 Upper Gulf Coasts
Tha 35 Around Chiang Mai
Tha Bo 48 Northeastern Thailand
Tha Bon 78 Far South

Tha Chalom 21 Samut Sakhon Town
Tha Champa 49 Northeastern Thailand
Tha Chamuang 64 Isthmus of Kra
Tha Chana 60 Upper Gulf Coasts
Tha Chang 22 Around Ayutthaya
Tha Chao Ngai 71 Phuket Province
Tha Charoen 41 Chiang Rai Province
Tha Chat Chai 64 Isthmus of Kra
Tha Chi 64 Isthmus of Kra
Tha Chin 21 Samut Sakhon Town
Tha Chumpon 18 Around Bangkok
Tha Daeng 17 Central Thailand
Tha Din Daeng 22 Around Ayutthaya
Tha Dua 35 Around Chiang Mai
Tha Duea 33 Chiang Mai,
    Mae Hong Son & Lamphun Provinces
Tha Faek 43 Lampang, Nan,
    Phrae, Uttaradit Provinces
Tha Hin 23 Lopburi Town
Tha It 43 Uttaradit Town
Tha Kam Cham 79 Far South
Tha Kasem 17 Central Thailand
Tha Khae 22 Around Ayutthaya
Tha Khaek 70 Phuket Province
Tha Kham 18 Around Bangkok
Tha Khan Tho 48 Northeastern Thailand
Tha Khanun 71 Phuket Province
Tha Kha-nun 26 Kanchanaburi Province
Tha Khlaeng 73 Phuket Town
Tha Khoi 78 Far South
Tha Khrai 35 Around Chiang Mai
Tha Khuan 73 Phuket Island
Tha Khum Ngoen 33 Chiang Mai, Mae
Hong Son & Lamphun Provinces
Tha Ko 33 Chiang Mai,
    Mae Hong Son & Lamphun Provinces
Tha Krachai 60 Upper Gulf Coasts
Tha Kradan 26 Kanchanaburi Province
Tha Kwian 35 Around Chiang Mai
Tha Lan 28 Southeastern Thailand
Tha Lao 60 Upper Gulf Coasts
Tha Lat 17 Central Thailand
Tha Len 71 Phuket Province
Tha Luk 35 Around Chiang Mai
Tha Mai 18 Around Bangkok
Tha Mai I 35 Around Chiang Mai
Tha Maka 60 Upper Gulf Coasts
Tha Maphrao 72 Phuket Island
Tha Muang 18 Around Bangkok
Tha Nam 79 Far South
Tha Nam Oi 24 Around Nakhon Sawan
Tha Nang Nom 79 Far South
Tha Ngiu 64 Isthmus of Kra
Tha Nod 78 Far South
Tha Nuea 33 Chiang Mai,
    Mae Hong Son & Lamphun Provinces
Tha Nun 70 Phuket Province
Tha Pha Pum 33 Chiang Mai,
    Mae Hong Son & Lamphun Provinces
Tha Phae 78 Far South
Tha Phlap 19 Around Bangkok
Tha Pho 78 Far South
Tha Phraya 18 Around Bangkok
Tha Phru 71 Phuket Province
Tha Pradu 30 Rayong Town
Tha Prat 48 Northeastern Thailand
Tha Rae 49 Northeastern Thailand
Tha Raeng 5 Greater Bangkok
Tha Rai 71 Phuket Province
Tha Rap 61 Phetchaburi (Phetburi) Town
Tha Rua 73 Phuket Island
Tha Ruea 18 Around Bangkok
Tha Sa-an 19 Around Bangkok
Tha Sae 60 Upper Gulf Coasts
Tha Sai 4 Greater Bangkok
Tha Sak 72 Phuket Island
Tha Sala 34 Around Chiang Mai
Tha Sano 78 Far South
Tha Sao 18 Around Bangkok
Tha Sila 48 Northeastern Thailand
Tha So 70 Phuket Province
Tha Som 28 Southeastern Thailand
Tha Song Yang 33 Chiang Mai,
    Mae Hong Son & Lamphun Provinces
Tha Ta Khro 18 Around Bangkok
Tha Ta Pao 63 Chumphon Town
Tha Taeng 70 Phuket Province
Tha Takiap 28 Southeastern Thailand
Tha Tako 32 Northern Thailand
Tha Talat 18 Around Bangkok
Tha Thewawong 29 Ko Si Chang
Tha Thong 79 Far South
Tha Thonglang 19 Around Bangkok
Tha Thuk Khwai 78 Far South
Tha Thung Luang 33 Chiang Mai,
    Mae Hong Son & Lamphun Provinces
Tha Ton 40 Chiang Rai Province
Tha Ton Kwao 35 Around Chiang Mai
Tha Tum 48 Northeastern Thailand

Tha Uthen 49 Northeastern Thailand
Tha Wa Su Kri 23 Ayutthaya Town
Tha Wang 65 Nakhon Si Thammarat Town
Tha Wang Mo Kaeng 71 Phuket Province
Tha Wang Pha 41 Chiang Rai Province
Tha Wang Phrao 33 Chiang Mai,
    Mae Hong Son & Lamphun Provinces
Tha Wang Tal 35 Around Chiang Mai
Tha Wasukri 22 Around Ayutthaya
Tha Wung 22 Around Ayutthaya
Tha Yai 71 Phuket Province
Tha Yang 60 Upper Gulf Coasts
Tha Yu 64 Isthmus of Kra
Thabawleikkyi 60 Upper Gulf Coasts
Thaen Kaeo 64 Isthmus of Kra
Thai Ban Mai 19 Around Bangkok
Thai Charoen 50 Around Phanom Rung
Thai Clana Suk 33 Chiang Mai,
    Mae Hong Son & Lamphun Provinces
Thai Hat 18 Around Bangkok
Thai Ko 19 Around Bangkok
Thai Muang 70 Phuket Province
Thai Talat 22 Around Ayutthaya
Thai U Dom 28 Southeastern Thailand
Thalang 64 Isthmus of Kra
Thalat Khae 48 Northeastern Thailand
Thalat Kruat 22 Around Ayutthaya
Thalat Luang 22 Around Ayutthaya
Thale Chup Son 23 Lopburi Town
Thale Noi 78 Far South
Tham Chalong 43 Lampang, Nan,
    Phrae, Uttaradit Provinces
Tham Phannara 64 Isthmus of Kra
Tham Sing 60 Upper Gulf Coasts
Tham Sua Nai 71 Phuket Province
Tham Thalu 79 Far South
Tham Waram 64 Isthmus of Kra
Thammarat 60 Upper Gulf Coasts
Thamniap 64 Isthmus of Kra
Thamsen 18 Around Bangkok
Thamyin 60 Upper Gulf Coasts
Than Bok Khorani 71 Phuket Province
Than Thong 33 Chiang Mai,
    Mae Hong Son & Lamphun Provinces
Than To 79 Far South
Thang Klang 22 Around Ayutthaya
Thang Phra 22 Around Ayutthaya
Thang Sai 71 Phuket Province
Thang Thanon 70 Phuket Province
Thani 44 New Sukhothai
Thankhiri 79 Far South
Thanon 79 Far South
Thanon Hak 50 Around Phanom Rung
Thanon Khat 18 Around Bangkok
Thanon Phetchabury
    9 Downtown Bangkok
Thanon Yai 22 Around Ayutthaya
Thanya Buri 19 Around Bangkok
Thao Ngoi 49 Northeastern Thailand
Thao Suranari Museum 50
    Nakhon Ratchasima City
Thao Suranari Monument 50
    Nakhon Ratchasima City
Thap Chang 79 Far South
Thap Khaek 71 Phuket Province
Thap Khlo 48 Northeastern Thailand
Thap Li 60 Upper Gulf Coasts
Thap Luang 18 Around Bangkok
Thap Phueng 33 Chiang Mai,
    Mae Hong Son & Lamphun Provinces
Thap Put 64 Isthmus of Kra
Thap Sai 28 Southeastern Thailand
Thap Sakae 60 Upper Gulf Coasts
Thap Salao 16 Central Thailand
Thap Than 24 Around Nakhon Sawan
Thap Yao 5 Greater Bangkok
That Phanom 49 Northeastern Thailand
That Thong 17 Central Thailand
Thawatchaburi 48 Northeastern Thailand
Thawi Mit 11 Lumphini
Thawi Watthana 4 Greater Bangkok
Thawon 50 Around Phanom Rung
The Luang 48 Northeastern Thailand
The Pha Rak 48 Northeastern Thailand
Theinkun 60 Upper Gulf Coasts
Thep Nimit 28 Southeastern Thailand
Thep Sadet 33 Chiang Mai,
    Mae Hong Son & Lamphun Provinces
Thep Sathit 48 Northeastern Thailand
Thepha 79 Far South
Thepha Sathani 79 Far South
Thepharak 19 Around Bangkok
Thepharam 35 Around Chiang Mai
Thepphamonkhon 18 Around Bangkok
Therawat 22 Around Ayutthaya
Thetke 60 Upper Gulf Coasts
Thi Ta Ro 16 Central Thailand
Thiang Thae 24 Around Nakhon Sawan
Tho Sung 72 Phuket Island

INDEX

Thoen Buri 33 Chiang Mai,
  Mae Hong Son & Lamphun Provinces
Thon Samrong 78 Far South
Thonburi 6 Central Bangkok
Thong Chai 60 Upper Gulf Coasts
Thong Fai 34 Around Chiang Mai
Thong Krut 66 Ko Samui
Thong Lang 71 Phuket Province
Thong Nai Pan 64 Isthmus of Kra
Thong Sala 60 Upper Gulf Coasts
Thong Thai 71 Phuket Province
Thongsala 68 Ko Pha-Ngan
Thung 35 Around Chiang Mai
Thung Bu Lang 78 Far South
Thung Bua 18 Around Bangkok
Thung Do 34 Around Chiang Mai
Thung Don 71 Phuket Province
Thung Faek 16 Central Thailand
Thung Fon 48 Northeastern Thailand
Thung Hok Fa 35 Around Chiang Mai
Thung Hong 43 Lampang,
  Nan, Phrae, Uttaradit Provinces
Thung Hua Chang 35 Around Chiang Mai
Thung Kaniang Taek 73 Phuket Island
Thung Kha 72 Phuket Island
Thung Khai 64 Isthmus of Kra
Thung Khi Sua 35 Around Chiang Mai
Thung Khlet 60 Upper Gulf Coasts
Thung Khli 24 Around Nakhon Sawan
Thung Khok 18 Around Bangkok
Thung Khru 4 Greater Bangkok
Thung Khuang 16 Central Thailand
Thung Khung Nang 78 Far South
Thung Khwai Kin
  28 Southeastern Thailand
Thung Khwang 18 Around Bangkok
Thung Klua 60 Upper Gulf Coasts
Thung Ko Yuan 78 Far South
Thung Kong 34 Around Chiang Mai
Thung Krathin 16 Central Thailand
Thung Kwao 33 Chiang Mai,
  Mae Hong Son & Lamphun Provinces
Thung Laeng 33 Chiang Mai,
  Mae Hong Son & Lamphun Provinces
Thung Luang 33 Chiang Mai,
  Mae Hong Son & Lamphun Provinces
Thung Luk Nok 18 Around Bangkok
Thung Maha Mek 13 Silom
Thung Mamao 60 Upper Gulf Coasts
Thung Manu 35 Around Chiang Mai
Thung Maphrao 64 Isthmus of Kra
Thung Mun Noi 35 Around Chiang Mai
Thung Nang Laeng 34 Around Chiang Mai
Thung Nao 43 Lampang, Nan,
  Phrae, Uttaradit Provinces
Thung Nari 78 Far South
Thung Ngam 33 Chiang Mai,
  Mae Hong Son & Lamphun Provinces
Thung Ngiu Tok 79 Far South
Thung Nui 78 Far South
Thung Pa Ha 34 Around Chiang Mai
Thung Pa Haew 34 Around Chiang Mai
Thung Pa Kha 35 Around Chiang Mai
Thung Pa Muang 34 Around Chiang Mai
Thung Pa Tong 34 Around Chiang Mai
Thung Pala 79 Far South
Thung Phao Nua 79 Far South
Thung Phaya Thai 10 Lumphini
Thung Phlap 60 Upper Gulf Coasts
Thung Pho 24 Around Nakhon Sawan
Thung Phraya 28 Southeastern Thailand
Thung Phueng 33 Chiang Mai,
  Mae Hong Son & Lamphun Provinces
Thung Phung 24 Around Nakhon Sawan
Thung Pi 33 Chiang Mai,
  Mae Hong Son & Lamphun Provinces
Thung Pong 34 Around Chiang Mai
Thung Prapat 17 Central Thailand
Thung Prong 48 Northeastern Thailand
Thung Raya 64 Isthmus of Kra
Thung Ri 16 Central Thailand
Thung Rin 78 Far South
Thung Rok Fa 35 Around Chiang Mai
Thung Ruang Tong 33 Chiang Mai,
  Mae Hong Son & Lamphun Provinces
Thung Sadao 28 Southeastern Thailand
Thung Sang Thong 50
  Around Phanom Rung
Thung Si Siat 60 Upper Gulf Coasts
Thung Si Udom 49 Northeastern Thailand
Thung Song 64 Isthmus of Kra
Thung Song Hong 5 Greater Bangkok
Thung Sukhla 28 Southeastern Thailand
Thung Tako 60 Upper Gulf Coasts
Thung Tam Sao 78 Far South
Thung Thong 18 Around Bangkok
Thung Tom 35 Around Chiang Mai
Thung Wa 70 Phuket Province
Thung Waen 34 Around Chiang Mai

Thung Wet 64 Isthmus of Kra
Thung Yai 78 Far South
Thung Yai Chi 28 Southeastern Thailand
Thung Yang Daeng 79 Far South
Thung Yao 35 Around Chiang Mai
Thung Yao Pa Taeng
  35 Around Chiang Mai
Ti Te 73 Phuket Island
Tin Doi 34 Around Chiang Mai
Tin Dong 34 Around Chiang Mai
Tin Khao 72 Phuket Island
Ting Rai 71 Phuket Province
To Lang 79 Far South
To Mo 79 Far South
To Non 79 Far South
To Yi 71 Phuket Province
Todeng 79 Far South
Tok Wat 72 Phuket Island
Ton Chan 35 Around Chiang Mai
Ton Chok 35 Around Chiang Mai
Ton Chot 78 Far South
Ton Din Nai 71 Phuket Province
Ton Du 35 Around Chiang Mai
Ton Haen 35 Around Chiang Mai
Ton Hai 35 Around Chiang Mai
Ton Hiaw 35 Around Chiang Mai
Ton Huat 34 Around Chiang Mai
Ton Kaeo 35 Around Chiang Mai
Ton Mamuang 73 Phuket Island
Ton Muang 72 Phuket Island
Ton Pho 22 Singburi Town
Ton Phuk 35 Around Chiang Mai
Ton Pin 35 Around Chiang Mai
Ton Phung 35 Around Chiang Mai
Ton Sae 70 Phuket Province
Ton Tan 18 Around Bangkok
Ton Yang 35 Around Chiang Mai
Ton Yang Luang 35 Around Chiang Mai
Tonbyawgyi 60 Upper Gulf Coasts
Tong Chai Nua 17 Central Thailand
Tong Kai 34 Around Chiang Mai
Tong Khaen 48 Northeastern Thailand
Tong Pha Phum 26 Kanchanaburi Province
Tong Yang 66 Ko Samui
Toong Kong Moo
  38 Around Mae Hong Son
Tourakom 48 Northeastern Thailand
Trai Trang 72 Phuket Island
Trakan Phut Phon
  49 Northeastern Thailand
Trang 79 Far South
Trat 31 Trat Town
Trok Sakae 17 Central Thailand
Tu Khun 72 Phuket Island
Tum Phlo 73 Phuket Island
Tun Pin 35 Around Chiang Mai
Tung Luang 18 Around Bangkok
Tung Samo 18 Around Bangkok
Tung Thong 26 Kanchanaburi Province
U Lok Si Mun 18 Around Bangkok
U Mong 35 Around Chiang Mai
U Taphao 24 Around Nakhon Sawan
U Thai Thong 48 Northeastern Thailand
U Thong 16 Central Thailand
Uan 43 Lampang, Nan, Phrae,
  Uttaradit Provinces
Ubon Ratchathani
  49 Northeastern Thailand
Ubonrat 48 Northeastern Thailand
Udom 48 Northeastern Thailand
Udom Thanya 24 Around Nakhon Sawan
Udon Thani 48 Northeastern Thailand
Um Phang 46 Um Phang
Uthai 22 Around Ayutthaya
U-Thai 48 Northeastern Thailand
Uthai Thani 25 Uthai Thani Town
Uttaradit 43 Uttaradit Town
Vadhana 15 Sukhumvit
Vieng Thong 49 Northeastern Thailand
Wa 32 Northern Thailand
Wa Na Mon 33 Chiang Mai,
  Mae Hong Son & Lamphun Provinces
Wa Tabaek 17 Central Thailand
Wa Wi 33 Chiang Mai,
  Mae Hong Son & Lamphun Provinces
Waeng 79 Far South
Waeng Noi 48 Northeastern Thailand
Waeng Yai 48 Northeastern Thailand
Wai Nieo 18 Around Bangkok
Waiang Nuea 33 Chiang Mai,
  Mae Hong Son & Lamphun Provinces
Wan Dao 18 Around Bangkok
Wan Din 43 Lampang, Nan, Phrae,
  Uttaradit Provinces
Wan Hsenlong 33 Chiang Mai,
  Mae Hong Son & Lamphun Provinces
Wan Hsinhkek 41 Chiang Rai Province
Wan Makhunglong 41 Chiang Rai Province
Wan Takhian 17 Central Thailand

Wan Yai 49 Northeastern Thailand
Wang Chan 33 Chiang Mai,
  Mae Hong Son & Lamphun Provinces
Wang Charoen 78 Far South
Wang Charoen Rat 78 Far South
Wang Chin 33 Chiang Mai,
  Mae Hong Son & Lamphun Provinces
Wang Chula 19 Around Bangkok
Wang Daeng 22 Around Ayutthaya
Wang Din 34 Around Chiang Mai
Wang Dong 34 Around Chiang Mai
Wang Hin 48 Northeastern Thailand
Wang Hin Ngon 16 Central Thailand
Wang Khanai 18 Around Bangkok
Wang Khlong Klang 71 Phuket Province
Wang Luang 42 Lampang, Nan,
  Phrae, Uttaradit Provinces
Wang Lung 33 Chiang Mai,
  Mae Hong Son & Lamphun Provinces
Wang Ma 24 Around Nakhon Sawan
Wang Mahakon 24 Around Nakhon Sawan
Wang Mai 9 Downtown Bangkok
Wang Man 24 Around Nakhon Sawan
Wang Manao 18 Around Bangkok
Wang Maprang 78 Far South
Wang Muang 48 Northeastern Thailand
Wang Mun 35 Around Chiang Mai
Wang Mut 48 Northeastern Thailand
Wang Na 24 Around Nakhon Sawan
Wang Nam Khiao 18 Around Bangkok
Wang Noi 19 Around Bangkok
Wang Nuea 33 Chiang Mai,
  Mae Hong Son & Lamphun Provinces
Wang Pha 78 Far South
Wang Phang 33 Chiang Mai,
  Mae Hong Son & Lamphun Provinces
Wang Phatthana 18 Around Bangkok
Wang Pong 35 Around Chiang Mai
Wang Prachan 78 Far South
Wang Rong 48 Northeastern Thailand
Wang Sai 79 Far South
Wang Sala 18 Around Bangkok
Wang Sam Mo 48 Northeastern Thailand
Wang San 16 Central Thailand
Wang Saphung 48 Northeastern Thailand
Wang Si Rat 24 Around Nakhon Sawan
Wang Sonbun 17 Central Thailand
Wang Tai 33 Chiang Mai,
  Mae Hong Son & Lamphun Provinces
Wang Takhian 28 Southeastern Thailand
Wang Takhrai 17 Central Thailand
Wang Tako 60 Upper Gulf Coasts
Wang Tha Chang
  28 Southeastern Thailand
Wang Than 35 Around Chiang Mai
Wang Thang 70 Phuket Province
Wang Thong 33 Chiang Mai,
  Mae Hong Son & Lamphun Provinces
Wang Thong Lang 7 Central Bangkok
Wang Tong 78 Far South
Wang Wiset 64 Isthmus of Kra
Wang Yai 79 Far South
Wang Yang 49 Northeastern Thailand
Wang Yao 26 Kanchanaburi Province
Wanon Niwat 48 Northeastern Thailand
Wapi Pathuai 48 Northeastern Thailand
Warin Chamrap 49 Northeastern Thailand
Waritchaphum 48 Northeastern Thailand
Wat Arun 8 Downtown Bangkok
Wat Bot 18 Around Bangkok
Wat Chan 45 Phitsanulok Town
Wat Lamut 18 Around Bangkok
Wat Luang 19 Around Bangkok
Wat Mai 72 Phuket Island
Wat Phleng 18 Around Bangkok
Wat Pradu 18 Around Bangkok
Wat Sam Praya 8 Downtown Bangkok
Wat Sing 24 Around Nakhon Sawan
Wat Son 78 Far South
Wat Taku 22 Around Ayutthaya
Wat Thep Sirin 9 Downtown Bangkok
Wat Thewadaram 64 Isthmus of Kra
Wat Tum 22 Around Ayutthaya
Wat Yang Ngam 18 Around Bangkok
Watak 33 Chiang Mai,
  Mae Hong Son & Lamphun Provinces
Watthana Nakhon 17 Central Thailand
Wiang 33 Chiang Mai,
  Mae Hong Son & Lamphun Provinces
Wiang Haeng 33 Chiang Mai,
  Mae Hong Son & Lamphun Provinces
Wiang Mok 33 Chiang Mai,
  Mae Hong Son & Lamphun Provinces
Wiang Nuea 42 Lampang Town
Wiang Pa Pao 33 Chiang Mai,
  Mae Hong Son & Lamphun Provinces
Wiang Sa 64 Isthmus of Kra
Wiang Ta 42 Lampang, Nan,
  Phrae, Uttaradit Provinces

Wichian Buri 48 Northeastern Thailand
Wihan Daeng 19 Around Bangkok
Wiphawadi 60 Upper Gulf Coasts
Wisai Nuea 60 Upper Gulf Coasts
Wo Kaeo 33 Chiang Mai,
  Mae Hong Son & Lamphun Provinces
Xanakham 48 Northeastern Thailand
Xebang-Nouan 49 Northeastern Thailand
Xieng Hon 41 Chiang Rai Province
Xonbuli 49 Northeastern Thailand
Ya Mi 71 Phuket Province
Ya Pai 20K 35 Around Chiang Mai
Ya Prasit 35 Around Chiang Mai
Ya Yai 73 Rawai
Yaha 79 Far South
Yai Cha 18 Around Bangkok
Yai Yam Wattana 50 Around Phanom Rung
Yala 79 Far South
Yan Khian 64 Isthmus of Kra
Yan Matsi 24 Around Nakhon Sawan
Yan Nawa 12 Silom
Yan Ri 33 Chiang Mai,
  Mae Hong Son & Lamphun Provinces
Yan Saba 73 Phuket Island
Yan Sue 22 Ang Thong Town
Yan Ta Khao 64 Isthmus of Kra
Yang Chum Noi 49 Northeastern Thailand
Yang Hom 41 Chiang Rai Province
Yang Huay Yao 34 Around Chiang Mai
Yang Kathung 17 Central Thailand
Yang Kham 48 Northeastern Thailand
Yang Lak Taeng 33 Chiang Mai,
  Mae Hong Son & Lamphun Provinces
Yang Lat 17 Central Thailand
Yang Mae Lan Kham
  34 Around Chiang Mai
Yang Mae Lan Ngoen
  34 Around Chiang Mai
Yang Moen 33 Chiang Mai,
  Mae Hong Son & Lamphun Provinces
Yang Muang 18 Around Bangkok
Yang Non 24 Around Nakhon Sawan
Yang Phra That 35 Around Chiang Mai
Yang Piang 33 Chiang Mai,
  Mae Hong Son & Lamphun Provinces
Yang Pu La 34 Around Chiang Mai
Yang Puan 35 Around Chiang Mai
Yang Sai 22 Around Ayutthaya
Yang Si Surat 48 Northeastern Thailand
Yang Talat 48 Northeastern Thailand
Yang Tan 43 Lampang, Nan, Phrae,
  Uttaradit Provinces
Yao 64 Isthmus of Kra
Yaong 48 Northeastern Thailand
Yap Hua na 43 Lampang, Nan, Phrae,
  Uttaradit Provinces
Yarang 79 Far South
Yaring 79 Far South
Yasothon 49 Northeastern Thailand
Yata 79 Far South
Yedwingyaung 60 Upper Gulf Coasts
Yilon 22 Around Ayutthaya
Yingo 79 Far South
Yisan 18 Around Bangkok
Yokkrabat 33 Chiang Mai,
  Mae Hong Son & Lamphun Provinces
Yong Sata 78 Far South
Yot Sunthon 14 Sukhumvit
Yothaka 19 Around Bangkok
Yu Charoen 11 Lumphini
Yuan 41 Chiang Rai Province
Yun 72 Phuket Island
Yung Thalai 18 Around Bangkok
Yupo 79 Far South
Zalun 60 Upper Gulf Coasts
Zalut 60 Upper Gulf Coasts
Zinchaung 60 Upper Gulf Coasts

Places of Interest & Nature Reserves

Airport of Division 9
  26 Kanchanaburi Province
Allied War Cemetery
  27 Kanchanaburi Town
An Pao Beach 71 Phuket Province
Ananta Samakhom Throne Hall
  9 Downtown Bangkok
Ancient City (Muang Boran)
  19 Around Bangkok
Ancient Palace 48 Northeastern Thailand
Anemone Reef Diving 71 Phuket Province
Ang Thon Marine National Park
  64 Around Samui
Ang Thong National Marine Park
  64 Isthmus of Kra
Anusarn Night Market
  37 Central Chiang Mai

nusawari Chai Samoraphum
  (Victory Monument) 10 Lumphini
o Cho Beach 28 Ko Samet
o Karang Beach 28 Ko Samet
o Kham Beach 28 Ko Samet
o Kiew Na Nai Beach 28 Ko Samet
o Kiu Na Nok Beach 28 Ko Samet
o Leuk Point Diving 69 Ko Tao
o Mae Ramphueng Beach
  60 Upper Gulf Coasts
o Molae 79 Tarutao Islands
o Nang Thara Beach 76 Ao Nang Beach
o Nuan Beach 28 Ko Samet
o Pa Cha Beach 28 Ko Samet
o Taloh Wao 79 Tarutao Islands
o Thian Beach 28 Ko Samet
o Toh Koh Beach 76 Ko Phi Phi Don
o Wai Beach 28 Ko Samet
o Wong Deuan Beach 28 Ko Samet
quarium 54 Sakon Nakhon Town
rchaeological Museum
  44 Satchanalai-Chaliang National Park
rmy Airport 50 Nakhon Ratchasima City
rt & Culture University Museum
  56 Khon Kaen Town
runothai Beach 64 Isthmus of Kra
yutthaya Elephant Palace and
  Elephant Kraal 23 Ayutthaya Town
yutthaya Planetarium 23 Ayutthaya Town
.N. Farm 32 Northern Thailand
aan Chang Elephant Trekking
  66 Ko Samui
aan Sao Nak 42 Lampang Town
aan Tai Elephant Trekking
  68 Ko Pha-Ngan
an Chiang 48 Northeastern Thailand
an Phu 48 Northeastern Thailand
an Tawai 35 Around Chiang Mai
ang Bao Delight 31 Ko Chang
ang Ben Beach 64 Isthmus of Kra
ang Niang Beach 70 Khao Lak
ang Po Beach 66 Ko Samui
ang Rak Beach 66 Ko Samui
ang Saen Beach 60 Upper Gulf Coasts
ang Sak Beach 70 Khao Lak
ang Tao Beach 74 Bang Tao Beach
ang Thao Beach 64 Isthmus of Kra
angkok Butterfly Garden and Insectarium
  6 Central Bangkok
angkok Folk Museum 13 Silom
angkok Immigration Office 13 Silom
angkok Information Center
  8 Downtown Bangkok
anteay Chhmar Protected Landscape 48
  ortheastern Thailand
at Cave 27 Sai Yok National Park
eacon Beach Diving
  70 Similan National Park
eacon Point Diving
  70 Similan National Park
eacon Reef Diving
  70 Similan National Park
ig Buddha Beach 66 Ko Samui
ig Golden Buddha 29 Pattaya
ird Garden 66 Ko Samui
o Lek Nam Phi 45 Pitsanulok,
  Sukhothai & Phichit Provinces
o Phut Beach 67 Mae Nam
o Sang Village 35 Around Chiang Mai
ok Krai Falls 64 Isthmus of Kra
oriphat Falls 64 Isthmus of Kra
orsan Village 40 Chiang Rai Province
ottle Art Museum 29 Pattaya
ottle Beach 68 Ko Pha-Ngan
oulder City Diving
  70 Similan National Park
oxing Stadium 40 Chiang Rai Town
reakfast Bend Diving
  70 Similan National Park
uddha Casting Foundry & Garden Birds
  of Thailand 45 Phichit Town
uddha Statue 66 Ko Samui
udha Rock Diving 69 Ko Tao
udo Su Ngai Padi, Forest & Waterfall
  79 Far South
udo-Sungai Padi National Park
  79 Far South
uffalo Fighting Stadium 67 Mae Nam
ujang Valley Archaeological Site
  78 Far South
ung Ta Lua Monument
  50 Nakhon Ratchasima City
ungboraped 24 Around Nakhon Sawan
ungy Jump 67 Chaweng
utterfly Garden 66 Ko Samui
ape Grachom Fai Diving 69 Ko Tao
at and Rat Sculpture 81 Songkhla Town
aves 69 Ko Tao
ha-am Beach 60 Upper Gulf Coasts

Chabad House of Chiang Mai
  37 Central Chiang Mai
Chae Son Waterfall 33 Chiang Mai,
  Mae Hong Son & Lamphun Provinces
Chai Nat Muni National Museum
  24 Around Nakhon Sawan
Chai Thale Khao Pilai 70 Phuket Province
Chakrapong Cave 29 Ko Si Chang
Chalalai Beach 79 Far South
Chalathat Beach 81 Songkhla Town
Chalee Mongkol At Royal Palace
  20 Nakhon Pathom Town
Chaloem Rattanakosin Sport Stadium
  77 Krabi Town
Champa Thong Waterfall 33 Chiang Mai,
  Mae Hong Son & Lamphun Provinces
Chang Lang Beach 78 Far South
Chantharakasem National Museum
  23 Ayutthaya Town
Chao Fah Park 77 Krabi Town
Chao Lay Cave 71 Phuket Province
Chao Phra Falls 78 Far South
Chao Phraya Suraya Lua Chai Monument
  42 Lampang Town
Chao Phraya Wichayen 23 Lopburi Town
Chao Sam Phraya National Museum
  23 Ayutthaya Town
Chao Samran Beach 60 Upper Gulf Coasts
Chat Trakan Waterfall
  32 Northern Thailand
Chaweng Beach 67 Chaweng
Chaweng North Beach 67 Chaweng
Che Bilang Pier 78 Far South
Chedi Daeng
  61 Phetchaburi (Phetburi) Town
Chedi Kho Waterfall
  46 Kamphaeng Phet & Tak Provinces
Chiang Dao Cave & Elephant Show
  40 Chiang Rai Province
Chiang Mai Airport 36 Central Chiang Mai
Chiang Mai Arts & Cultural Center
  36 Central Chiang Mai
Chiang Mai National Museum
  36 Central Chiang Mai
Chiang Mai Stadium 36 Central Chiang Mai
Chiang Mai University
  35 Around Chiang Mai
Chiang Mai University Art Museum
  36 Central Chiang Mai
Chiang Mai Zoo, Aquarium
  35 Around Chiang Mai
Chiang Saen National Museum
  40 Chiang Saen
Chinese Cultural Area 81 Songkhla Town
Chitralada Royal Palace
  9 Downtown Bangkok
Chong Banphot Falls 78 Far South
Christmas Point Diving
  70 Similan National Park
Chulaphon Submarine Park Conservation
  Center & Lodge 64 Isthmus of Kra
Chumphon Pinnacle Diving
  64 Around Samui
Chumsaeng Goddess Shrine
  24 Around Nakhon Sawan
Chun Saeng Falls 64 Isthmus of Kra
Cinnamon Bay Diving
  70 Similan National Park
City Pillar Shine 41 Phayao Town
City Pillar Shrine 59 Udon Thani Town
City Wall & The North Gate
  65 Nakhon Si Thammarat Town
City Walls 43 Lampang, Nan,
  Phrae, Uttaradit Provinces
Cliff Gate 33 Chiang Mai,
  Mae Hong Son & Lamphun Provinces
Clock Tower
  31 Chanthaburi (Chanburi) Town
Clocktower 77 Trang Town
Coconut Home Beach 71 Phuket Province
Coine & Royal Decorations Museums
  8 Downtown Bangkok
Co-op 64 Isthmus of Kra
Coral Garden Diving
  70 Similan National Park
Coral Reef 64 Isthmus of Kra
Corrections Museum
  8 Downtown Bangkok
Crocodile Cave 79 Tarutao Islands
Crocodile Farm 66 Ko Samui
Crocodile World & Sea Aquarium
  73 Phuket Town
Daen Maha Mongkol Meditation Center
  26 Kanchanaburi Province
Daeng Waterfall 68 Ko Pha-Ngan
Dai Chong Thong Waterfall
  26 Kanchanaburi Province
Dao Wadeung Cave
  26 Kanchanaburi Province

Deep Six Diving 70 Similan National Park
Democracy Monument
  8 Downtown Bangkok
Den Ha Crematorium 40 Chiang Rai Town
Diamond Cave 76 Railay
Doi Ang Khang 33 Chiang Mai,
  Mae Hong Son & Lamphun Provinces
Doi Inthanon National Park 33 Chiang Mai,
  Mae Hong Son & Lamphun Provinces
Doi Khun Tan 33 Chiang Mai,
  Mae Hong Son & Lamphun Provinces
Doi Luang Chiang Dao 33 Chiang Mai,
  Mae Hong Son & Lamphun Provinces
Doi Pha Hom Pok 33 Chiang Mai,
  Mae Hong Son & Lamphun Provinces
Doi Phak Long National Park 42 Lampang,
  Nan, Phrae, Uttaradit Provinces
Doi Sawan Waterfall 43 Lampang,
  Nan, Phrae, Uttaradit Provinces
Doi Suthep 34 Around Chiang Mai
Doi Suthep Doi Pui National Park
  34 Around Chiang Mai
Don Hoi Lot 18 Around Bangkok
Don Muang Airport 5 Greater Bangkok
Don Port 60 Upper Gulf Coasts
Don Wai Market 18 Around Bangkok
Donald Duck Bay Diving
  70 Similan National Park
Dusit Zoo 9 Downtown Bangkok
East Railay Beach 77 Railay
Elephant Gate 66 Ko Samui
Elephant Head Diving
  70 Similan National Park
Elephant Jungle Trekking 31 Ko Chang
Elephant Training Centre 33 Chiang Mai,
  Mae Hong Son & Lamphun Provinces
Elephant Trekking 76 Ko Lanta
Erawan Cave 48 Northeastern Thailand
Erawan Shrine 10 Lumphini
Erawan Waterfall
  26 Kanchanaburi Province
Eskimo Roll 43 Nan
Family Zoo 66 Ko Samui
Fang Hot Spring 33 Chiang Mai,
  Mae Hong Son & Lamphun Provinces
Fantasy Reef Diving
  70 Similan National Park
Fishing Area 79 Tarutao Islands
Fitness Park 73 Phuket Town
Floating Market 18 Around Bangkok
Floating Markets 6 Central Bangkok
Fountain 59 Udon Thani Town
Freedom Adventures 76 Ko Lanta
Friendship Bridge
  48 Northeastern Thailand
Full Moon Party 68 Hat Rin
Garang Herg Diving 71 Phuket Province
Go-Cart Center 29 Pattaya
Gold Mine 79 Far South
Golden Mermaid Sculpture
  81 Songkhla Town
Golden View 69 Ko Tao
Governor's Mansion Museum
  59 Nong Khai Town
Green Rock Diving 69 Ko Tao
Gubu-Barn Klong Ton Beach 79 Far South
Gunung Jerai 78 Far South
H.M. Kings Project
  26 Kanchanaburi Province
Haad Rin Beach 65 Around Samui
Hala Bala Forest 79 Far South
Half Moon Festival 68 Ko Pha-Ngan
Hall of Railway Heritage
  6 Central Bangkok
Hariphunchai National Museum
  39 Lamphun Town
Hat Ao Khoei 64 Isthmus of Kra
Hat Bai Lan 30 Ko Chang
Hat Chao Mai National Park 78 Far South
Hat Kai Bae 30 Ko Chang
Hat Kai Mook 30 Ko Chang
Hat Khlong Makok 30 Ko Chang
Hat Khlong Nin Beach 76 Ko Lanta
Hat Maharat 78 Far South
Hat Nai Plao Beach 64 Isthmus of Kra
Hat Noppharat Thara Mu Ko Phi Phi
  National Park 64 Isthmus of Kra
Hat Phlai Dam 64 Isthmus of Kra
Hat Phra Ae Beach 76 Ko Lanta
Hat Praphat 64 Isthmus of Kra
Hat Sai Khao 30 Ko Chang
Hat Thai Muang National Park
  70 Phuket Province
Hat Thung Nang Dam 64 Isthmus of Kra
Hat Thung Thaleh Beach 76 Ko Lanta
Hat Wai Chek 31 Ko Chang
Hat Yao 31 Ko Chang
Hellfire Pass 26 Kanchanaburi Province
Heroines Monument 72 Phuket Island

Hew Khwaay Tok 66 Ko Samui
Hideaway Diving 70 Similan National Park
Highway Information Service Center
  64 Isthmus of Kra
Hill Tribe Plaster Puppet Museum
  40 Chiang Rai Town
Hilltribe Museum & Education Center
  40 Chiang Rai Town
Him Ngan Bay Diving 69 Ko Tao
Hin Dat Hot Spring
  26 Kanchanaburi Province
Hin Dot Diving 76 Ko Phi Phi Don
Hin Khom Beach 76 Ko Phi Phi Don
Hin Lad Falls 65 Around Samui
Hin Lad River Stone 66 Ko Samui
Hin Lat Waterfall 66 Ko Samui
Hin Ngam Beach 64 Isthmus of Kra
Hin Rup Ruea Bai 70 Similan National Park
Hin Wong Beach 69 Ko Tao
Hin Wong Pinnacle Diving 69 Ko Tao
Hin Yippon Diving 64 Around Samui
Hin-Ta & Hin-Yai (Grandfather &
  Grandmother Rock) 67 Lamai
Historical Sites 79 Tarutao Islands
Ho Phra Phut Tha Angkirot
  30 Rayong Town
Honeymoon Bay Diving
  70 Similan National Park
Hong Moon Mung Khon KaenCity Museum
  57 Khon Kaen Town
Horseback Riding 66 Ko Samui
Hot Spring 39 Around Mae Hong Son
Hot Springs 33 Chiang Mai,
  Mae Hong Son & Lamphun Provinces
Hua Dong Handicraft 42 Phrae Town
Hua Hin Golf Center 62 Hua Hin
Hua Lamai Beach 67 Lamai
Hua Lin 36 Central Chiang Mai
Huai Mae Sai Waterfall 33 Chiang Mai,
  Mae Hong Son & Lamphun Provinces
Huai To Falls 64 Isthmus of Kra
Huai To Waterfall 71 Phuket Province
Huai Yang Waterfall 60 Upper Gulf Coasts
Huay Kaeo Waterfall
  34 Around Chiang Mai
Huay Mae Khamin Waterfall
  26 Kanchanaburi Province
Humanality Climb 76 Railay
Hutan Lipur Puncak Janing 79 Far South
Island Discovery 68 Ko Pha-Ngan
Island Safari & Elephant Trek 66 Ko Samui
Jamboree 15 Sukhumvit
Jan Som Bay 69 Ko Tao
Jao Pho Phraya Lae Monument
  56 Chaiyaphum Town
Jeath War Museum
  27 Kanchanaburi Town
Jim Thompson's House
  9 Downtown Bangkok
John Suwan Rock 69 Ko Tao
Jomtien Beach 29 Pattaya
June Jeua Beach 69 Ko Tao
June Jeua Beach Diving 69 Ko Tao
Jungle Bungy Jump 72 Phuket Island
Jungle Rafts 26 Kanchanaburi Province
Jutee Beach 73 Phuket Island
Kachong Falls 78 Far South
Kaeng Krachan 60 Upper Gulf Coasts
Kaeng Krung 64 Isthmus of Kra
Kaeng Krung Falls 64 Isthmus of Kra
Kaeng Krung National Park
  60 Upper Gulf Coasts
Kaeng Tana 49 Northeastern Thailand
Kaeo Cave 60 Upper Gulf Coasts
Kalare Night Bazaar 37 Central Chiang Mai
Kalim Beach 75 Patong Beach
Kamala Beach 75 Kamala Beach
Kamphaeng Phet Historical Park
  44 Pitsanulok, Sukhothai &
  Phichit Provinces
Kamphaeng Phet National Museum 47
  Kamphaeng Phet Town
Kamphaeng Phet Regional Museum 47
  Kamphaeng Phet Town
Kang Sopa Waterfall 32 Northern Thailand
Kangsadan (Crescent Moon) Beach
  29 Pattaya
Karon Beach 72 Karon & Kata Beaches
Karon Noi Beach 72 Phuket Island
Kat Rin Kham Night Bazaar
  36 Central Chiang Mai
Kata Beach 64 Isthmus of Kra
Kata Noi Beach 72 Karon & Kata Beaches
Kata Yai Beach 72 Karon & Kata Beaches
Katam 36 Central Chiang Mai
Kathu Waterfall 72 Phuket Island
Kha On Falls 60 Upper Gulf Coasts
Khae Khae Beach 79 Far South
Khanom Beach 64 Isthmus of Kra

Khao Chamao & Khao Wong N. P.
  28 Southeastern Thailand
Khao Chao Mueang View Point
  64 Isthmus of Kra
Khao Chong 78 Far South
Khao Chong Krajok 63
  Prachuap Khiri Khan Town
Khao Hua Lan Forest Park
  64 Isthmus of Kra
Khao Khieo Zoo 60 Upper Gulf Coasts
Khao Kho Royal Palace
  32 Northern Thailand
Khao Kradong Forest Park
  48 Northeastern Thailand
Khao Kriap Cave 64 Isthmus of Kra
Khao Kuoi Cave 71 Phuket Province
Khao Lak Beach 70 Khao Lak
Khao Lak Falls 64 Isthmus of Kra
Khao Lak National Park 70 Khao Lak
Khao Lak-Lam Ru National Park
  64 Isthmus of Kra
Khao Lak-Lam Ru National Park Office
  70 Khao Lak
Khao Luang National Park
  64 Isthmus of Kra
Khao Nam Khang National Park
  79 Far South
Khao Nan National Park
  64 Isthmus of Kra
Khao Pang Waterfall
  26 Kanchanaburi Province
Khao Patthawi 24 Around Nakhon Sawan
Khao Phaeng Ma
  48 Northeastern Thailand
Khao Phang Forest Park 64 Isthmus of Kra
Khao Phanom Benja National Park
  71 Phuket Province
Khao Phra Taew Royal Wildlife
  Forest Preserve 73 Phuket Island
Khao Phra Thaew National Park
  72 Phuket Island
Khao Phra Wihan National Park
  49 Northeastern Thailand
Khao Pra-Bang Kram Wildlife Sanctuary
  64 Isthmus of Kra
Khao Pu - Khao Ya National Park 78
  Far South
Khao Ra Viewpoint 68 Ko Pha-Ngan
Khao Sa Bap National Park
  28 Southeastern Thailand
Khao Sakae Krong 25 Uthai Thani Town
Khao Sakaekrong
  24 Around Nakhon Sawan
Khao Sam Muk 60 Upper Gulf Coasts
Khao Sam Roi Yot 60 Upper Gulf Coasts
Khao Sam Yot 60 Upper Gulf Coasts
Khao Tang Kuan (Monkey Mountain)
  81 Songkhla Town
Khao Tha Phet 64 Isthmus of Kra
Khao Wang 20 Ratchaburi (Ratburi) Town
Khao Yai National Park
  28 Southeastern Thailand
Khe Lang Parks 42 Lampang Town
Khlang Phara Mangrove Forest
  64 Isthmus of Kra
Khlong Chack Beach 71 Phuket Province
Khlong Lan National Park 46
  Kamphaeng Phet & Tak Provinces
Khlong Muang Beach 71 Phuket Province
Khlong Nakha 64 Isthmus of Kra
Khlong Nakha Wildlife Sanctuary
  60 Upper Gulf Coasts
Khlong Non Si Waterfall 31 Ko Chang
Khlong Nueng Waterfall 31 Ko Chang
Khlong Phanom National Park
  64 Isthmus of Kra
Khlong Phlu Waterfall 31 Ko Chang
Khlong Thom Falls 64 Isthmus of Kra
Khlong Tron National Park
  48 Northeastern Thailand
Kho Khot Kra 64 Isthmus of Kra
Khok Khathiam Air Base
  22 Around Ayutthaya
Khom Beach 68 Ko Pha-Ngan
Khon Kaen National Museum
  57 Khon Kaen Town
Khontee Beach 68 Hat Rin
Khorat Zoo 48 Northeastern Thailand
Khu Khak Beach 70 Khao Lak
Khuean Srinakarin
  26 Kanchanaburi Province
Khuean Vachiralongkorn
  26 Kanchanaburi Province
Khun Chae Waterfall 33 Chiang Mai,
  Mae Hong Son & Lamphun Provinces
Khun Kon Waterfall 33 Chiang Mai,
  Mae Hong Son & Lamphun Provinces
Khun Tan Tunnel 33 Chiang Mai,
  Mae Hong Son & Lamphun Provinces

King Cruiser Diving 71 Phuket Province
King Mengrai Monument
  40 Chiang Rai Town
King Narai the Great Monument
  23 Lopburi Town
King Prajadhipok Museum
  9 Downtown Bangkok
King Rama I Monument 51 Buriram Town
King Rama IX Park 73 Phuket Town
King Rama IX Royal Park
  7 Central Bangkok
King Rama V Boulder 69 Ko Tao
King Rama V Monument
  9 Downtown Bangkok
King Rama V the Great Monument
  43 Uttaradit Town
King Ramkhamhaeng Monument
  44 Sukhothai Historical Park
King Taksin Monument 12 Silom
King Vajiravudh Museum
  8 Downtown Bangkok
Klai Kangwon Palace 62 Hua Hin
Kloeng Thaw Waterfall
  26 Sangkhlaburi
Klong Jark Bay Beach 76 Ko Lanta
Klong Khang Beach 76 Ko Lanta
Klri Phet Waterfall 31 Ko Chang
Ko Bida Nai Diving 71 Phuket Province
Ko Bida Nok Diving 71 Phuket Province
Ko Dok Mai Diving 71 Phuket Province
Ko Hah Diving 71 Phuket Province
Ko Kwang Beach 76 Ko Lanta
Ko Lamphu Public Park
  65 Surat Thani Town
Ko Lanta Commanity Museum 76 Ko Lanta
Ko Phetra National Marine Park
  78 Far South
Ko Racha Yai Diving 71 Phuket Province
Ko See Diving 71 Phuket Province
Ko Wao Diving 64 Around Samui
Ko Waterfall 33 Chiang Mai,
  Mae Hong Son & Lamphun Provinces
Ko Yamasan Diving 71 Phuket Province
Kok Chong Kata Safari
  72 Karon & Kata Beaches
Kolae Boatmaking Village 79 Far South
Kong Nui 68 Ko Pha-Ngan
Kong Yai 68 Ko Pha-Ngan
Korat Royal Thai Air Force
  49 Greater Nakhon Ratchasima
Kosa Bowl 57 Khon Kaen Town
Kroeng Krawia Waterfall
  26 Kanchanaburi Province
Kruad Beach 68 Ko Pha-Ngan
Krung Ching Falls 64 Isthmus of Kra
Ku Huang 36 Central Chiang Mai
Kuala Kedah Fort 78 Far South
Kudi Dao Priest's Camp Site
  61 Phetchaburi (Phetburi) Town
Kui Buri National Park
  60 Upper Gulf Coasts
Kulen Prum Tep Wildlife Sanctuary
  49 Northeastern Thailand
La Po Ret 64 Isthmus of Kra
La Po Waterfall 79 Tarutao Islands
Laem Ka Beach 73 Rawai
Laem Khwai Rap Wildlife Sanctuary
  78 Far South
Laem Phrom Thep 64 Isthmus of Kra
Laem Rua Taek 28 Ko Samet
Laem Singh Beach 74 Kamala Beach
Laem Son National Park 64 Isthmus of Kra
Laem Thian Pinnacle Diving 69 Ko Tao
Laem Trong Beach 76 Ko Phi Phi Don
Laem Yung Cave 71 Phuket Province
Laeng Tham Sai Thai 71 Phuket Province
Lak Meuang 8 Downtown Bangkok
Lam Plok Falls 78 Far South
Lamai Beach 67 Ko Samui
Lampang Airport 42 Lampang Town
Lampang Lanna Museum
  42 Lampang Town
Lampao 48 Northeastern Thailand
Lampi Falls 71 Phuket Province
Lang Khaay Bay Diving 69 Ko Tao
Lang Sod Beach 76 Ko Lanta
Lanta Old Town 76 Ko Lanta
La-ong Rung Waterfall 79 Far South
Lawa Cave 26 Kanchanaburi Province
Lighthouse Bay 69 Ko Tao
Lion King Climb 76 Railay
Living Thailand Cultural Center
  66 Ko Samui
Lizard Garden 66 Ko Samui
Lo Bi Beach 71 Phuket Province
Lo Pa Ret Beach 71 Phuket Province
Lo Samah Bay Diving 71 Phuket Province
Lod Nua Cave 71 Phuket Province
Loh Moo Dee Beach 76 Ko Phi Phi Don

Loha Prasart (Metal Castle)
  8 Downtown Bangkok
Long Beach 76 Ko Phi Phi Don
Long Phae 43 Lampang, Nan, Phrae,
  Uttaradit Provinces
Lookout 10 Lumphini
Lopburi Zoo 23 Lopburi Town
Lu Du Waterfall 79 Tarutao Islands
Luang Phu Ong Tu
  48 Northeastern Thailand
Luang Po Ban Laem 60 Upper Gulf Coasts
Lum Nam Pai WS
  39 Around Mae Hong Son
Lumphini Boxing Stadium 14 Sukhumvit
Mae Chok Hot Spring 33 Chiang Mai,
  Mae Hong Son & Lamphun Provinces
Mae Had Beach 68 Ko Pha-Ngan
Mae Hong Son Airport
  38 Mae Hong Son Town
Mae Kam Waterfall 43 Lampang, Nan,
  Phrae, Uttaradit Provinces
Mae Kasa Waterfall 46
  Kamphaeng Phet & Tak Provinces
Mae Laka Cave 33 Chiang Mai,
  Mae Hong Son & Lamphun Provinces
Mae Lamun Forestry Past
  26 Kanchanaburi Province
Mae Man Reservoir 42 Phrae Town
Mae Nam Beach 67 Mae Nam
Mae Ping 33 Chiang Mai,
  Mae Hong Son & Lamphun Provinces
Mae Ping River Cruise
  37 Central Chiang Mai
Mae Pool Waterfall 42 Lampang,
  Nan, Phrae, Uttaradit Provinces
Mae Ram Phueng Beach 28 Ban Phe
Mae Sa Elephant Camp
  34 Around Chiang Mai
Mae Sa Valley 34 Around Chiang Mai
Mae Sakud Waterfall
  39 Around Mae Hong Son
Mae Sariang Museum 38 Mae Sariang
Mae Surin Noi Waterfall 33 Chiang Mai,
  Mae Hong Son & Lamphun Provinces
Mae Surin Waterfall National Park
  39 Around Mae Hong Son
Mae Ya Waterfall 33 Chiang Mai,
  Mae Hong Son & Lamphun Provinces
Mae Yai Falls 64 Isthmus of Kra
Magic Banyan Trees 51 Phimai
Maha Wirawong National Museum
  50 Nakhon Ratchasima City
Mahaena Bay 69 Ko Tao
Mahamongkon Park 43 Uttaradit Town
Mai Khao Beach 72 Phuket Island
Mai Pai Bay Beach 76 Ko Lanta
Mambo Cabaret Show 15 Sukhumvit
Mango Bay Diving 69 Ko Tao
Mao Ta Phut Industrial Port
  28 Southeastern Thailand
Map Ta Phut Port 60 Upper Gulf Coasts
Marble Inscription of King Rama IX
  75 Patong Beach
Marine National Park Education Centre
  64 Isthmus of Kra
Maya Bay Diving 71 Phuket Province
Mengrai Maharat Came
  40 Chiang Rai Town
Mini Siam 29 Pattaya
Mo Mamuang Beach 78 Far South
Mo Paeng Waterfall 33 Chiang Mai,
  Mae Hong Son & Lamphun Provinces
Mong Kala Khiri Wong Cave
  26 Kanchanaburi Province
Monkey at Work (Coconut-picking)
  66 Ko Samui
Monkey Beach 76 Ko Phi Phi Don
Moslem Cultural Area 81 Songkhla Town
Mountain Viewpoint 66 Ko Samui
Mountain View Point 69 Ko Tao
Mountain Viewpoint 68 Ko Pha-Ngan
Mu Ko Chumphon National Park
  64 Isthmus of Kra
Mu Ko Dong 79 Tarutao Islands
Mu Ko Lanta National Park 76 Ko Lanta
Mu Ko Phetra National Park 78 Far South
Muang Kaew 44 Pitsanulok,
  Sukhothai & Phichit Provinces
Muang Ngam Beach 79 Far South
Muang Paeng Hot Spring 33 Chiang Mai,
  Mae Hong Son & Lamphun Provinces
Muang Tam 48 Northeastern Thailand
Mukdahan National Park
  49 Northeastern Thailand
Municipal Zoo 20 Nakhon Pathom Town
Museum Gift & Snack Shop 51 Phimai
Museum of Siam 8 Downtown Bangkok
Museum of World Insects and
  Natural Wonders 36 Central Chiang Mai

Muslim Village 66 Ko Samui
Na Kha Le Beach 72 Phuket Island
Na Muang Falls 65 Around Samui
Na Muang Waterfall 2 66 Ko Samui
Naga Pearl Farm 66 Ko Samui
Nai Harn Beach 70 Phuket Province
Nai Thon Beach 72 Phuket Island
Nai Yang Beach 72 Phuket Island
Nakhon Sawan Airport
  24 Around Nakhon Sawan
Nam Kading National Biodiversity
  and Conservation Area
  49 Northeastern Thailand
Nam Nao National Park
  48 Northeastern Thailand
Nam Tak Bang Pae Waterfall
  73 Phuket Island
Nam Tok Beach 68 Ko Pha-Ngan
Nam Tok Chipo National Park 79 Far Sou
Nam Tok Jonlongle 79 Tarutao Islands
Nam Tok Kapo Forest Park
  64 Isthmus of Kra
Nam Tok Kham Cha-I Park
  49 Northeastern Thailand
Nam Tok Mae Surin 33 Chiang Mai,
  Mae Hong Son & Lamphun Provinces
Nam Tok Ngao National Park
  64 Isthmus of Kra
Nam Tok Sai Khao National Park 79
  Far South
Nam Tok Si Khit National Park
  64 Isthmus of Kra
Nam Tok Tam Nak Tot 79 Tarutao Island
Nam Tok Than Sadet National Park
  64 Isthmus of Kra
Namuang Waterfall I 66 Ko Samui
Nan National Museum 43 Nan
Nan Tak Ton Sai Waterfall
  73 Phuket Island
Nang Khruan Waterfall 46
  Kamphaeng Phet & Tak Provinces
Nang Rong Waterfall 17 Central Thailand
Nang Thong Beach 70 Khao Lak
Nang Yom Waterfall 30 Ko Chang
Nang Yuan Pinnacle Diving 69 Ko Tao
Nangyuan Terrace 69 Ko Tao
Narai National Museum 23 Lopburi Town
Nara-that Beach 79 Far South
Narsillion Climb 77 Railay
National Art Museum 23 Ayutthaya Town
National Gallery 8 Downtown Bangkok
National Museum 8 Downtown Bangkok
National Museum of Roi Et 54 Roi Et Tow
National Park 71 Phuket Province
National Stadium 9 Downtown Bangkok
Native Handicrafts Center
  73 Phuket Island
New Heaven 69 Ko Tao
Night Bazaar 45 Phichit Town
Night Safari 34 Around Chiang Mai
Nok Nam Khu Khut Park 78 Far South
Nong Chong Kham Public Park
  38 Mae Hong Son Town
Nong Thin Public Park 59 Nong Khai Tow
Nopparat Thara Beach 76 Ao Nang Beac
Nopparat Thara National Park
  76 Ao Nang Beach
Noppharat Thara Beach
  71 Phuket Province
North Point Diving
  70 Similan National Park
Nui Bay Beach 76 Ko Lanta
Nung Krerngkawia and Nong Namsap
  Wild life Reservation
  26 Kanchanaburi Province
Ob Khan National Park
  34 Around Chiang Mai
Ob Luang 33 Chiang Mai,
  Mae Hong Son & Lamphun Provinces
October 14 Memorial
  8 Downtown Bangkok
Oil Well 44 Pitsanulok, Sukhothai &
  Phichit Provinces
Old Chiang Mai Cultural Center and
  Sbun-Nga Textile Museum
  36 Central Chiang Mai
Old Chiang Rai Airport 40 Chiang Rai Tow
Old Community Area 41 Phayao Town
Old Mon Temple Wat Samprasop
  26 Sangkhlaburi
Old Royal Palace 23 Ayutthaya Town
Oldtimer Museum 34 Around Chiang Ma
Om Com 31 Chanthaburi (Chanburi) Tow
One, Two, Three Wall 77 Railay
Ongshu Cave 26 Kanchanaburi Province
OTOP 65 Nakhon Si Thammarat Town
Overlap Stone 66 Ko Samui
Pa Mai Beach 79 Far South
Pacific Island Club 72 Phuket Island

ak Bang Na Thap Beach 79 Far South
ak Bara Port 64 Isthmus of Kra
ak Lam Wat Khao Kha Kaeng Chot
   26 Kanchanaburi Province
ak Meng Beach 78 Far South
ak Nan Village 43 Lampang, Nan,
   Phrae, Uttaradit Provinces
ak Weep Beach 70 Khao Lak
aka Timo Beach 79 Far South
alm Beach 29 Pattaya
along Bay Diving 71 Phuket Province
anare Beach 79 Far South
ansea Beach 74 Kamala Beach
apiyong Cliff 79 Tarutao Islands
aradise Beach 28 Ko Samet
aradise Waterfall 68 Ko Pha-Ngan
ark Entrance and Headquarters
   26 Kanchanaburi Province
ark@Pai 38 Pai
asteur Institute 13 Silom
atjamit Fort 12 Silom
atong Beach 75 Patong Beach
attaya Beach 78 Ko Lipe
attaya View Point 29 Pattaya
earl Culture Farm 71 Phuket Province
ee Wee Rock Diving 69 Ko Tao
erlis State Park 78 Far South
ha Chana Dai 49 Northeastern Thailand
ha Laem National Park
   49 Northeastern Thailand
ha Pueng Substation
   26 Kanchanaburi Province
ha That 26 Kanchanaburi Province
ha That Cave 26 Kanchanaburi Province
ha Wang Chan Cave
   26 Kanchanaburi Province
ha Ya Nak (Body) 81 Songkhla Town
ha Ya Nak (Tail) 81 Songkhla Town
hae Muang Phi 43 Lampang,
   Nan, Phrae, Uttaradit Provinces
haeng Waterfall 68 Ko Pha-Ngan
haengkhanoon 66 Ko Samui
ha-Ngan Safari & Elephant Trekking 68
   Ko Pha-Ngan
hangnga Bay National Marine Park
   71 Phuket Province
hanom Rung Historical Park
   50 Around Phanom Rung
hanom Sawai Forest Park
   48 Northeastern Thailand
hi Hua To Cave 71 Phuket Province
hi Le Diving 71 Phuket Province
hi Mai Stone Castle
   48 Northeastern Thailand
hichit Crocodile Auditorium
   45 Phichit Town
hilatelic Museum 37 Central Chiang Mai
himai Historical Park 51 Phimai
himai National Museum 51 Phimai
ho Khun Ngam Muang Monument
   41 Phayao Town
hom Pier Fortress 23 Ayutthaya Town
hra Borommathat Chaiya
   64 Isthmus of Kra
hra Cave 32 Northern Thailand
hra Chao Kawila Monument
   37 Central Chiang Mai
hra Chedi Si Song Rak
   32 Northern Thailand
hra Kayang Cave 64 Isthmus of Kra
hra Nakhon Khiri Historical
   Park (Khao Wang)
   61 Phetchaburi (Phetburi) Town
hra Nang Beach 71 Phuket Province
hra Nang Cave 71 Phuket Province
hra Nang Chamthewi Statue
   39 Lamphun Town
hra Pathom Chedi National Museum
   20 Nakhon Pathom Town
hra Phuttabat (Buddha Footprint)
   17 Central Thailand
hra Prang Sam Yod
   48 Northeastern Thailand
hra Prang Sam Yot 23 Lopburi Town
hra Ratchawang Ban Peun 61
hetchaburi (Phetburi) Town
hra Sabai Cave 33 Chiang Mai,
   Mae Hong Son & Lamphun Provinces
hra Sawan Falls 78 Far South
hra Sumen Fort 8 Downtown Bangkok
hra Tamnak Thaksin Ratchaniwet
   79 Far South
hra Thaen Sila-at 43 Lampang, Nan,
hrae, Uttaradit Provinces
hra That Khao Moi 43 Lampang, Nan,
   Phrae, Uttaradit Provinces
hranang Cave 76 Railay
hranang Cave Beach 76 Railay
hranangnai Cave 76 Railay

Phra-ngoen Garden
   65 Nakhon Si Thammarat Town
Phraram Cave 33 Chiang Mai,
   Mae Hong Son & Lamphun Provinces
Phrat That Chae Heng 43 Lampang, Nan,
Phrae, Uttaradit Provinces
Phratat Chomphet
   61 Phetchaburi (Phetburi) Town
Phraya Chaiyabun Monument
   42 Phrae Town
Phraya Nakhon Cave 60 Upper Gulf Coasts
Phraya Phichai Dap Hak Monument
   43 Uttaradit Town
Phraya Ratsadanu Pradit Mahisom
   Phakdi Monument 77 Trang Town
Phraya Rattanasetthi Monument
   63 Ranong Town
Phraya Singhanatracha Monument
   38 Mae Hong Son Town
Phraya Surin Phakdi Si Narong
   Changwang Monument 52 Surin Town
Phu Hin Rong Kla
   48 Northeastern Thailand
Phu Khlao Wildlife Conservation Area
   48 Northeastern Thailand
Phu Kradueng National Park
   48 Northeastern Thailand
Phu Luang 48 Northeastern Thailand
Phu Phra Bat Historical Park
   48 Northeastern Thailand
Phu Rua 32 Northern Thailand
Phu Ruea National Park
   48 Northeastern Thailand
Phu Sa Dok Bua National Park
   49 Northeastern Thailand
Phu Soi Dao National Park
   48 Northeastern Thailand
Phu Wua Wildlife Sanctuary
   48 Northeastern Thailand
Phuchong Nayoi National Park
   49 Northeastern Thailand
Phuket Famous Sunset View
   72 Phuket Island
Phuket Fantasea 75 Kamala Beach
Phuket Gibbon Rehabilitation Center
   73 Phuket Island
Phuket International Airport
   72 Phuket Island
Phuket Marine Biological Research Centre
   & Phuket Aquarium 73 Phuket Island
Phuket Pearl Farm 73 Phuket Island
Phuket Seashell Museum 73 Rawai
Phuket Thai Hua Museum 73 Phuket Town
Phuket Zoo 72 Phuket Island
Phuphalom Forest Park
   48 Northeastern Thailand
Phuphing Rajanivet Palace
   34 Around Chiang Mai
Phutsa Beach 28 Ko Samet
Phutthamonthon 4 Greater Bangkok
Pimai Ruins 48 Northeastern Thailand
Pirate's Waterfall 79 Tarutao Islands
Pla Ba Waterfall 48 Northeastern Thailand
Planetarium Science Museum
   15 Sukhumvit
Police Museum 9 Downtown Bangkok
Pong Ba Diat Waterfall 33 Chiang Mai,
   Mae Hong Son & Lamphun Provinces
Portuguese Village 23 Ayutthaya Town
Prachuap Khiri Khan Beach
   63 Prachuap Khiri Khan Town
Pran Khiri Beach 60 Upper Gulf Coasts
Prang Khaek 23 Lopburi Town
Prap Hor Monument 59 Nong Khai Town
Prasat Ban Khok Ngio
   50 Around Phanom Rung
Prasat Ban Pluang
   51 Around Phanom Rung
Prasat Hin Ban Phluang
   48 Northeastern Thailand
Prasat Hin Phanom Rung
   48 Northeastern Thailand
Prasat Hin Phanomwan
   48 Northeastern Thailand
Prasat Meuang Singh Historical Park
   26 Kanchanaburi Province
Prasat Preah Wihan
   49 Northeastern Thailand
Prasat Ta Meuan 50 Around Phanom Rung
Prathat Wiang Haeng 33 Chiang Mai,
   Mae Hong Son & Lamphun Provinces
Prathat Doi Kaeo 33 Chiang Mai,
   Mae Hong Son & Lamphun Provinces
Prathat Khru Ba Si Wichai 33 Chiang Mai,
   Mae Hong Son & Lamphun Provinces
Prathat Klong Khao Noi
   49 Northeastern Thailand
Prathat Mon Phaya Kaichae 33 Chiang Mai,
   Mae Hong Son & Lamphun Provinces

Prathat Wat Fa Wiang In 33 Chiang Mai,
   Mae Hong Son & Lamphun Provinces
Pratu Chang Pheuak
   36 Central Chiang Mai
Pratu Chiang Mai 36 Central Chiang Mai
Pratu Suan Dok 36 Central Chiang Mai
Pratu Suan Prung 36 Central Chiang Mai
Pratu Tha Phae 36 Central Chiang Mai
Pratubjai House 42 Phrae Town
Prince Prajak Monument
   59 Udon Thani Town
Princess Bay Diving
   70 Similan National Park
Princess Mother '90 Museum
   40 Chiang Rai Town
Princess Mother '90 Park
   40 Chiang Rai Town
Pu Kai 70 Similan National Park
Public Fitness Park 73 Phuket Town
Puek Tiean Beach 60 Upper Gulf Coasts
Punyaban Falls 64 Isthmus of Kra
Pu-Ya Shrine 59 Udon Thani Town
Queen Sirikit Botanic Garden
   34 Around Chiang Mai
Rad Pubs Complex 57 Khon Kaen Town
Railay Beach 76 Railay
Raksawarin Floral Park 64 Isthmus of Kra
Ram Khamhaeng National Park
   44 Pitsanulok, Sukhothai &
   Phichit Provinces
Ram Khamhaeng National Park 47
   Kamphaeng Phet & Tak Provinces
Rama VI Statue (King Mongkutklao)
   13 Silom
Ramkhamhaeng National Museum
   44 Sukhothai Historical Park
Rangsit Stadium 19 Around Bangkok
Ranong Mineral Hot Springs
   63 Ranong Town
Rap Ro Cave 64 Isthmus of Kra
Ratchaburi National Museum 20
Ratchaburi (Ratburi) Town
Ratchadamnoen Boxing Stadium
   9 Downtown
Ratchaprapa Dam 64 Isthmus of Kra
Rattana Rangsarn Throne Hall
   62 Ranong Town
Rawai Beach 73 Rawai
Rawai Rest Area 72 Phuket Island
Rayong Aquarium 28 Ban Phe
Rock Climbing 77 Railay
Rocky Bay (Thong Rang) 67 Ko Samui
Rocky Bay Diving 70 Similan National Park
Rocky Point Diving
   70 Similan National Park
Roi Et Aquarium 54 Roi Et Town
Rose Garden 18 Around Bangkok
Royal Barges 8 Downtown Bangkok
Royal Barges National Museum
   8 Downtown Bangkok
Royal Flora Ratchapruek
   34 Around Chiang Mai
Royal Palace 8 Downtown Bangkok
Royal Thai Airforce Base - Wing 53
   63 Prachuap Khiri Khan Town
Sa Bua Beach 64 Isthmus of Kra
Sa Kaeo Circle 23 Lopburi Town
Sa Pan Waterfall 32 Northern Thailand
Saampan Waterfall 68 Ko Pha-Ngan
Sadet Beach 68 Ko Pha-Ngan
Sadet Cave 71 Phuket Province
Safari Park 26 Kanchanaburi Province
Safarine 27 Kanchanaburi Town
Sai Kaew Beach 28 Ko Samet
Sai Khu Falls 60 Upper Gulf Coasts
Sai Nuan Beach Diving 69 Ko Tao
Sai Rung Waterfall 70 Khao Lak
Sai Thong National Park
   48 Northeastern Thailand
Sai Tong Beach 69 Ko Tao
Sai Yok Cave 27 Sai Yok National Park
Sai Yok National Park
   27 Sai Yok National Park
Sai Yok Noi Waterfall
   26 Kanchanaburi Province
Sai Yok Yai Waterfall
   27 Sai Yok National Park
Sail Rock Diving 65 Around Samui
Sairee Beach 69 Ko Tao
Sak Yai Forest Park 43 Lampang,
   Nan, Phrae, Uttaradit Provinces
Sakai Village 79 Far South
Sakhon Nakhon Gate City Monument
   54 Sakon Nakhon Town
Sakom Beach 79 Far South
Salad Beach 68 Ko Pha-Ngan
Sam Phraya Beach 60 Upper Gulf Coasts
Sam Rong Kiat Waterfall
   49 Northeastern Thailand

Samila Beach 81 Songkhla Town
Samila Sea Sport 81 Songkhla Town
Samira Beach 79 Far South
Samphran Elephant Ground & Zoo
   18 Around Bangkok
Samran Beach 78 Far South
Samran Pinnacle Diving 65 Around Samui
Samrong Boxing Stadium
   5 Greater Bangkok
Samui Airport 66 Ko Samui
Samui Aquarium & Tiger Zoo 66 Ko Samui
Samui Everest Viewpoint 66 Ko Samui
Samui Gallery Hill 66 Ko Samui
Samui Go Kart Track 67 Mae Nam
Samui Highlands 66 Ko Samui
Samui Monkey Theatre 66 Ko Samui
Samui Shell Museum 66 Ko Samui
San Phra Kan 23 Lopburi Town
Sanam Chan Royal Palace
   20 Nakhon Pathom Town
Sanctuary of Truth 29 Pattaya
Santiburi Samui Country Club 66 Ko Samui
Sao Ching Cha (Giant Swing)
   8 Downtown Bangkok
Sao Din Gorge (Hom Chom) 43 Lampang,
   Nan, Phrae, Uttaradit Provinces
Saphan Lao Waterfall
   26 Kanchanaburi Province
Saranrom Royal Garden
   8 Downtown Bangkok
Sawan Park 25 Nakhon Sawan Town
Scuba Diving 79 Tarutao Islands
Sea Gypsy Village 76 Ko Phi Phi Don
Secret Statuary Garden 66 Ko Samui
Seekantang Beach 64 Isthmus of Kra
Sergeant Major Thawee Folk Museum
   45 Phichit Town
Sericulture 49 Northeastern Thailand
Shark Fin Reef Diving
   70 Similan National Park
Shark Island Diving 69 Ko Tao
Shark Point Diving 71 Phuket Province
Shell Fossil Cemetery 71 Phuket Province
Shell Fossil Cemetery 64 Isthmus of Kra
Ship Wreck Diving 69 Ko Tao
Shooting Ranch 66 Ko Samui
Shrine of the Serene Light 73 Phuket Town
Si Nakhon Khuean Khan Botanical Park
   6 Central Bangkok
Si Phangnga 64 Isthmus of Kra
Si Satchanalai Historical Park
   33 Chiang Mai, Mae Hong Son &
   Lamphun Provinces
Si Satchanalai National Park 44
Satchanalai-Chaliang National Park
Si Thep Ruins 17 Central Thailand
Siam Natural History Museum
   67 Mae Nam
Sichon Beach 64 Isthmus of Kra
Similan National Park Office
   70 Similan National Park
Simueang Park 30 Rayong Town
Siracha Tiger Zoo 60 Upper Gulf Coasts
Siri Phum Waterfall 33 Chiang Mai,
   Mae Hong Son & Lamphun Provinces
Sirinat Marine National Park 72
   Phuket Island
Sirinat Nat'l Park 64 Isthmus of Kra
Sirithon Falls 79 Far South
Snake Farm 66 Ko Samui
Som Pa - Friendly Monument
   54 Kalasin Town
Som Paen Beach 64 Isthmus of Kra
Somdej Phranaresuan Shrine &
   Monument 58 Nong Bua Lam Phu Town
Somdet Phra Jao Taksin Maharat Shrine
   46 Kamphaeng Phet & Tak Provinces
Somdet Phra Srinagarindra Park
   71 Phuket Province
Somedet Ya Park 41 Phayao Town
Son Beach 68 Ko Pha-Ngan
Son Ngam Beach 71 Phuket Province
Song Rua 66 Ko Samui
Songkhla Aquarium 81 Songkhla Town
Songkhla National Museum
   81 Songkhla Town
Songkran Niyosane Forensic Medicine
   Museum 8 Downtown Bangkok
Soontornpoo Monument
   28 Southeastern Thailand
South West Rock Diving 64 Around Samui
Souvenir Center 40 Chiang Rai Town
Springs 27 Sai Yok National Park
Sra Kaew Pond 71 Phuket Province
Sra Keaw Cave 71 Phuket Province
Sramanora River Stone 68 Ko Pha-Ngan
Sramanora Waterfall 68 Ko Pha-Ngan
Sri Gurusingh Sabha
   8 Downtown Bangkok

Sri Phum 36 Central Chiang Mai
Statue of Mae Thorani
    8 Downtown Bangkok
Statue of Pone Kingpetch 62 Hua Hin
Stonehenge Diving
    70 Similan National Park
Suan Ampon 9 Downtown Bangkok
Suan Hin Maharat 42 Phrae Town
Suan Mai Falls 64 Isthmus of Kra
Suan Rukhachat Bokharani Forest Garden
    71 Phuket Province
Suan Som Mueang Long 42 Phrae Town
Sukho Cave 26 Kanchanaburi Province
Sukhothai Historical Park
    44 Sukhothai Historical Park
Sun Ta Then Waterfall
    28 Southeastern Thailand
Sunantha Falls 64 Isthmus of Kra
Sundowner Horse Ranch 66 Ko Samui
Sunlight Beach 78 Ko Lipe
Sunset Beach 68 Hat Rin
Sunset View 28 Ko Samet
Surin Airport 52 Surin Town
Surin Beach 74 Kamala Beach
Surin Elephant Show Stadium
    52 Surin Town
Susan Hoi Lan Pi 32 Northern Thailand
Suspension Bridge 27
    Sai Yok National Park
Suvarnabhumi Int'l Airport
    60 Upper Gulf Coasts
Suvarnabhumi International Airport
    5 Greater Bangkok
T.A.T 66 Ko Samui
Ta Thong Port 64 Around Samui
Taa Toh Rock Diving 69 Ko Tao
Tai Rom Yen National Park
    64 Isthmus of Kra
Tai Ton 17 Central Thailand
Takhli Airport 24 Around Nakhon Sawan
Taksin Monument
    31 Chanthaburi (Chanburi) Town
Talingngam Beach 66 Ko Samui
Talo Kapo Beach 79 Far South
Talot Cave 79 Far South
Tam Nok Nang Cave 79 Tarutao Islands
Tam Wa Priest's Camp Site
    61 Phetchaburi (Phetburi) Town
Tammalang Border Crossing Point
    78 Far South
Tamnak Keow Museum
    56 Chaiyaphum Town
Tanote Bay Diving 69 Ko Tao
Tanote View 69 Ko Tao
Tao Nai Chian 50 Around Phanom Rung
Tao Sawai 50 Around Phanom Rung
Taphraya National Park
    48 Northeastern Thailand
Tarun Cave 79 Tarutao Islands
Tarutao Islands National Marine Park
    79 Tarutao Islands
TAT 9 Downtown Bangkok
Tat Mok Waterfall 32 Northern Thailand
TAT Office 23 Ayutthaya Town
Tat Phranba Waterfall
    48 Northeastern Thailand
Tat Ton National Park
    48 Northeastern Thailand
Temple 64 Isthmus of Kra
Temple Ruins 49 Northeastern Thailand
Tesco Lotus Supercenter 66 Ko Samui
Tex Rock Climbing 76 Railay
Tha Nun Beach 70 Phuket Province
Tha Pom (Khlong Song Nam)
    71 Phuket Province
Tha Thong Port 64 Isthmus of Kra
Tha Thung Na Dam
    26 Kanchanaburi Province
Thaan Rua 66 Ko Samui
Thai Boat Museum 23 Ayutthaya Town
Thai Boxing Garden 62 Hua Hin
Thai Human Imagery Museum
    18 Around Bangkok
Thai Life Waterfall 68 Ko Pha-Ngan
Thai Muang Beach 70 Phuket Province
Thaiwand Wall 76 Railay
Thalang National Museum
    73 Phuket Island
Thale Ban National Park 78 Far South
Tham Daowadung
    26 Kanchanaburi Province
Tham Duean Tham Dao
    32 Northern Thailand
Tham Kaew Cave 71 Phuket Province
Tham Khao Ngoen 64 Isthmus of Kra
Tham Lot 33 Chiang Mai, Mae Hong Son
    & Lamphun Provinces
Tham Mae Hu 33 Chiang Mai,
    Mae Hong Son & Lamphun Provinces

Tham Mae Usu 33 Chiang Mai,
    Mae Hong Son & Lamphun Provinces
Tham Men 71 Phuket Province
Tham Nak Cave 71 Phuket Province
Tham Petch Cave 71 Phuket Province
Tham Pha Thai 33 Chiang Mai,
    Mae Hong Son & Lamphun Provinces
Tham Phang Beach 29 Ko Si Chang
Tham Phra Sabai 33 Chiang Mai, Mae
    Hong Son & Lamphun Provinces
Tham Pla National Park
    38 Around Mae Hong Son
Tham Sra Tuan Thong Cave
    71 Phuket Province
Tham Thalu Fa Cave 71 Phuket Province
Tham To Luang Cave 71 Phuket Province
Tham Waree Rin Cave 71 Phuket Province
Than Bokkhorani National Park
    64 Isthmus of Kra
Than Mayom Waterfall 31 Ko Chang
Than Ngam Park 48 Northeastern Thailand
Than Prapar Waterfall 68 Ko Pha-Ngan
Than Prawet Waterfall 68 Ko Pha-Ngan
Than Sader Waterfall 68 Ko Pha-Ngan
Than Sawan Waterfall
    41 Chiang Rai Province
Than Thip Waterfall
    48 Northeastern Thailand
Than To National Park 79 Far South
Thanrattana Waterfall
    48 Northeastern Thailand
Thao Suranari Monument
    48 Northeastern Thailand
Thaplan National Park
    28 Southeastern Thailand
The Boulders Diving
    70 Similan National Park
The Coleridge Institute 66 Ko Samui
The Lakeland Water Cable Ski 29 Pattaya
The Marine Scientific Institute
    60 Upper Gulf Coasts
The Morning Edge Diving
    70 Similan National Park
The Royal Turf Club 9 Downtown Bangkok
Thian Beach 68 Ko Pha-Ngan
Thong Lang Beach 68 Ko Pha-Ngan
Thong Nai Pan Noi Beach 68 Ko Pha-Ngan
Thong Nai Pan Yai Beach 68 Ko Pha-Ngan
Thong Nang Waterfall 68 Ko Pha-Ngan
Thong Reng Beach 68 Ko Pha-Ngan
Thorani Fountain 8 Downtown Bangkok
Three Pagodas Pass 26 Sangkhlaburi
Thung Nang Dam Pier 64 Isthmus of Kra
Thung Salaeng Luang National Park
    48 Northeastern Thailand
Thung Tuek Archaeological Site
    64 Isthmus of Kra
Thung Wua Laen Beach 64 Isthmus of Kra
Tiger Cave 76 Ko Lanta
Tiger Temple 26 Kanchanaburi Province
Toh-Bo Cliff 79 Tarutao Islands
Ton Nga Chang Falls 78 Far South
Ton Nga Chang Wildlife Sanctuary
    78 Far South
Ton Phet Falls 64 Isthmus of Kra
Ton Pling Waterfall 70 Khao Lak
Ton Sai Bay Beach 76 Railay
Ton Te Falls 78 Far South
Ton Tok Falls 78 Far South
Tourism Authority of Thailand
    9 Downtown Bangkok
Tourism Authority of Thailand (TAT)
    65 Surat Thani Town
Tourism Information Office
    63 Chumphon Town
Tourist Information Centre (TAT)
    77 Krabi Town
Tra Khro Waterfall
    48 Northeastern Thailand
Trat Airport 28 Southeastern Thailand
Triple Coconut Tree 66 Ko Samui
Triple Coconut Tree 66 Ko Samui
Trok Ban Chin 46 Tak Town
Tropical Zoo 66 Ko Samui
Tub Tim Beach 28 Ko Samet
Turtle Rock Diving
    70 Similan National Park
Twin Coconut Tree 68 Ko Pha-Ngan
Twin Rock Diving 69 Ko Tao
Two Views 69 Ko Tao
Ubon National Museum
    53 Ubon Ratchathani Town
Ubon Ratchathani Airport (UBP)/ Ubon
    Royal Thai Air Force Base 53
    Ubon Ratchathani Town
Udon Thani Int'l Airport
    49 Greater Udon Thani.
Udon Thani Provincial Museum
    59 Udon Thani Town

Um Phang Airstrip 46 Mae Sot
Uncle Nim's Waterfall & Magic Garden
    66 Ko Samui
Underwater World Pattaya 29 Pattaya
U-Tapao Int'l Airport
    28 Southeastern Thailand
Uttaradit Provincial Culture Hall
    43 Uttaradit Town
Vat Phra Keo 48 Northeastern Thailand
Vichaiprasit 8 Downtown Bangkok
View Point 28 Ko Samet
Viewpoint 27 Sai Yok National Park
Viking Cave 71 Phuket Province
Visitor Center & Park Headquarters
    27 Sai Yok National Park
Vongburi House 42 Phrae Town
Votive Candle Statue
    53 Ubon Ratchathani Town
Wainam Beach 68 Ko Pha-Ngan
Walking Buddha Statue 54 Roi Et Town
Wang Ba Dan Cave
    26 Kanchanaburi Province
Wang Long Diving 76 Ko Phi Phi Don
Wang Mai Daeng Waterfall
    68 Ko Pha-Ngan
Wang Phetburi Mountain
    60 Upper Gulf Coasts
Wang Sai Waterfall 68 Ko Pha-Ngan
Wang Sam Seiyn 29 Pattaya
Wang Saotong Falls 65 Around Samui
Wang Takrai N. P.
    48 Northeastern Thailand
Wang Yai Waterfall
    49 Northeastern Thailand
Wangkaeo Wangthong Waterfall
    33 Chiang Mai, Mae Hong Son &
    Lamphun Provinces
Wangsaotong 66 Ko Samui
Wangthong Waterfall 68 Ko Pha-Ngan
Wanorn 66 Ko Samui
Wasu-Kri Beach 79 Far South
Wat Aranyakhet 46 Mae Sot
Wat Arun Ratchawararam (Temple of
    Dawn) 8 Downtown Bangkok
Wat Bowonniwet 8 Downtown Bangkok
Wat Jin Sanjao Pu-Ya 59 Udon Thani Town
Wat Pha Narai Maha Rat
    51 Nakhon Ratchasima City
Wat Pho 8 Downtown Bangkok
Wat Pho Chai 48 Northeastern Thailand
Wat Phra Kaew (The Emerald Buddha)
    8 Downtown Bangkok
Wat Phra Kaew Museum
    8 Downtown Bangkok
Wat Phra That Hariphunchai
    35 Around Chiang Mai
Wat Phra That Phanom 55 That Phanom
Wat Sri Khom Kham Cultural Home Centre
    41 Phayao Town
Water Gardens Fantasia Lagoon
    50 Nakhon Ratchasima City
Water Park 47 Kamphaeng Phet Town
Waterfalls 79 Tarutao Islands
West Railay Beach 76 Railay
Whale Skeleton 69 Ko Tao
White Elephant Monument
    36 Central Chiang Mai
White Rock Diving 69 Ko Tao
Wieng Ko Sat 42 Lampang, Nan, Phrae,
    Uttaradit Provinces
Wild Life Park 66 Ko Samui
Wild Life Preservation Center
    28 Southeastern Thailand
Wildlife Sanctuary 64 Isthmus of Kra
Wine de Samui 66 Ko Samui
Wiphawadi Falls 64 Isthmus of Kra
Wonder World Fun Park 7 Central Bangkok
Wong Amat Beach 29 Pattaya
Wongwien 22 July 9 Downtown Bangkok
Wood Carving Village 42 Lampang, Nan,
    Phrae, Uttaradit Provinces
Wood Carving Village 33 Chiang Mai,
    Mae Hong Son & Lamphun Provinces
Woodland Park View 66 Ko Samui
WWII Museum 27 Kanchanaburi Town
Yacht Haven Phuket Marina
    72 Phuket Island
Ya-le Monument 20 Nakhon Pathom Town
Yang Beach 68 Ko Pha-Ngan
Yao (East) Beach 68 Ko Pha-Ngan
Yao Beach 66 Ko Samui
Yao Khao Viewpoint 66 Ko Samui
Yong Hua Wreck Diving 78 Ko Lipe
Yong Ling Beach 78 Far South
Yong Waterfall 64 Isthmus of Kra
Yuan Beach 68 Ko Pha-Ngan
Yuttha Navi Ko Chang 31 Ko Chang